GW01458824

Chemi
About Us

A. H. Johnstone, B.Sc., Ph.D., F.R.S.C.
Senior Lecturer in Chemistry, University of Glasgow

T. I. Morrison, T.D., M.Sc., F.R.S.C.
Adviser in Secondary Education, Angus Division, Tayside

N. Reid, B.Sc., Ph.D., Dip.Ed., F.R.S.C.
Principal Teacher of Chemistry, Armadale Academy, Lothian

Heinemann Educational Books
London and Edinburgh

Heinemann Educational Books Ltd
22 Bedford Square, London WC1B 3HH

LONDON EDINBURGH MELBOURNE AUCKLAND
HONG KONG SINGAPORE KUALA LUMPUR NEW DELHI
IBADAN NAIROBI JOHANNESBURG
EXETER (NH) KINGSTON PORT OF SPAIN

British Library Cataloguing in Publication Data
Johnstone, Alex
  Chemistry about us.
  1. Chemistry
  I. Title   II. Morrison, T I
  III. Reid, N
  540   QD33

ISBN 0-435-64499-8

Acknowledgement   The cover photographs were kindly
supplied by Shell UK Ltd.

Filmset in Monophoto by Eta Services (Typesetters) Ltd, Beccles, Suffolk
Printed and bound in Great Britain by
Richard Clay (The Chaucer Press) Ltd, Bungay, Suffolk

Contents

PERIODIC TABLE OF

1	2
1.008 **H** Hydrogen 1 — 1	

6.939 **Li** Lithium 3 — 2)1	9.012 **Be** Beryllium 4 — 2)2

22.990 **Na** Sodium 11 — 2)8)1	24.312 **Mg** Magnesium 12 — 2)8)2

1	2							
39.102 **K** Potassium 19 2)8)8)1	40.080 **Ca** Calcium 20 2)8)8)2	44.956 **Sc** Scandium 21 2)8)9)2	47.900 **Ti** Titanium 22 2)8)10)2	50.942 **V** Vanadium 23 2)8)11)2	51.996 **Cr** Chromium 24 2)8)13)1	54.938 **Mn** Manganese 25 2)8)13)2	55.847 **Fe** Iron 26 2)8)14)2	58.933 **Co** Cobalt 27 2)8)15)2
85.470 **Rb** Rubidium 37 2)8)18)8)1	87.620 **Sr** Strontium 38 2)8)18)8)2	88.905 **Y** Yitrium 39 2)8)18)9)2	91.220 **Zr** Zirconium 40 2)8)18)10)2	92.906 **Nb** Niobium 41 2)8)18)12)1	95.940 **Mo** Molybdenum 42 2)8)18)13)1	[99] **Tc** Technetium 43 2)8)18)14)1	101.070 **Ru** Ruthenium 44 2)8)18)15)1	102.905 **Rh** Rhodium 45 2)8)18)16)1
132.905 **Cs** Caesium 55 2)8)18)18)8)1	137.340 **Ba** Barium 56 2)8)18)18)8)2	138.910 **La** Lanthanum 57 2)8)18)18)9)2	178.490 **Hf** Hafnium 72 2)8)18)32)10)2	180.948 **Ta** Tantalum 73 2)8)18)32)11)2	183.850 **W** Tungsten 74 2)8)18)32)12)2	186.200 **Re** Rhenium 75 2)8)18)32)13)2	190.200 **Os** Osmium 76 2)8)18)32)14)2	192.200 **Ir** Iridium 77 2)8)18)32)15)2
[223] **Fr** Francium 87 2)8)18)32)18)8)1	[226] **Ra** Radium 88 2)8)18)32)18)8)2	227* **Ac** Actinium 89 2)8)18)32)18)9)2						

Lanthanides

138.910 **La** Lanthanum 57 2)8)18)18)9)2	140.120 **Ce** Cerium 58 2)8)18)20)8)2	140.907 **Pr** Praseodymium 59 2)8)18)21)8)2	144.240 **Nd** Neodymium 60 2)8)18)22)8)2	[147] **Pm** Promethium 61 2)8)18)23)8)2	150.350 **Sm** Samarium 62 2)8)18)24)8)2
227* **Ac** Actinium 89 2)8)18)32)18)9)2	232.038 **Th** Thorium 90 2)8)18)32)18)10)2	[231] **Pa** Protactinium 91 2)8)18)32)20)9)2	238.030 **U** Uranium 92 2)8)18)32)21)9)2	[237] **Np** Neptunium 93 2)8)18)32)23)8)2	[242] **Pu** Plutonium 94 2)8)18)32)24)8)2

Key:
- Atomic weight
- Symbol
- Name
- Atomic number
- Electronic structure

[ ] This is the mass number of the isotope with the longest known half life of the element indicated.
* This is the mass number of the most stable or best known isotope of the element indicated.

	3	4	5	6	7	0

ELEMENTS

							4.003 **He** Helium 2 [2]

3	4	5	6	7	0
10.811 **B** Boron 5 2)3	12.011 **C** Carbon 6 2)4	14.007 **N** Nitrogen 7 2)5	15.999 **O** Oxygen 8 2)6	18.998 **F** Fluorine 9 2)7	20.183 **Ne** Neon 10 2)8
26.982 **Al** Aluminium 13 2)8)3	28.086 **Si** Silicon 14 2)8)4	30.974 **P** Phosphorus 15 2)8)5	32.064 **S** Sulphur 16 2)8)6	35.453 **Cl** Chlorine 17 2)8)7	39.948 **Ar** Argon 18 2)8)8

			3	4	5	6	7	0
58.710 **Ni** Nickel 28 2)8)16)2	63.540 **Cu** Copper 29 2)8)18)1	65.370 **Zn** Zinc 30 2)8)18)2	69.720 **Ga** Gallium 31 2)8)18)3	72.590 **Ge** Germanium 32 2)8)18)4	74.922 **As** Arsenic 33 2)8)18)5	78.960 **Se** Selenium 34 2)8)18)6	79.909 **Br** Bromine 35 2)8)18)7	83.800 **Kr** Krypton 36 2)8)18)8
106.400 **Pd** Palladium 46 2)8)18)18	107.870 **Ag** Silver 47 2)8)18)18)1	112.400 **Cd** Cadmium 48 2)8)18)18)2	114.820 **In** Indium 49 2)8)18)18)3	118.690 **Sn** Tin 50 2)8)18)18)4	121.750 **Sb** Antimony 51 2)8)18)18)5	127.600 **Te** Tellurium 52 2)8)18)18)6	126.904 **I** Iodine 53 2)8)18)18)7	131.300 **Xe** Xenon 54 2)8)18)18)8
195.090 **Pt** Platinum 78 2)8)18)32)17)1	196.967 **Au** Gold 79 2)8)18)32)18)1	200.590 **Hg** Mercury 80 2)8)18)32)18)2	204.370 **Tl** Thallium 81 2)8)18)32)18)3	207.190 **Pb** Lead 82 2)8)18)32)18)4	208.980 **Bi** Bismuth 83 2)8)18)32)18)5	[210] **Po** Polonium 84 2)8)18)32)18)6	[210] **At** Astatine 85 2)8)18)32)18)7	[222] **Rn** Radon 86 2)8)18)32)18)8

151.960 **Eu** Europium 63 2)8)18)25)8)2	157.250 **Gd** Gadolinium 64 2)8)18)25)9)2	158.924 **Tb** Terbium 65 2)8)18)27)8)2	162.500 **Dy** Dysprosium 66 2)8)18)28)8)2	164.930 **Ho** Holmium 67 2)8)18)29)8)2	167.260 **Er** Erbium 68 2)8)18)30)8)2	168.934 **Tm** Thulium 69 2)8)18)31)8)2	173.040 **Yb** Ytterbium 70 2)8)18)32)8)2	174.970 **Lu** Lutetium 71 2)8)18)32)9)2
[243] **Am** Americium 95 2)8)18)32)25)8)2	[247] **Cm** Curium 96 2)8)18)32)25)9)2	[249] **Bk** Berkelium 97 2)8)18)32)27)8)2	[251] **Cf** Californium 98 2)8)18)32)28)8)2	[254] **Es** Einsteinium 99 2)8)18)32)29)8)2	[253] **Fm** Fermium 100 2)8)18)32)30)8)2	[256] **Md** Mendelevium 101 2)8)18)32)31)8)2	254* **No** Nobelium 102 2)8)18)32)32)8)2	[257] **Lw** Lawrencium 103 2)8)18)32)32)9)2

Introduction for pupils

The title of this book has been chosen because of its double meaning, which depends upon where you place the emphasis.

Chemistry *About* Us suggests that chemistry has something to do with our surroundings: the air we breathe; the food we eat; the house in which we live; in fact, every material in the world. This is certainly the case. Everything you can touch, taste, smell, or see is chemical. A knowledge of chemistry helps us to understand the material world in which we live.

The title can also be read as Chemistry About *Us*, which makes it more personal. Our bodies are very complicated chemical factories which can be better understood by a study of chemistry. How we eat and grow, how we repair our injuries or find energy to work and play are of great importance to us.

There is another sense in which Chemistry is About *Us*. A very large range of jobs is based upon chemistry. Obviously industry concerned with oil or dyestuffs is chemical, but so also are farming, the food preparation and catering industries, the iron and steel industry, the cosmetics and plastics industries. Plumbing, painting, interior design, fabrics, and the rag trade all have their base in chemistry. In this sense Chemistry is About *Us* because it affects the way we live, the prosperity of our country, and the kind of jobs we may do.

We hope that as you work through this book you will have found out how and why Chemistry is About Us.

Important introduction for teachers

Please read this carefully

The structure of this book is a departure from the normal. The content of the Scottish 'O' Grade syllabus has been the subject of an intensive research programme over the past ten years and this book is based upon its findings. This has affected content, presentation, order, language, and use of bold type. Considerable space has been devoted to revision sections and discussion material.

Content

Our research showed that pupils at all stages were complaining about the same areas of the syllabus—energetics, the mole, balancing equations, ionic equations, and parts of the organic chemistry. These problems persisted well into university study. The factor common to all of these areas was that they were being taught in a fashion which overwhelmed the short-term memory. Pupils were being asked to recall material, sometimes from lessons of a year ago, and to add to this a portion of new material and vocabulary. For example, in the conductivity experiments simultaneous recall of the following ideas was required: conductivity depends upon ions, their concentration, their mobility, the process of neutralization, graph drawing and intepretation. It is little wonder that this material, by its very nature, left many pupils baffled instead of providing the enlightenment for which it was designed.

This led to a dilemma. Pupils could simultaneously cope with these ideas if their concept of conductivity was well developed; but how could this development of understanding occur? Certainly not by experiments which *initially* required the understanding to be present.

We have no control over the syllabus content, but, by manipulation of order and method, we have sought to minimize these problems. For example, we do not begin with the large tract of atomic theory and bonding which used to occupy the first month or six weeks of the course. We introduce only the minimum of theory to enable us to start upon the experimental investigations. Simple atomic theory and covalent bonding is all that is required to cope satisfactorily with the organic chemistry. Additional theory of bonding, balancing of equations, oxy-anions, and ionic equations are introduced *only* when required. Theory is the 'sound track' down the side of the 'film' rather than a formidable introductory block which has to be learned out of context and recalled up to a year later. Teachers may find it difficult to accept unbalanced inorganic equations in the earlier part of the book. It does not seem unreasonable to us to use these at the same stage as we are using unbalanced organic equations. In line with our philosophy of introducing a new idea only when it is necessary, we have begun to justify equation balancing only when considering stoichiometry. At that stage we encourage pupils to practise balancing equations by going back and checking which of the equations in their earlier work need balancing. This is in line with the memorandum on equations (*Memorandum No. 13*, Dundee: National Curriculum Development Centre, 1971) issued by the Scottish Certificate of Education Examination Board and the National Curriculum Development Centre. There is experimental evidence that this departure has been found helpful to pupils.

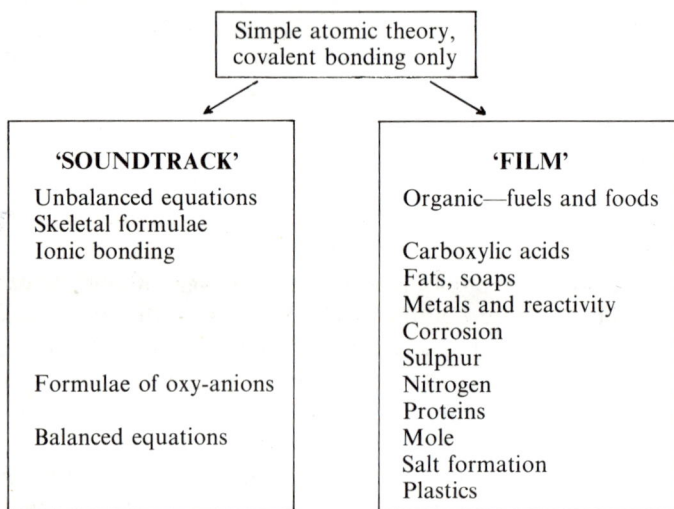

```
                    ┌──────────────────────────┐
                    │  Simple atomic theory,   │
                    │  covalent bonding only   │
                    └──────────────────────────┘
                       ↙                    ↘
┌─────────────────────────────┐   ┌─────────────────────────────┐
│        'SOUNDTRACK'         │   │           'FILM'            │
│  Unbalanced equations       │   │  Organic—fuels and foods    │
│  Skeletal formulae          │   │                             │
│  Ionic bonding              │   │  Carboxylic acids           │
│                             │   │  Fats, soaps                │
│                             │   │  Metals and reactivity      │
│                             │   │  Corrosion                  │
│                             │   │  Sulphur                    │
│  Formulae of oxy-anions     │   │  Nitrogen                   │
│                             │   │  Proteins                   │
│  Balanced equations         │   │  Mole                       │
│                             │   │  Salt formation             │
│                             │   │  Plastics                   │
└─────────────────────────────┘   └─────────────────────────────┘
```

Language

Our research has revealed that language problems for pupils lie not so much in the technical words (although these are by no means easy) as in normal English words which change their meaning or have a more precise meaning in science. Words like 'volatile', 'correspond', and 'strong' are more troublesome than 'titrate', 'pipette', or 'alkali' because the pupil already knows what they mean in common parlance and mistakenly assumes that their meaning is unchanged in science. New technical words are being met for the first time and so they have, for the student, only one meaning.

We have tried to take account of this and to explain changes of meaning where we are aware of a possible conflict. In addition we have compiled a glossary of new technical words at the end of each chapter. We have attempted to make the sentence structure simple and so keep the text within the reading age of pupils in the top half of the ability range.

However, we would not care to be accused of teaching in baby language. By offering explanations we hope that we are contributing to the widening and strengthening of the pupil's language.

Revision sections

At the end of each group of chapters we have inserted a revision section. These are not just collections of questions. They have a variety of formats designed to direct the pupil back into the text to consolidate his or her ideas, and to rectify misconceptions. It is recommended that these should be seen as diagnostic aids as well as providing exercise for pupils, and that action should be taken to clear up misunderstandings before the next group of chapters is attempted. The answers to the problems are set out in full at the back of the book so that pupils can see, if they have gone wrong, how to put things right.

Discussion sections

These eleven sections appear under the heading 'Chemistry in Action' and have been introduced at appropriate places in the text. The main text says little about industrial or social chemistry, but this has been balanced by the discussion sections. Chemistry is so often presented as 'cut and dried', whereas in reality chemistry has many unresolved problems—problems of theory, application, and social consequence. We believe young people should be made aware of this and introduced to the means by which decisions are made about chemistry and its application.

Our research has shown quite clearly that telling pupils about problems leaves them largely unmoved and uncommitted in their attitudes towards them. However, when pupils are invited, through structured discussion, to take part in the decision process, considerable impact is made. This is *not* an attempt to brainwash pupils, but to allow them to come to their own informed decisions. There are often no 'right' answers to these problems. This is meant to be an antidote to the way that science is normally taught—as if everything had been handed down on Sinaiatic tablets! We strongly recommend that these discussion sections should be tackled *on the way*, at the appropriate points in the book. Most of them can be done in one period or less and they allow the pupils to apply what they have just learned to realistic situations.

Practical work

In the interests of keeping the book within reasonable bounds, details of practical work have been largely omitted. Details of all experiments can be found in our earlier series *Chemistry Takes Shape* (London: Heinemann Educational Books, 1966; 1970). An appendix listing sources of practical work is to be found at the back of the book (page 255).

Use of bold type

This is particularly important in the organic sections. Our work has shown that pupils tend to concentrate upon the chain in organic molecules and fail to see the 'parts which do the work'—the functional groups. This is understandable in the hydrocarbons section where the chain length is the important thing from the point of view of separation and uses, but for the bulk of organic chemistry the chains are relatively unimportant. We have therefore used bold type to highlight the functional group and to focus attention on it and away from the chain. We have taken the unusual step of highlighting the $-\overset{\displaystyle H}{\underset{\displaystyle H}{\overset{|}{\underset{|}{C}}}}-OH$ part of alcohols and not just the —OH. This then allows us to link the oxidation of alcohols to acids more realistically. The end carbon on the chain becomes the carbon of the carboxyl group because two hydrogen atoms have been removed and replaced by oxygen: $-\overset{\displaystyle O}{\overset{\|}{C}}-OH$. This will also lay a proper foundation for the study of carboxyl compounds at 'H' Grade. This approach may raise problems for nomenclature, but these can be overcome by stressing that the name depends upon the total number of carbon atoms in the longest continuous chain of the molecule.

Revision questions

A companion book, *Testing Your Chemistry* by C. A. Wood (to be published by Heinemann Educational Books in 1981), provides a large number of questions for revision and examination preparation. Sections in this question book fit exactly with the chapters in *Chemistry About Us*.

We hope that you and your pupils will enjoy and profit from this new attempt to present chemistry in a palatable and attractive form.

How to use this book

Since this book contains no details of experiments it is unsuitable as a laboratory bench work-book and is probably most useful as reinforcement for normal class work. It is designed to be used by the individual pupil in that the revision sections will send different pupils back into different parts of the text, depending upon their particular weaknesses.

The 'Chemistry in Action' sections are planned to be used to promote group discussion. What normally passes for 'discussion' in a science lesson is the teacher holding the central position and drawing answers from the class. Each pupil may, however, contribute only a few words (or none at all) and probably not in continuous English.

The discussion sections in the book are designed to allow pupils to have their say in small peer groups. The teacher should not be the central figure, but should act as a catalyst as he moves from group to group. At first sight teachers might feel that the discussion material is too difficult. From our experimental work we have had to conclude that teachers tend to underestimate their pupils' ability to discuss logically and to arrive at sound conclusions.

May we recommend that you allow your pupils to try these exercises without your intervention (unless they enlist your help). We are sure that you will be pleasantly surprised by their response.

1

The building blocks

1.1

Quite early in your study of science you came across the idea that everything in the world is made up of tiny particles, and that these are constantly moving. In a solid the movement is quite small; in a liquid the particles roll over each other; while in gases the particles are moving about rapidly, colliding with each other and with the walls of the container.

This simple picture helped us to explain the differences between the behaviour of solids, liquids, and gases. However, the idea is too simple and leaves many other things unexplained. In this chapter we shall look more closely at these particles to see how they differ from each other. Why are particles of hydrogen different from particles of sulphur? Why do some particles form bigger clusters than others? Why do particles have different sizes and masses? These are some of the questions we shall attempt to answer.

1.2

Before we go much further we shall have to decide upon the meaning of four words which we are going to use often in this chapter. These are

element,   compound,   atom,   and   molecule

You will have met them before but let us refresh your memory of them.

On p. vi you will find a copy of a chart called the **Periodic Table**. On it are listed the names and symbols of about one hundred substances called **elements**. These are the hundred kinds of 'brick' out of which everything in the world is made. On the chart you will notice substances such as hydrogen, oxygen, iron, carbon, sodium, and chlorine, but you will find no mention of sugar or salt, Polythene or petrol, or any of the thousand common materials you could name. The reason for this is quite simple. The particles of sugar are made by joining together particles of carbon, hydrogen, and oxygen in a certain way. Salt particles consist of particles of sodium and chlorine joined together. Polythene and petrol particles are the result of joining carbon particles and hydrogen particles in two different cluster patterns.

1

The basic 'brick' substances are called **elements**, and the materials made by joining together two or more of these elements are called **compounds**. In a way, the elements are like the letters of the alphabet and the compounds are like the words made by combining the letters.

Although there are only about one hundred elements there are millions of compounds, in the same way that twenty-six letters can give us many thousands of words, or thirteen basic notes can give a Beethoven symphony or the song at the top of the charts.

The other two words, atom and molecule, are related to the ideas of element and compound. Each element is made up of one kind of particle called an **atom**, and so there must be about one hundred different kinds of atom.

Atoms can form clusters and these clusters are called **molecules**. If all the atoms in the cluster are the same these are **molecules of elements**, but if the clusters contain atoms of more than one kind these are called **molecules of compounds**.

Figure 1.1 collects all of these ideas together.

There are millions of compounds and so there must be millions of kinds of molecules.

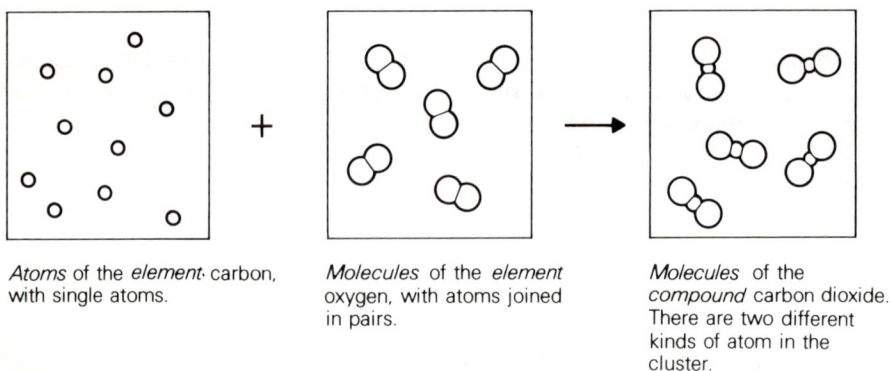

Atoms of the element carbon, with single atoms.

Molecules of the element oxygen, with atoms joined in pairs.

Molecules of the compound carbon dioxide. There are two different kinds of atom in the cluster.

Figure 1.1

1.3

In the next chapter we shall see how atoms join to form molecules, but for the moment we shall look more closely at the atoms themselves.

About a century ago scientists were content to think of atoms as very small spheres. They knew that all the atoms of any one element had about the same mass and that the mass of atoms ranged from the lightest ones of hydrogen to heavy ones (such as uranium) which were more than two hundred times the mass of hydrogen atoms.

In the 1890s a group of physicists began to explore atoms in more detail and found unexpected patterns which helped to explain many of the facts which had puzzled chemists for a long time. They discovered that atoms are made up of even smaller particles and that these particles are built into the atom in a regular way.

These 'sub-atomic particles', as they are called, are the **proton**, the **neutron**, and the **electron**.

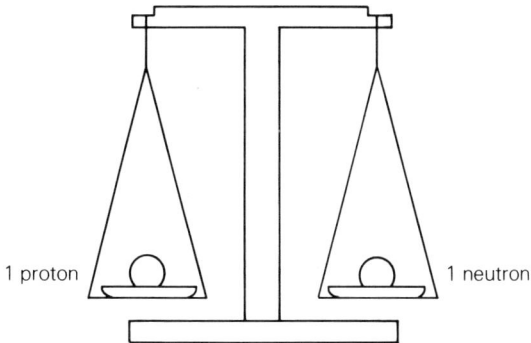

Figure 1.2

Protons and neutrons have almost the same mass (Fig. 1.2), but the protons carry a single positive electrical charge. Neutrons have no charge. Electrons have only a tiny mass compared with protons or neutrons. It needs about 1850 electrons to equal the mass of one proton (Fig. 1.3).

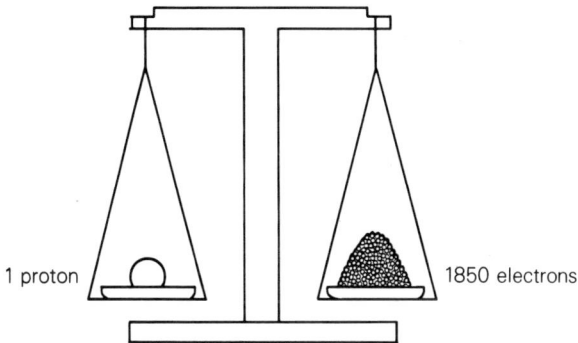

Figure 1.3

Electrons each carry a single negative electrical charge.

The heavier particles sit together in the middle of the atom (the **nucleus**) while the light electrons move round the nucleus and at some distance from it.

Summing up so far

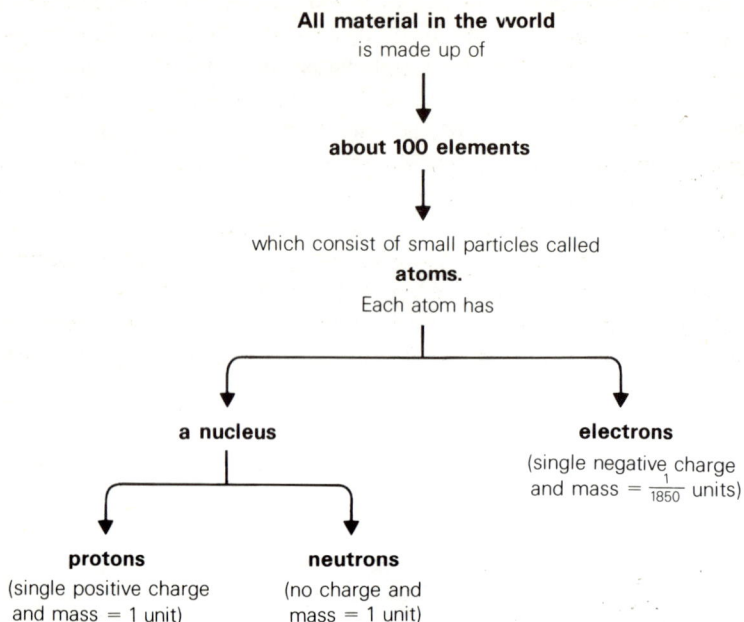

Figure 1.4

It is worth stopping for a moment to think about Fig. 1.4 in another way.

From three basic particles (the proton, neutron, and electron) are made the 100 types of atoms in the natural world. These in turn can be joined in different patterns to give us the molecules which go to make the millions of things we find in the world, from buttons to space ships and from footballs to elephants.

1.4

We are now in a position to understand some of the patterns in the Periodic Table which we looked at earlier. Here is a small section of the Table for you to look at as we try to make sense of it (Fig. 1.5).

1 **H** Hydrogen 1							4 **He** Helium 2
7 **Li** Lithium 3	9 **Be** Beryllium 4	11 **B** Boron 5	12 **C** Carbon 6	14 **N** Nitrogen 7	16 **O** Oxygen 8	19 **F** Fluorine 9	20 **Ne** Neon 10
23 **Na** Sodium 11	24 **Mg** Magnesium 12	27 **Al** Aluminium 13	28 **Si** Silicon 14	31 **P** Phosphorus 15	32 **S** Sulphur 16	35.5 **Cl** Chlorine 17	40 **Ar** Argon 18

Figure 1.5

The first element is hydrogen and you can see that its atoms have a mass nearly equal to one unit. These atoms must, therefore, contain one **proton** (positive charge; mass = 1) balanced electrically by one **electron** (negative charge; mass = 1/1850). This is usually represented by the symbols ^1_1H. The lower number gives the number of protons while the upper number gives the overall mass.

The next element at the top right-hand corner of the Table is helium and we can see that its mass is four units. Its atoms each contain two protons and two electrons to balance the charges. The extra mass is made by adding two neutrons to the nucleus. This would be represented by ^4_2He (two protons and overall mass of four). The mass of the electrons is so tiny that it is ignored.

The element lithium comes next, with three protons and an overall mass of seven units. The extra mass must be made up by four neutrons (Fig. 1.6).

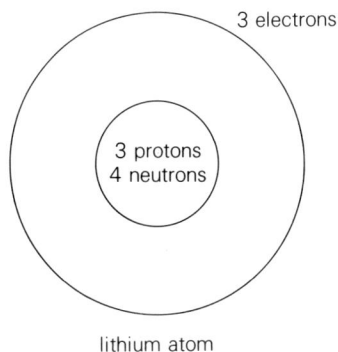

3 electrons

3 protons
4 neutrons

lithium atom

Figure 1.6

We could go on in this way through the whole Table, building up by one proton, one electron, and a few neutrons each time.

To make sure that you have got the idea clearly try the following questions. The answers will be found on p. 7.

1 How many protons, neutrons, and electrons are present in $^{20}_{10}Ne$; $^{31}_{15}P$; $^{56}_{26}Fe$; $^{238}_{92}U$?
2 Using the Periodic Table on p. vi, find the correct answers for the blank spaces in Table 1.1.

Table 1.1

Element	Symbol	Number of protons	Number of electrons	Number of neutrons
Magnesium	$^{24}_{12}Mg$			
		22		26
	64	29		

The number of protons in an atom is usually called the **atomic number.** The total mass of the atom is usually called the **mass number**.

atomic number = number of protons = number of electrons

mass number = number of protons + number of neutrons

(The mass of the electrons is ignored because they are so light.)

number of neutrons = mass number − atomic number

3 Complete Table 1.2 before you finish this chapter.

Table 1.2

Element	Symbol	Atomic number	Mass number	Number of neutrons
Gold	$^{197}_{79}Au$			
Plutonium		94	242	

New words you have met in this chapter

Element	a substance made up of one kind of atom. There are about 100 elements known.
Compound	a substance made up of different elements joined together. There are millions of compounds.
Atoms	the simple particles which make up elements. There are about 100 different kinds of them.
Molecule	a cluster of atoms joined together. If all the atoms in the cluster are the same, the clusters are molecules of elements. If there are different kinds of atom in the cluster, the clusters are molecules of compounds.
Proton	a sub-atomic particle with a single positive electrical charge and a mass of one unit on the atomic scale. It is found in the nucleus of an atom.
Neutron	a sub-atomic particle with no charge and a mass of one unit on the atomic scale. It is found in the nucleus of an atom.
Electron	a sub-atomic particle with a single negative charge and a mass of 1/1850 on the atomic scale. It is found outside the nucleus of an atom.
Atomic number	number of protons or number of electrons in a neutral atom.
Mass number	number of protons plus the number of neutrons in the nucleus of an atom.

1 $^{20}_{10}$Ne has 10 protons, 10 electrons, and 10 neutrons.

   $^{31}_{15}$P has 15 protons, 15 electrons, and 16 neutrons.

   $^{56}_{26}$Fe has 26 protons, 26 electrons, and 30 neutrons.

   $^{238}_{92}$U has 92 protons, 92 electrons, and 146 neutrons.

2

Element	Symbol	Number of protons	Number of electrons	Number of neutrons
Magnesium	$^{24}_{12}$Mg	12	12	12
Titanium	$^{48}_{22}$Ti	22	22	26
Copper	$^{64}_{29}$Cu	29	29	35

3 *The answer to question 3 is on page 12.*

2

Finding space for electrons

2.1

If you rub your hair with a rubber balloon, electrons are transferred from one material to the other. When you move the balloon away from your head your hair is attracted to it and your hair really stands on end. The *opposite* charges on the hair and the rubber *attract* each other (Fig. 2.1).

Figure 2.1

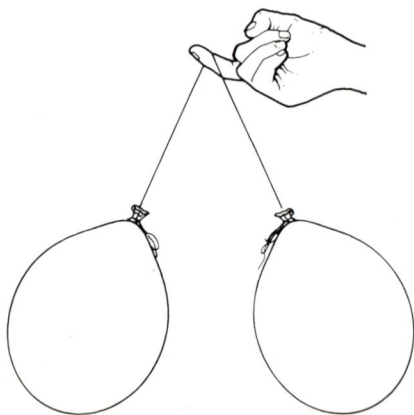

Figure 2.2

If you now take two balloons attached together by a metre of cotton thread and rub them both on your hair they will both have the *same* charge. When you hold the balloons up by the middle of the thread you will see that they stand away from each other (Fig. 2.2) because the *same* charge on each causes *repulsion* between them.

Rules

    Objects with the **opposite** electrical charge **attract** each other.

    Objects with the **same** electrical charge **repel** each other.

These rules must also apply to the positive and negative particles which make up an atom. Protons (positive) must attract the electrons (negative). Electrons must repel each other.

2.2

In the simplest atom (hydrogen) we have one proton and one electron. Since they are of opposite charge they must attract each other. We would therefore expect the proton and the electron to be stuck together, but experimental evidence shows that the electron is moving about and that this movement would tend to carry the electron away from the proton.

What happens is that the attraction of the proton for the electron just balances its moving urge to escape and so the electron is kept moving round the proton but at some distance from it (Fig. 2.3).

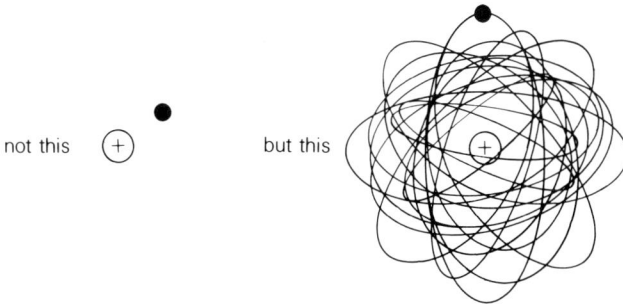

Figure 2.3

When we consider the next kind of atom, helium, we find that there is a nucleus consisting of two protons and two neutrons (held together) with two electrons moving round them (Fig. 2.4).

Scientists do not fully understand why the positive protons stay together in the nucleus, but experiment shows that they do.

The freely moving electrons, however, tend to repel each other because of their negative charge; but even they, under certain conditions, can overcome this repulsion and form pairs. (They *cannot* form groups of three or more.)

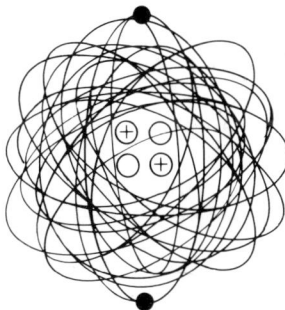

Figure 2.4

2.3

In atoms with many electrons there could soon be overcrowding of electrons round the nucleus with a great deal of repulsion between them. To avoid this, the electrons fit round the nucleus in layers (or **shells**).

Each layer has limited space for electrons. The layer nearest the nucleus can take only two electrons, the next can accept eight, the next can take 18, and so on.

2.4

Turn back to the Periodic Table and let us see how these rules begin to apply.

In hydrogen there is only one electron and it will take its place in the layer nearest the nucleus. This is represented as 1). Helium, with its two electrons to fit in, can find space for them in the same inner layer. This is represented as 2). Lithium has to make room for three electrons and so one of these must be placed in the next layer because the innermost layer is full. This is represented as 2)1. As we go across the Periodic Table from lithium to fluorine and neon we are filling up the eight spaces in the second layer. Carbon must have its six electrons arranged as 2)4, fluorine must have its nine electrons arranged 2)7, and neon completes the layer at 2)8.

At sodium we must begin another new layer because the inner two layers are full. We have eleven electrons to get in as 2)8)1. The filling continues to argon, whose 18 electrons will be arranged as 2)8)8.

Summing up so far

Table 2.1

H 1)							He 2)
Li 2)1	Be 2)2	B 2)3	C 2)4	N 2)5	O 2)6	F 2)7	Ne 2)8
Na 2)8)1	Mg 2)8)2	Al 2)8)3	Si 2)8)4	P 2)8\5	S 2)8)6	Cl 2)8)7	Ar 2)8)8

2.5

In Section 2.3 it was mentioned that the third layer could hold 18 electrons and so far we have filled in only 8 electrons—as far as argon. Where are the other 10?

When any layer is the outside layer it can only take 8 electrons, but when a new layer outside it starts to fill, it is no longer the outer layer and can then fill in the remainder of its quota of electrons.

Go back to the Periodic Table and follow this passage.

Potassium is the beginning of the fourth layer and its 19 electrons are arranged 2)8)8)1. Calcium is 2)8)8)2. Then from scandium to zinc there are ten elements in which the extra ten spaces in the third layer are progressively filled while the outer layer remains with two electrons.

Scandium is 2)8)9)2 and zinc is 2)8)18)2—the third layer is now full.

By the time we get to krypton the fourth layer has filled to eight electrons; krypton is 2)8)18)8.

Similar patterns follow for all of the other elements in the Table. We have now gone far enough to see the orderly and tidy way the electrons fit into atoms. These **electronic arrangements** (or **configurations**) are shown in detail in Table 2.1 for elements 1 to 18.

2.6

Before we leave this section on atomic structure there is one other matter which must be cleared up. In each box in the Periodic Table the atomic number (bottom left-hand number) is always a whole number corresponding to the number of protons in the atoms of each element. The other number at the top of each box is, in most cases, nearly a whole number, but not quite. The number for fluorine is 18.998, for bromine it is 79.909, and for uranium 238.030. This number is *not* the **mass number** (p. 6), but is called the **atomic mass**.

Although all atoms of the same element have the same number of protons (and electrons), they do not all have the same number of neutrons. For example, most chlorine atoms are $^{35}_{17}Cl$, that is, they have 17 protons, 17 electrons, and *18 neutrons*. But some chlorine atoms are a little heavier, $^{37}_{17}Cl$. They still have 17 protons and 17 electrons, but they have *20 neutrons*. In a sample of chlorine gas there are about three times as many $^{37}_{17}Cl$ atoms as there are $^{37}_{17}Cl$ atoms and so the *average* mass of chlorine atoms is

$$\frac{(3 \times 35) + (1 \times 37)}{4} = 35.5$$

These atoms of the *same element* which differ only in mass (that is, in the number of neutrons) are called **isotopes**. You may have come across this name in connection with radioactivity, but most isotopes are not radioactive.

At this stage we suggest that you attempt questions 1, 2, and 3 in the revision section on p. 24. The answers will be found on p. 239.

New words you have met in this chapter

Shells — the layers into which electrons fit in an atom. The one closest to the nucleus has room for 2 electrons, the next can take 8, and the third can take a maximum of 18, although to start with it is quite stable with 8.

Electronic configurations — the arrangements of electrons in the shells round an atom. For example, the electronic configuration for chlorine ($^{35}_{17}Cl$) is 2)8)7.

Atomic mass (or atomic weight) — the average mass of an atom of a given element. The atoms of an element do not all have the same mass (see **isotopes**). The unit in which these masses are measured is related to the mass of the isotope $^{12}_{6}C$ which is taken to have a mass of exactly 12 units.

Isotopes — atoms of the same element having the same number of protons but having different numbers of neutrons. Or in other words, isotopes have the same atomic number but different mass numbers. For example, $^{12}_{6}C$ has 6 protons and 6 neutrons while $^{14}_{6}C$ has 6 protons and 8 neutrons. They are still atoms of the element carbon.

Answer to question 3 on page 6.

Element	Symbol	Atomic number	Mass number	Number of neutrons
Gold	$^{197}_{79}Au$	79	197	118
Plutonium	$^{242}_{94}Pu$	94	242	148

3

From atoms to molecules

3.1

We are now almost in a position to understand how atoms join together to form molecules. Before we tackle this, here is an experiment you can do in your imagination. Let us concentrate on one of the electron layers (shells) in an atom and think about how these electrons might position themselves.

If we have only one electron it can probably wander anywhere within the layer. Two electrons in the same layer will tend to keep as far apart as possible on opposite sides of the nucleus (Fig. 3.1).

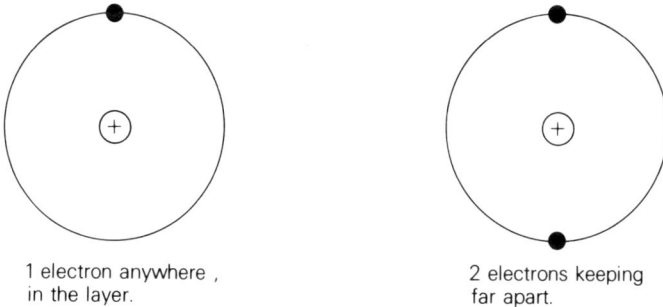

1 electron anywhere, in the layer.

2 electrons keeping far apart.

Figure 3.1

How will three electrons in the same layer arrange themselves to keep as far apart as possible? They will tend to be at the corners of a regular triangle (Fig. 3.2).

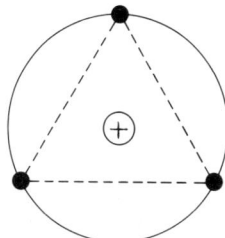

Figure 3.2

13

What if there are four electrons to be fitted into the same shell? If you use the tip of the thumb and forefinger of one hand to represent two electrons and do the same with the other hand to represent the other two how will they arrange themselves to be as far apart as possible (Fig. 3.3)?

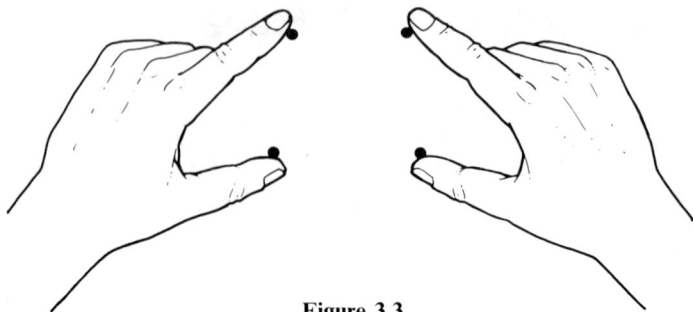

Figure 3.3

They will give us one electron at each corner of a regular tetrahedron (Fig. 3.4).

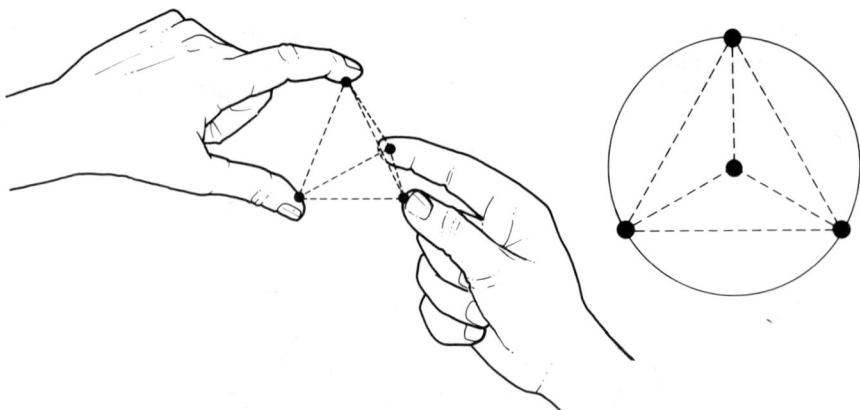

Figure 3.4

Electrons are constantly on the move and so we can never be sure exactly where they are. These geometrical figures are probably a bit *too* exact. It would be fairer to smudge the lines a bit and to say that there is a good chance of finding the electrons somewhere in these cloudy regions (Fig. 3.5).

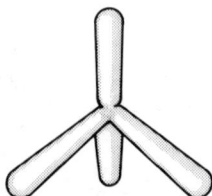

Figure 3.5

What happens when we have five electrons to fit in? We could find another geometrical shape, but what actually happens is that two electrons are prepared to pair up with each other. The five electrons form one pair, completely occupying one of the 'cloudy' regions in Fig. 3.6, and the other three spread out, one to each of the three remaining 'clouds'.

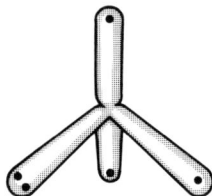

Figure 3.6

In the six-electron case we get two pairs and two singles; and in the seven-electron case we find three pairs and one single. The eight-electron case makes all the four 'clouds' full.

3.2

This ability of two electrons to share a 'cloud' is the basic reason for atoms joining to form molecules.

If we think of two chlorine atoms side by side, each has the electronic arrangement 2)8)7. Only the electrons on the outer layer are involved in the joining process.

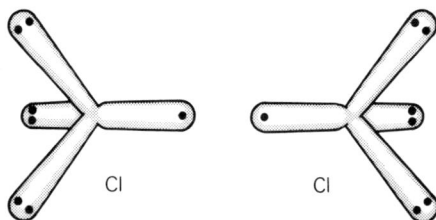

Figure 3.7

The seven outer electrons are arranged as three pairs and one single electron (Fig. 3.7). If the single electron in one atom shares a 'cloud' with the single electron in the other atom we end up with all of the electron 'clouds' fully occupied and the two atoms have been joined into a molecule (Fig. 3.8).

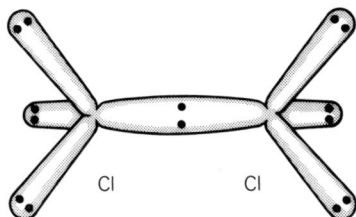

Figure 3.8

Do not think of these 'clouds' as solid objects. They are only volumes in space where the electrons are most likely to be. They are only a way of saying that we cannot be sure exactly where electrons are at any one time.

If at 10 o'clock on a Tuesday morning someone were to ask your mother where you were, she would probably not be able to say that you would be in the third seat from the left in the second row in Maths Room 3. She would probably say that you were at school and, for all practical purposes, that would be good enough. In the same way we say that electrons are probably within the cloud but we never know exactly where.

Returning to our chlorine molecule, we might ask how two electrons sharing a cloud between the nuclei hold the atoms together. We must remember that the nuclei are positively charged and would tend to repel each other. However, a pair of negative electrons situated between them would provide an 'electrical glue' to hold them together (Fig. 3.9).

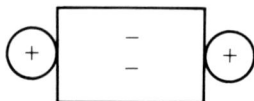

Figure 3.9

In the case of oxygen we have six outer electrons—two pairs and two singles (Fig. 3.10).

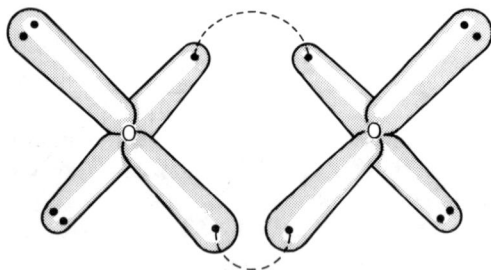

Figure 3.10

They could combine well by sharing two pairs of electrons (Fig. 3.11).

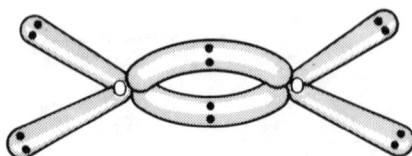

Figure 3.11

Nitrogen has five outer electrons with one pair and three singles. The combination of two nitrogen atoms would be as shown in Fig. 3.12.

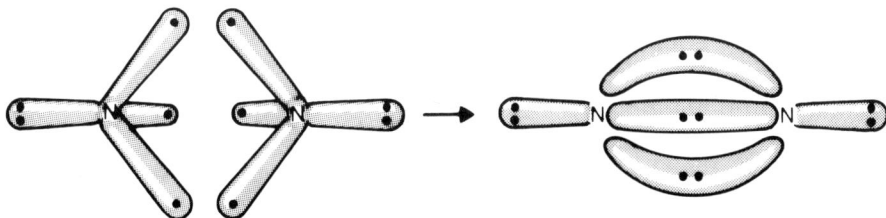

Figure 3.12

It would be a nuisance to draw these clouds all the time and so a shortened version has been introduced. A single straight line is taken to stand for a pair of shared electrons or, as it is more commonly called, a **chemical bond**.

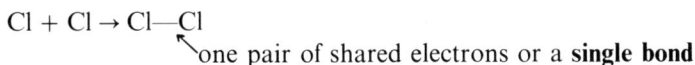

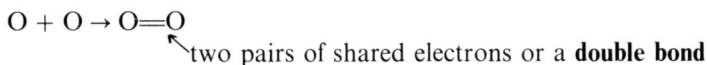

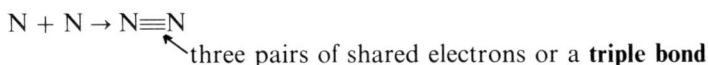

$$Cl + Cl \rightarrow Cl\text{---}Cl$$

↖one pair of shared electrons or a **single bond**

$$O + O \rightarrow O\text{=}O$$

↖two pairs of shared electrons or a **double bond**

$$N + N \rightarrow N\text{≡}N$$

↖three pairs of shared electrons or a **triple bond**

3.3

So far we have examined the combination of identical atoms to give molecules of elements. Most molecules are those of compounds in which *different* kinds of atoms are joined. Are there any simple rules for this combination?

We shall work out a few examples in detail and then look for a short cut to speed up the process.

A hydrogen atom has only one electron in the innermost layer, in which there is room for two electrons. A chlorine atom has seven electrons in its outer shell, leaving room for one electron. When these two atoms meet they can share their 'single' electrons to form a bond (Fig. 3.13).

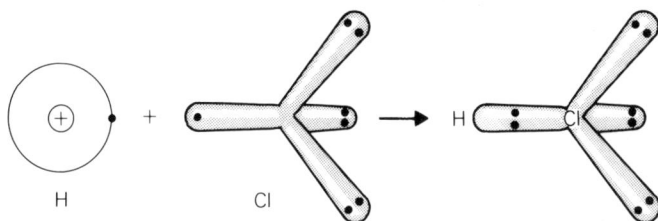

Figure 3.13

In this case, *one* atom of hydrogen exactly 'satisfies' *one* atom of chlorine. When an oxygen atom meets a hydrogen atom we might get the arrangement shown in Fig. 3.14.

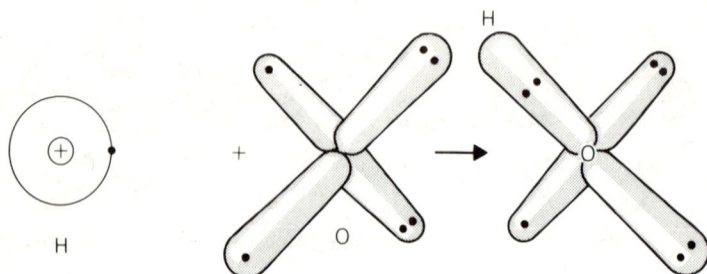

Figure 3.14

But this is incomplete because the oxygen still has room for one more electron. This could be supplied by another hydrogen atom, which would give us the situation shown in Fig. 3.15.

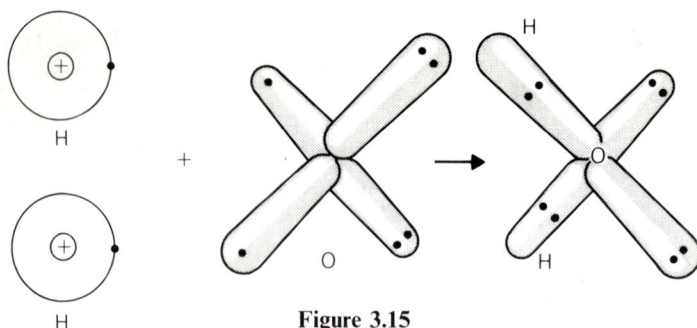

Figure 3.15

To 'satisfy' *one* oxygen atom *two* hydrogen atoms are required to make a molecule of hydrogen oxide (water) or H_2O. This method of writing a chemical substance in symbols is called a **formula**. Numbers written below the line refer to the number of atoms of the element *in front of* the number.

By a similar method we could show that when nitrogen and hydrogen combine, *three* hydrogen atoms are required for each nitrogen atom.

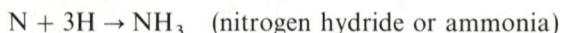

$$N + 3H \rightarrow NH_3 \quad \text{(nitrogen hydride or ammonia)}$$

When carbon and hydrogen combine, four hydrogen atoms are required for each carbon atom because carbon atoms have four single electrons on their outer layer which can pair up with four hydrogen atoms.

$$C + 4H \rightarrow CH_4 \quad \text{(methane)}$$

Let us take one last example before we look back for a pattern which will simplify our reasoning. You will have heard of the gas, carbon *dioxide*. Its name suggests that there are two oxygen atoms for each carbon atom (Fig. 3.16).

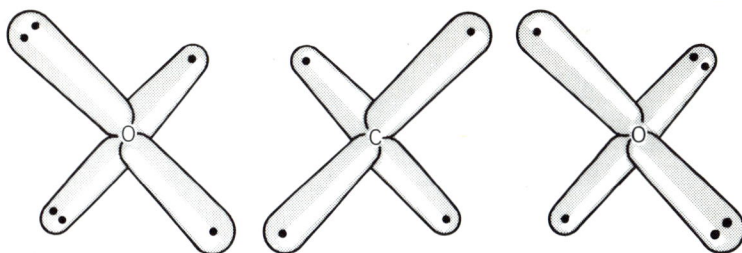

Figure 3.16

Each oxygen atom has two single electrons able to share with the four single electrons in the carbon (Fig. 3.17).

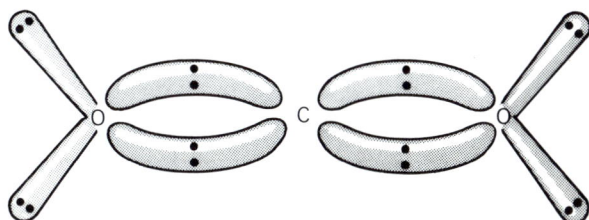

Figure 3.17

Written in the shortened version this gives us O=C=O with the carbon atom forming a **double bond** (sharing 4 electrons) with each oxygen atom.

3.4

If we now look back over the examples in Section 3.3 you will be able to see that hydrogen, with its one single electron, always forms one bond.

Oxygen, with its *two single* electrons, forms *two* bonds.

Nitrogen, with its *three single* electrons, forms *three* bonds.

Carbon, with its *four single* electrons, forms *four* bonds.

Any combination between elements to form compounds must depend upon the number of bonds which each can make. Representing the bonds by straight lines we have

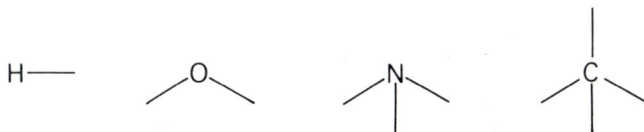

These bonds will stick out in space depending upon the position of the single electrons on the outer layer of each atom.

The one electron on hydrogen can point in any direction. The two single electrons on oxygen will form bonds sticking out at an angle to each other, because oxygen atoms also have two pairs of electrons in the outside layer to make room for (Fig. 3.18).

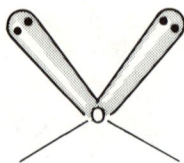

Figure 3.18

In nitrogen the bonds will be arranged like the legs of a tripod, leaving room for the other electron pair cloud. Sometimes wedge shapes are used to show the bonds sticking out from or into the page.

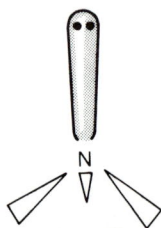

Figure 3.19

In carbon the four bonds will point to the corners of a regular tetrahedron (Fig. 3.20).

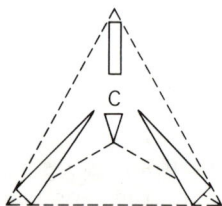

Figure 3.20

3.5

Go back to the Periodic Table (p. vi) and look down each of the long columns. You will notice that the number of electrons on the outside layer of all the elements in one column is the same. For example, in the column beginning with hydrogen, all the elements have one electron on their outside layer. This means that all of these will be able to form one bond with other elements. In column 2 (beginning with beryllium) all of the elements have two single electrons on the outside layer and so all of them can make two bonds with other elements. In column 3 (beginning with boron) every element will be able to make three bonds and in column 4 (beginning with carbon) they will all be able to make four bonds.

Summing up so far

The column number (1–4) in the Periodic Table tells us the number of bonds an element can make.

When we come to column 5 (nitrogen) we have atoms with five electrons. These are arranged as one pair and *three singles* and so elements in this column usually make *three single bonds*.

In column 6 (oxygen) we have atoms with six electrons arranged as two pairs and *two singles* and so elements in this column usually make *two bonds*.

Column 7 (fluorine) contains elements making *one* bond and column 8 contains elements which usually make no bonds and these are mainly unreactive elements.

For columns 5 to 8 the number of electrons free to make bonds is eight *minus* the column number (Fig. 3.21).

1	2			3	4	3	2	1	0
		Special cases, but most form at least 2 bonds				$8-5$ $=3$	$8-6$ $=2$	$8-7$ $=1$	$8-8$ $=0$

Figure 3.21

3.6

We can now use the Periodic Table to simplify our work in deciding the most likely combining patterns between elements. If we know the column numbers of the two elements, we know the number of bonds they usually form. By linking these bonds together we can find out how many atoms of one element 'satisfy' an atom of the other.

Here are some examples. It does not matter if you have never heard of the elements before, the rules still apply.

(a) **Phosphorus chloride**

Phosphorus (P) is in column 5 and so it can make $8 - 5 = 3$ bonds
Chlorine (Cl) is in column 7 and so it can make $8 - 7 = 1$ bond

Three chlorine atoms will be needed for one phosphorus atom, giving

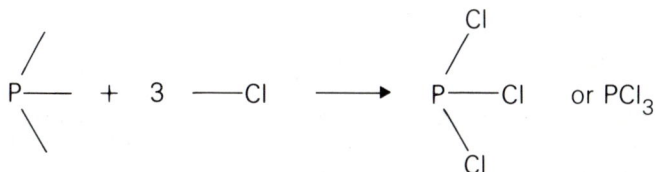

P— + 3 —Cl $\longrightarrow$ Cl–P—Cl or PCl_3
                                          |
                                          Cl

Remember that the little number tells how many atoms there are of the element *in front of it*. This group of symbols representing a molecule is called a **formula**.

(b) **Silicon fluoride**

Silicon (Si) — 4 bonds
Fluorine (F) — 1 bond

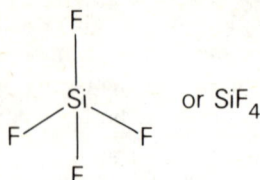

$$\begin{array}{c} F \\ | \\ F - Si - F \\ | \\ F \end{array} \quad \text{or SiF}_4$$

(c) **Aluminium oxide**

Aluminium (Al) — 3 bonds
Oxygen (O) — 2 bonds

This is a little more difficult. Two Al atoms can make six bonds and three O atoms can make six bonds. This gives

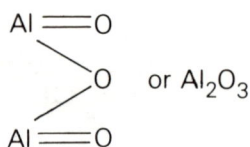

$$\begin{array}{c} Al = O \\ \diagdown \\ O \quad \text{or Al}_2O_3 \\ \diagup \\ Al = O \end{array}$$

(d) **Beryllium chloride**

Beryllium (Be) — 2 bonds
Chlorine (Cl) — 1 bond

This gives $BeCl_2$.

(e) **Magnesium nitride**

Magnesium (Mg) — 2 bonds
Nitrogen (N) — 3 bonds

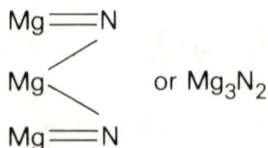

$$\begin{array}{c} Mg = N \\ \diagup \\ Mg \quad \text{or Mg}_3N_2 \\ \diagdown \\ Mg = N \end{array}$$

Notice that the names of compounds with two elements in them end with the letters **-ide**.

The number of bonds which an element can form is sometimes known as its **valency**. Thus elements in column 1 and column 7 would be called **monovalent**, those in columns 2 and 6 would be **divalent**, those in columns 3 and 5 would be **trivalent**, and those in column 4 **tetravalent**.

In this chapter we have seen that bonds between atoms are a result of sharing a pair of electrons and this is true for the vast majority of compounds.

New words you have met in this chapter

A chemical bond   the sharing of a pair of electrons between two atoms. There can be single, double, or triple bonds.

Formula   a group of chemical symbols which represent a molecule. Small numbers in formulae refer to the number of atoms of the kind *just before the symbol*.

H_2SO_4 would mean two atoms of hydrogen, one atom of sulphur, and four atoms of oxygen joined together.

Ending -ide   the names of compounds containing *two* kinds of elements often end in **-ide**.

Valency   the valency of an element is the number of bonds which one of its atoms can make.

Answers to this section will be found on page 239.

1 Divide the following substances under the two headings 'elements' and 'compounds'.

iron, starch, Nylon, petrol, tin, lead, Terylene, sulphur, silver, salt, water, alcohol, methane.

Use the Periodic Table to help you.

2 From the diagrams below select the ones which represent molecules of compounds.

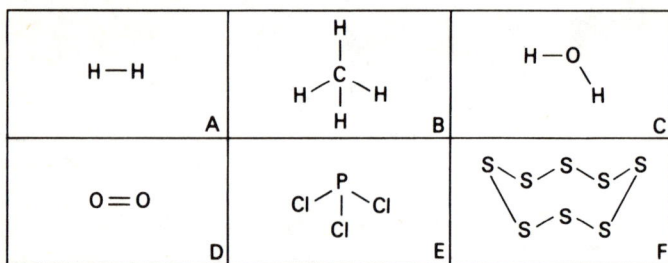

H—H
 	
 A
	H
	|
	H—C—H
	|
	H
	 B
		H—O
		    \\
		      H
		 C

O=O D	P Cl—|—Cl Cl E	S–S–S–S–S S–S–S F

3 (a) Select from boxes A–L the atoms which are isotopes of the atom in box A.

(b) Select from the boxes atoms with 20 neutrons.

(c) Select from the boxes atoms with more than 90 electrons.

(d) Select the atoms which have an equal number of protons, electrons and neutrons.

234 **U** 92 A	39 **K** 19 B	234 **Pa** 91 C	14 **N** 7 D
56 **Fe** 26 E	108 **Ag** 47 F	24 **Mg** 12 G	37 **Cl** 17 H
234 **Th** 90 I	238 **V** 92 J	40 **Ca** 20 K	32 **S** 16 L

4 What will be the electron arrangement in an atom with 12 electrons? What will be the arrangement in another atom with 19 electrons?

5 With the help of the Periodic Table, work out the formulae for the following compounds.

    (a) carbon sulphide   (b) germanium oxide   (c) sodium selenide

    (d) lithium iodide   (e) strontium bromide (f) magnesium nitride

    (g) caesium oxide   (h) silicon hydride

What shape would you expect for the molecule in (a) and that in (h)?

Exploring the Periodic Table

Below you will see a Periodic Table with most of the first eighty-six elements. Each element has a date shown above it. This is the date when a chemist first succeeded in obtaining a fairly pure sample of the element.

Of course, some elements have been known to man for thousands of years and so we do not know for sure when they were discovered. These eleven elements have been marked with a star. One or two of the eleven were used in mixtures. For example, copper and tin mixtures are known as bronze.

A – very common in the world
B – common in the world
C – fairly rare in the world
D – very rare in the world
* – known for several thousand years

1766 **H** 1 A																	1895 **He** 2 D
1817 **Li** 3 C	1828 **Be** 4 C											1808 **B** 5 C	* **C** 6 B	1772 **N** 7 B	1772 **O** 8 B	1771 **F** 9 B	1898 **Ne** 10 D
1807 **Na** 11 A	1808 **Mg** 12 A											1825 **Al** 13 A	1823 **Si** 14 C	1669 **P** 15 B	* **S** 16 B	1774 **Cl** 17 B	1894 **Ar** 18 C
1807 **K** 19 A	1808 **Ca** 20 A	1876 **Sc** 21 C	1791 **Ti** 22 A	1830 **V** 23 B	1798 **Cr** 24 B	1774 **Mn** 25 B	* **Fe** 26 A	1735 **Co** 27 C	1751 **Ni** 28 B	* **Cu** 29 B	* **Zn** 30 B	1875 **Ga** 31 C	1886 **Ge** 32 C	1649 **As** 33 C	1817 **Se** 34 C	1826 **Br** 35 C	1898 **Kr** 36 D
1861 **Rb** 37 C	1808 **Sr** 38 B	1843 **Y** 39 C	1789 **Zr** 40 B	1801 **Nb** 41 C	1782 **Mo** 42 C	1937 **Tc** 43	1844 **Ru** 44 D	1803 **Rh** 45 D	1803 **Pd** 46 D	* **Ag** 47 D	1817 **Cd** 48 C	1863 **In** 49 C	* **Sn** 50 B	1450 **Sb** 51 C	1782 **Te** 52 D	1811 **I** 53 D	1898 **Xe** 54 D
1860 **Cs** 55 C	1808 **Ba** 56 B	1839 **La** 57 C	1922 **Hf** 72 C	1802 **Ta** 73 C	1783 **W** 74 C	1925 **Re** 75 D	1803 **Os** 76 D	1803 **Ir** 77 D	* **Pt** 78 C	* **Au** 79 D	1861 **Hg** 80 D	1861 **Tl** 81 C	* **Pb** 82 B	1450 **Bi** 83 D	1898 **Po** 84 D	1940 **At** 85 D	1900 **Rn** 86 D

Here are some questions for you to discuss. This is best done if you **form a group** with two or three from your class. When you agree on an answer, one of the group can write it down.

1 In 1869, a Russian chemist called Mendeleev hit upon the idea of the Periodic Table. In his first table, how many elements would he have had?

2 List all the elements which you know are gases at room temperature. In general, where do these elements lie in the Periodic Table? Write down the date of discovery of each. Can you see any pattern in these dates?

3 List all the elements, the symbols of which begin with 'C'. Suggest a symbol for an imaginary element, called 'Caledonium'. Make sure that your new symbol is not already being used for another element.

4 Can you name the metal in each of the following substances?
stannic fluoride; ferrous sulphide; strontianite; wolframite; argentite.
You may find the symbols helpful.

5 The following elements occur in large amounts in the sea:
  hydrogen and oxygen (making up the water), carbon, sodium, magnesium,
  sulphur, chlorine, potassium, calcium, and bromine.
  Can you suggest *why* these elements are present in the sea, while elements like
  iron, lead, aluminium, and phosphorus are not?

6 The Romans did not discover sodium, magnesium, or potassium. List the
  metals which they would have known. In what way do the metals on your list
  differ from sodium, magnesium, and potassium?

7 Look for element 22. It is very common, but you may never have seen a piece
  of it. It is grey, shiny, hard, very strong, and very light for its size. Have a
  few guesses why the metal is not used in large quantities. You might like to
  find out more about this metal from other books.

8 Do you know what elements are used for? Try to list one use for each of
  the elements whose numbers are listed below:

  7, 8, 10, 13, 15, 17, 20, 25, 50, 74, 82.

  You may need help from books or from your teacher.

4

Carbon at the centre

In a play some of the characters have a larger part than others; in a song some notes are used more often than others. In chemistry some elements are used much more often than others in making compounds.

The element which appears in most compounds is carbon. One of the reasons for this is that carbon atoms can join not only with atoms of different elements, but with other carbon atoms.

4.1 Linking atoms of carbon

Two of the ways in which carbon atoms can join with one another are shown in Fig. 4.1.

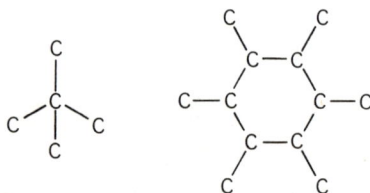

Figure 4.1

These two arrangements form two quite different substances. One of them you will have heard of, but the other is less well-known although it is as close to you as the tip of your pencil! The two forms of carbon are called diamond and graphite.

The diamond structure

Try to think what the lines in the diamond structure represent. Carbon is in column 4 of the Periodic Table and each carbon atom, therefore, has four electrons which are available to make bonds. Each atom can link with four other carbon atoms (Fig. 4.2).

Each bond is composed of one pair of shared electrons—one electron coming from each of the carbon atoms it links together.

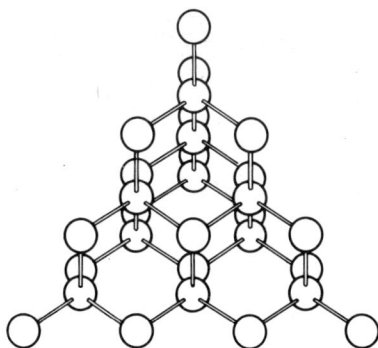

Figure 4.2

These four pairs of shared electrons form a tetrahedral structure in space, as was explained in Chapter 3 and if you look at Fig. 4.2, or better still, build a model in class, you will see tetrahedra over and over again in this structure.

Each carbon atom, except those on the surface of the crystal, is joined by single bonds to four other carbon atoms.

This is the arrangement of carbon atoms which is present in diamond, a transparent, glittering, hard substance with a high melting point. It is the hardest substance which has been found in the Earth's crust. This is not surprising since it is made up of many millions of carbon atoms joined together in the form of tetrahedra to make a structure which is rigid and strong in all directions.

The graphite structure

Here the carbon atoms are arranged in parallel layers or planes like floors in a block of flats. The atoms in each plane are linked to three other carbon atoms (not four as in diamond) to give layers made up, like a honeycomb, in groups of six carbon atoms.

You will see in Fig. 4.3 how a six-sided ring (hexagon) structure can be formed from three simpler units. Each hexagon is surrounded by six other hexagons in the same layer.

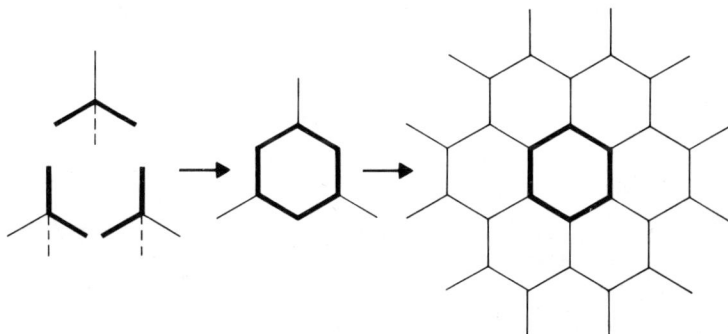

Figure 4.3

Each line in the diagram represents one pair of shared electrons, or one bond. Only three of the four electrons which are available for bonding in each carbon atom are used to make bonds. This means that each carbon atom has one electron near it which is not being used for bonding atoms together. In a lump of graphite, therefore, there will be many millions of these electrons which are free to move about. If these electrons can be made to move in one direction we will have an electric current. Graphite can therefore be a conductor of electricity. Diamond, which has all its electrons involved in making bonds, is an electrical insulator.

Graphite is a black, glossy, slippery, and fairly soft solid; quite clearly a different substance from diamond, although both are made entirely of carbon atoms. The 'lead' in your pencil is mainly graphite; you certainly will not write with a diamond!

Diamond and graphite are said to be **polymorphs** of carbon, that is, they are carbon in different shapes (poly = many; morph = shape).

Carbon can also combine with other elements. It has, for example, a strong 'attraction' for oxygen, as we shall see in the next section.

4.2 Carbon and its oxides

When chemical reactions take place they are accompanied by changes in heat energy. Either heat energy is released and the temperature rises, or heat energy is absorbed.

When carbon burns in a plentiful supply of oxygen, heat energy is released and the oxide of carbon, called carbon dioxide, is formed (Fig. 4.4). This is the reaction which takes place in a coal fire. Coal is mainly carbon.

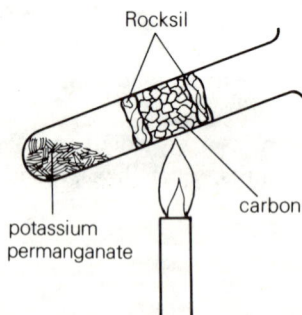

Figure 4.4

We can sum up this reaction in the following way, in what is called a **chemical equation**.

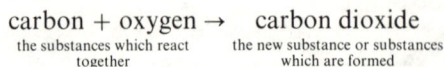

carbon + oxygen → carbon dioxide

the substances which react together   the new substance or substances which are formed

Carbon dioxide is invisible but it can be detected easily. If some of the gas is collected and shaken up with clear lime water (calcium hydroxide solution) a distinct cloudiness or chalkiness appears. This is a simple test to prove the presence of carbon dioxide gas.

If there is a shortage of oxygen when carbon is being burnt, there is a possibility that another oxide of carbon will also be made. This is called carbon *monoxide* and it is a very poisonous gas. It has been responsible for many accidental deaths and it is all the more dangerous because it has no smell.

However, if more oxygen is available later, carbon monoxide can be made to combine with it to form carbon dioxide.

$$\text{carbon monoxide} + \text{oxygen} \rightarrow \text{carbon dioxide}$$

One of the commonest ways of doing this is to burn the gas in oxygen. Carbon monoxide often occurs in coke fires and it burns with a blue flame at the surface, where more air (and therefore oxygen) is available. You may have seen this effect above a workman's fire.

Despite its poisonous nature, carbon monoxide is very useful. Because it is short of oxygen it will take oxygen away from other substances such as metal oxides (ores).

$$\text{metal oxide} + \text{carbon monoxide} \rightarrow \text{metal} + \text{carbon dioxide}$$

This is the way in which iron is extracted from its ore, iron oxide.

When a metal oxide is changed in this way it is said to have been **reduced**. The carbon monoxide is a **reducing agent**.

Electrons in reserve

It is fairly easy to work out that in carbon dioxide, $O{=}C{=}O$, carbon shows its usual valency of four and oxygen has valency two.

The bonding in carbon monoxide, however, is less easy to understand. Only two of the four bonding electrons in each carbon atom are used in this case. The unused pair of electrons remains in reserve and is ready to form a bond with oxygen if some becomes available later. This makes carbon monoxide a good reducing agent, that is, a substance which will take oxygen from other substances.

Carbon monoxide as a fuel

Gases which burn are often used as fuels. Two common fuels are called water gas and producer gas and both contain some carbon monoxide.

Water gas   When *steam* is passed through hot coke (carbon), water gas is formed. In the laboratory it can be made on a small scale as shown in Fig. 4.5.

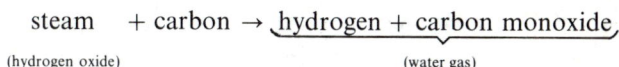

$$\text{steam} + \text{carbon} \rightarrow \underline{\text{hydrogen} + \text{carbon monoxide}}$$
(hydrogen oxide)   (water gas)

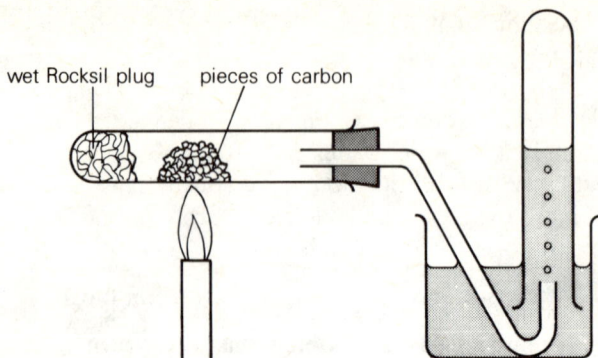

Figure 4.5

Producer gas This is a different mixture. It is formed when *air* is passed through hot coke and is a mixture of nitrogen and carbon monoxide.

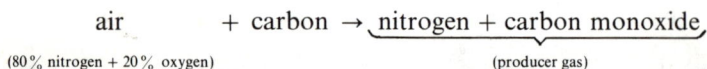

$$\underset{\text{(80\% nitrogen + 20\% oxygen)}}{\text{air}} + \text{carbon} \rightarrow \underset{\text{(producer gas)}}{\underbrace{\text{nitrogen + carbon monoxide}}}$$

In water gas both gases in the mixture are flammable, whereas in producer gas only the carbon monoxide can burn, that is only the carbon monoxide can combine with oxygen and give out heat.

4.3 Chains and rings

A carbon atom has four electrons which can be used to form bonds with other atoms. Each of the two atoms joined by one bond gives one electron to the shared pair.

If a carbon atom is joined to hydrogen atoms only, the molecule formed is called a **hydrocarbon**. Figure 4.6 shows the molecule of the simplest hydrocarbon, which is called methane. We first mentioned this structure in Chapter 3.

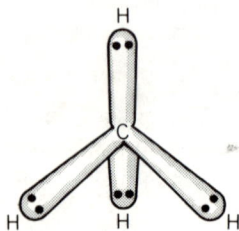

Figure 4.6

Usually this three-dimensional, tetrahedral molecule is represented by flattening it on to the page as shown below. Each line indicates one bond, that is one pair of shared electrons. The carbon atom forms four bonds and each hydrogen atom forms one bond.

Many more hydrocarbon molecules are known because carbon atoms can combine with one another to form chains—a trick which few other elements can do at all and none nearly as well as carbon.

There can be many hundred of carbon atoms in some chains.

It is possible for the ends of a chain to join (like a snake biting its tail) and form a ring.

Once again it is more convenient to flatten out the three-dimensional structure. Chains of carbon atoms are usually represented as while rings, which commonly contain six carbon atoms joined together, are represented as

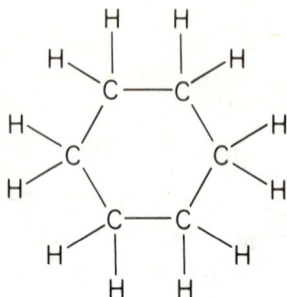

The ability of carbon atoms to join together to form chains and rings is the main reason for there being so many carbon-containing compounds in the world. Even the number of hydrocarbons is huge—and they involve only the elements carbon and hydrogen!

Carbon forms more compounds than do all the other elements added together. Most carbon-containing compounds are referred to as **organic** compounds.

If the remaining bonding electrons in the carbon atoms form bonds with hydrogen atoms, a large number of hydrocarbons can be formed, each with a different chain length. Some of the simplest ones are shown below.

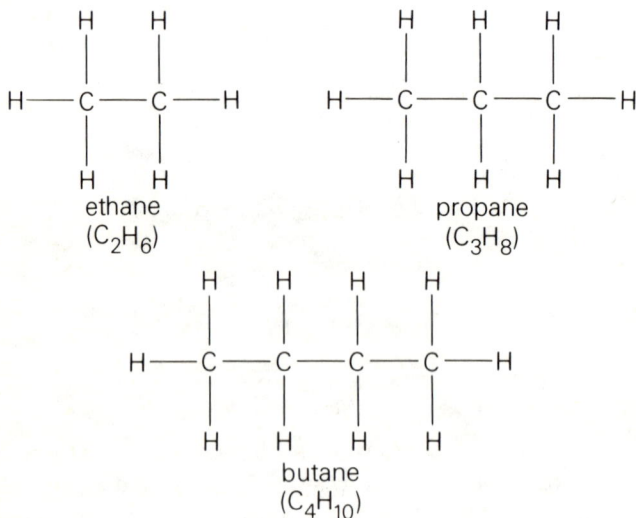

Can you suggest what the formula of the next member of the series might be?

About sixty members of this series are known and in all of these each carbon atom forms four bonds while each hydrogen atom forms one. All have a similar chemical behaviour and together they form a 'family' of compounds known as a **homologous series** (*homologous* = same name).

The four simplest members of the series are called meth*ane* (CH_4), eth*ane* (C_2H_6), prop*ane* (C_3H_8), and but*ane* (C_4H_{10}). They have fairly simple molecules and all are gases. 'Calor' or 'Rural' gas (which you may have used on a camping holiday) is mainly butane with a small amount of propane.

The molecules of the next half-dozen members in the series are more complicated. These compounds have a higher boiling point and are liquid at room temperature. There is probably a sample of hex*ane* in your laboratory. Oct*ane* is one of the components of petrol.

Compounds high in the series, with even larger molecules, are waxy solids like candle wax. They have an even higher boiling point.

This particular homologous series is called the **alkanes** and the name of each compound in the series ends in **-ane**.

There are many other homologous series of compounds in chemistry. Each series has a general formula from which the formula of any member of the series can be worked out. The general formula for the alkane series is C_nH_{2n+2}. The letter 'n' gives the position of the hydrocarbon in the series. For instance, the third member of the series, propane, will have the formula C_3H_{6+2}, that is C_3H_8. The sixth member, *hexane*, will have the formula C_6H_{12+2} or C_6H_{14}.

All the alkanes are fuels. Methane is the main constituent of the natural gas which comes from the Earth's crust in many regions. It occurs in coal mines and, although it burns quite quietly, a mixture of methane and air can be explosive. It is for this reason that miners are not permitted to use matches while at work.

How do we know that hydrocarbons contain carbon and hydrogen?

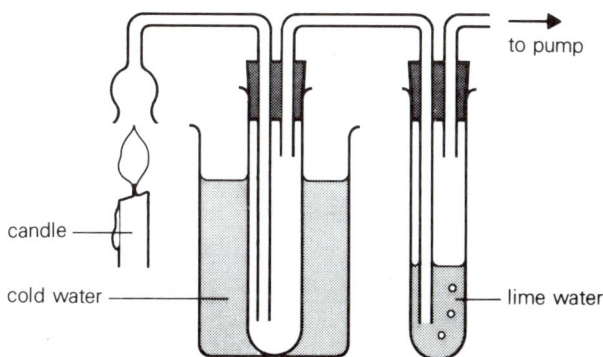

Figure 4.7

When air is drawn through the apparatus in Fig. 4.7 for a few minutes, nothing forms in the first test-tube and the lime water in the second remains clear.

However, once the candle (made of hydrocarbons) is lit, a colourless liquid (water) forms in the first test-tube. The lime water in the second turns cloudy, indicating the presence of carbon dioxide. The candle wax is the only possible source of the hydrogen in the water and the carbon in the carbon dioxide.

The oxygen in the water and the carbon dioxide could have come from the wax, or from the air, or from both. It can be shown by other experiments that *all* the oxygen comes from the air and that the wax contains carbon and hydrogen only.

Apart from the fact that they burn and release energy, the alkanes are not chemically reactive. They are quite unaffected by acids and alkalis. This unreactivity is explained by the fact that all four of the electrons on the outer layer of the carbon atoms are occupied in making bonds with hydrogen atoms or with another carbon atom. The alkanes all contain carbon atoms joined by single bonds to hydrogen or to carbon. Hydrocarbons with this structure are said to be **saturated**.

4.4 Breaking and making bonds

When hydrocarbons burn in air to form carbon dioxide and water, the existing bonds are broken and new ones are made (Fig. 4.8).

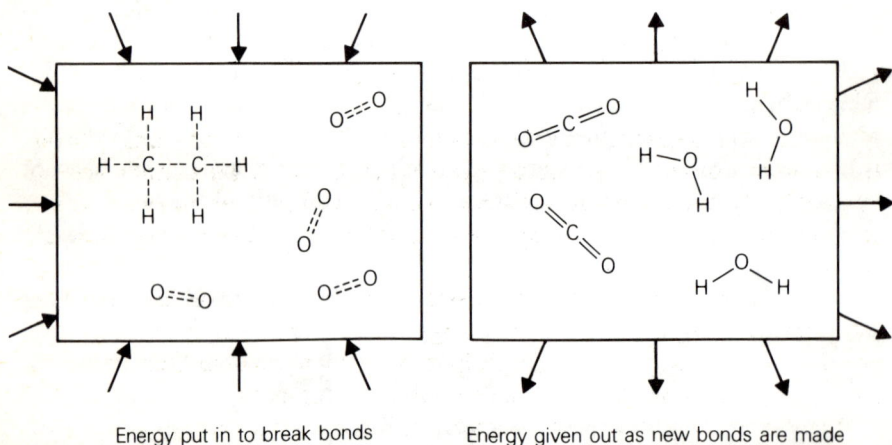

Energy put in to break bonds   Energy given out as new bonds are made

Figure 4.8

Carbon to hydrogen, carbon to carbon, and oxygen to oxygen bonds are *broken*. This *requires* energy. On the other hand, carbon to oxygen and hydrogen to oxygen bonds are *made*. The formation of these new bonds *liberates* energy.

More energy is released when the new bonds are made than is used to break the existing bonds. Hence the overall effect is of energy being given out. A reaction which gives out heat is said to be **exothermic.**

Chemistry is very largely about the breaking of existing bonds and the formation of new ones.

4.5 Variety in a molecule

In some of the more complicated alkane molecules the atoms can be re-arranged to form yet more members of the series, but in all of the molecules the basic rules are obeyed. Each carbon atom must make four bonds ('has a valency of four') and each hydrogen atom must make one bond ('has a valency of one').

For example, the normal butane molecule is given by Formula 1. However, the four carbon atoms and ten hydrogen atoms can be arranged to give another compound (Formula 2) while still keeping to the bonding rules. Check these two formulae to see if the rules apply.

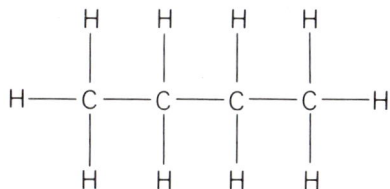 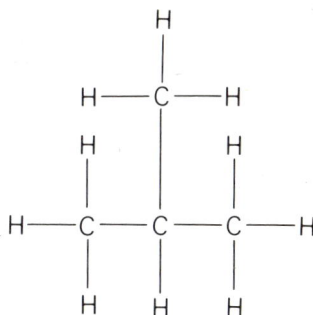

Formula 1   **Formula 2**

It is worth making models of these two forms of butane and comparing them.

Butane with Formula 1 and butane with Formula 2 have the same molecular formula (C_4H_{10}) but each has a different arrangement of these atoms in space, that is, a different *structural* formula. They are known as **isomers** (*iso* = equal; *meros* = part).

As the length of an alkane chain increases, the number of isomers increases. In butane there are only two ways of arranging the four carbon atoms and the ten hydrogen atoms. Pentane, however, has three isomers, hexane has five, and octane, the eighth member of the alkane series, has eighteen.

All the isomers of one particular alkane are very similar to one another. In the laboratory they look the same, they smell the same, and they have very similar chemical behaviour. The isomers of a compound are, therefore, very difficult to separate. However, chemists have devised a very interesting method of doing this which makes use of a technique known as gas chromatography. Your teacher may be able to show you such a separation in the laboratory.

4.6 Breaking the chains

The chain of carbon atoms in a saturated hydrocarbon is difficult to break. Once it has been broken, the atoms must be re-arranged in order to ensure that each carbon atom is still making four bonds and that each hydrogen atom is still making only one bond.

The carbon chains in a saturated hydrocarbon oil (e.g. medicinal paraffin) can be broken by allowing the substance to come into contact with a hot surface. This process is called **cracking**.

A suitable arrangement for carrying out this experiment is shown in Fig. 4.9. Your teacher will discuss the necessary precautions with you.

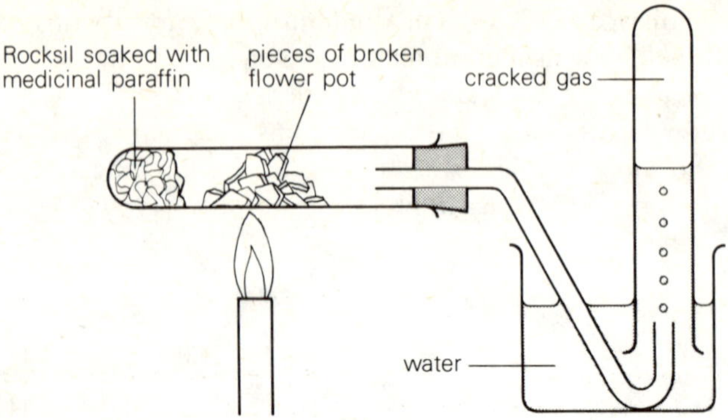

Rocksil soaked with medicinal paraffin

pieces of broken flower pot

cracked gas

water

Figure 4.9

When a few drops of bromine water are shaken with the liquid before cracking, the brown colour of the bromine does not fade. On cracking, a gas is made. When this is shaken with bromine water the brown colour rapidly disappears.

Medicinal paraffin is a saturated compound, as are all alkanes. None of them has any effect on bromine water. Since each carbon atom already has four single bonds and each hydrogen atom has one, it is difficult for any other atom, such as bromine, to enter this saturated molecule.

But consider what happens when the molecule is cracked, that is, a carbon chain is broken.

A molecule such as

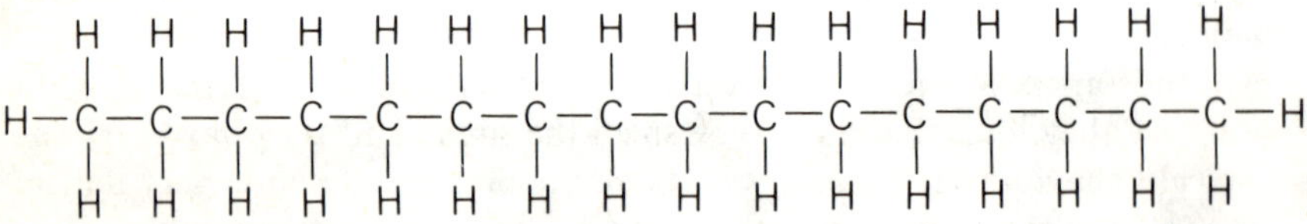

can be broken down in several ways. One possibility is shown below.

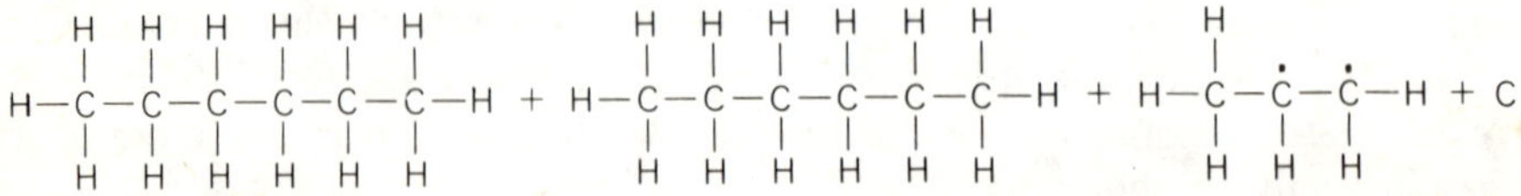

The broken bonds leave two electrons which are no longer being used for bonding. These pair together to form a carbon-to-carbon double bond. We first met the idea of a double bond in Chapter 3.

The possible products are hexane, another hydrocarbon with a double bond, plus carbon which is deposited as soot.

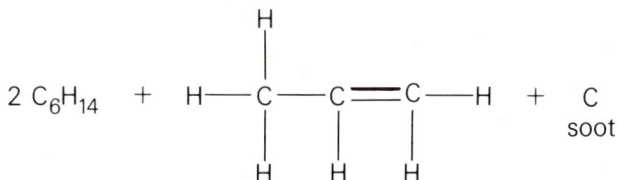

$$2\ C_6H_{14} \quad + \quad \underset{\displaystyle \overset{|}{H}}{\overset{\displaystyle \overset{H}{|}}{H-C-C=C-H}} \quad + \quad \underset{\text{soot}}{C}$$

The new compound, C_3H_6, is likely to be a gas since it contains only a very short chain of carbon atoms, but it also contains a carbon-to-carbon double bond. Nevertheless, the total number of bonds formed by each carbon atom is still four and by each hydrogen atom, one. Check the formula for yourself.

A compound like this, which contains carbon atoms linked by a double bond, is said to be **unsaturated**. There are four electrons, that is two pairs, between the two carbon atoms.

If this compound is exposed to an element like bromine, which could accept an electron to form a bond, it is likely that the bromine will be attracted to this double bond, where the extra electrons are concentrated.

The reaction which takes place between bromine and an unsaturated compound can be represented as

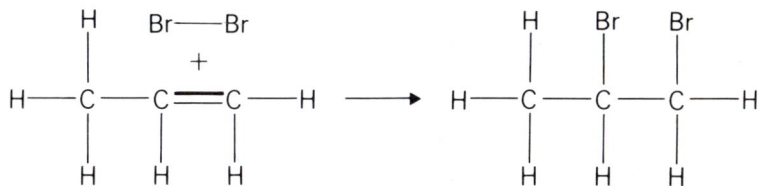

This new substance is colourless. It is also now a saturated compound containing only single carbon-to-carbon bonds.

4.7 Ring alkanes

The carbon chain of an alkane can be arranged as a ring compound. For example, pentane can give a ring compound, cyclopentane (*cyclo* = circle or ring).

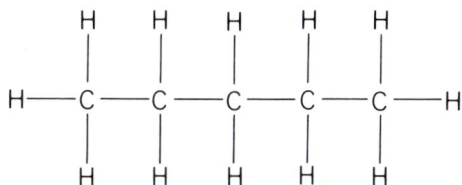

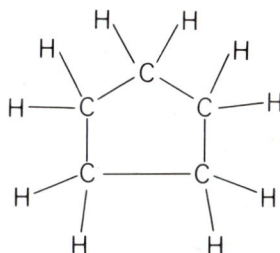

pentane   cyclopentane

When the ring is formed two hydrogen atoms have to be lost from the molecule in order to keep each carbon atom with only four bonds and each hydrogen atom with only one. Although the molecular formula of pentane is C_5H_{12}, the molecular formula of *cyclo*pentane is C_5H_{10}.

New words you have met in this chapter

Polymorphs	different forms of the same element or compound. They often have different crystal shapes and different properties.
Reducing agent	a substance which takes oxygen away from other substances.
Hydrocarbon	a compound containing hydrogen and carbon only.
Organic compounds	compounds of carbon, with the exception of the oxides of carbon and carbonates.
Homologous series	a family of compounds all having the same general formula, e.g. C_nH_{2n+2}. The individual members are known as homologues.
Alkanes	a homologous series of hydrocarbons having the general formula C_nH_{2n+2}. All of their names end in **-ane**. The series begins methane, ethane, propane, butane, pentane, etc.
Saturated*	these hydrocarbons have only single bonds. Each carbon atom makes four single bonds and each hydrogen atom makes one. They do not react with bromine dissolved in water.
Unsaturated*	these hydrocarbons have double or even triple bonds between some of the carbon atoms. They react with bromine water to saturate the molecule by returning to single bonds.
Cracking	when a long chain molecule is strongly heated it breaks into smaller fragments, some of which are unsaturated.
Exothermic	a reaction is exothermic if energy (usually heat energy) is given out.

* Please note that in everyday language the words 'saturated' and 'unsaturated' normally indicate the presence of water. In organic chemistry the words indicate the absence or presence of double (or triple) bonds.

5

Hidden hydrocarbons

5.1 Oil

Oil is the common name for petroleum and is a most important source of hydrocarbons. It is found below the Earth's surface in many parts of the world. It may be necessary to drill down six or seven kilometres before the oil is reached.

Oil was formed many millions of years ago from dead sea animals and plants which collected on the floor of the ocean and were covered by layers of rock fragments, silt, and mud. Decay of the soft parts was slow because there was little dissolved oxygen at the bottom of the sea. The mud accumulated and over the years was pressed together by an increasing amount of sediment. This pressure, together with the heat from the interior of the Earth and the action of bacteria, formed oil from the slowly decaying plant and animal material. The sediment thus became an oil-bearing rock. Usually the oil is held in the tiny spaces between the rock grains as water is held in a sponge (Fig. 5.1). There are no pools of oil.

Figure 5.1

It is not really surprising that oil is formed from plants and animals when you think that some of the oil which we use, other than as a fuel, comes from plants and animals. Cod liver oil, olive oil, and castor oil are some examples.

5.2

The oil which we get from the Earth is a mixture of many hydrocarbons and without the work of the chemist, whose ingenuity has made it possible to separate this mixture into its various hydrocarbons, it would be useless. This process of separation is called **distillation**.

When the oil is heated sufficiently it turns into a vapour. The vapour is cooled and, as the temperature falls, condenses to give a series of liquid hydrocarbons (Fig. 5.2).

41

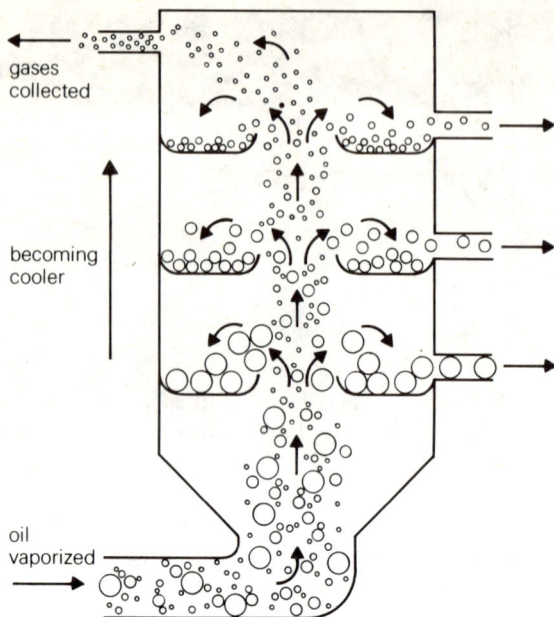

gases
collected

becoming
cooler

oil
vaporized

Figure 5.2

Distillation sorts out the mixture of hydrocarbons, which we call oil, into collections (fractions) of hydrocarbons with different chain lengths. This is rather like the separation of a mixture of people into groups with different ages at the entrance to a football ground—juveniles, adults, and pensioners (Fig. 5.3).

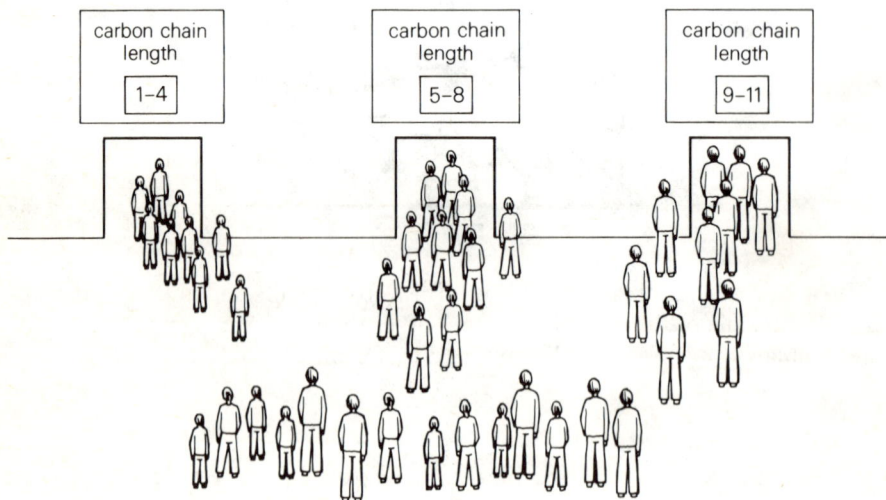

carbon chain
length

1–4

carbon chain
length

5–8

carbon chain
length

9–11

Figure 5.3

You may have carried out a small scale distillation of oil in the laboratory, using the apparatus in Fig. 5.4. You were probably able to obtain three or four different distillates (or fractions) as the temperature was altered.

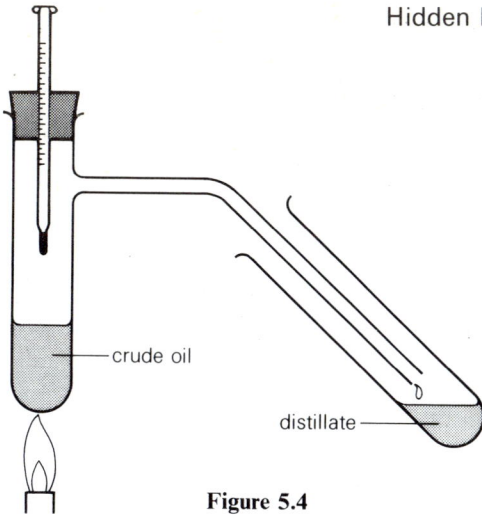

Figure 5.4

Figure 5.5 shows some of the substances which are obtained from oil by distillation in a refinery, together with the approximate number of carbon atoms in the molecules of each.

Fraction	Use	Number of carbon atoms per molecule
Gases		1–4
Petrol		4–12
Kerosene (paraffin)		9–16
Diesel oil		15–25
Lubricating oil		20–70
Fuel oil		>10
Bitumen		>70

Figure 5.5

You will notice that most of these substances are used as fuels. It is worth remembering that the energy released when these hydrocarbons from oil are burned was obtained from the Sun hundreds of millions of years ago and has, since then, been stored in the oil underground.

5.3 The demand for petrol

The quantity of petrol which can be obtained from the distillation of oil does not meet our demands (see Fig. 5.6). This creates a problem for the chemist. How is he to increase the proportion of petrol produced to match the level of the demand?

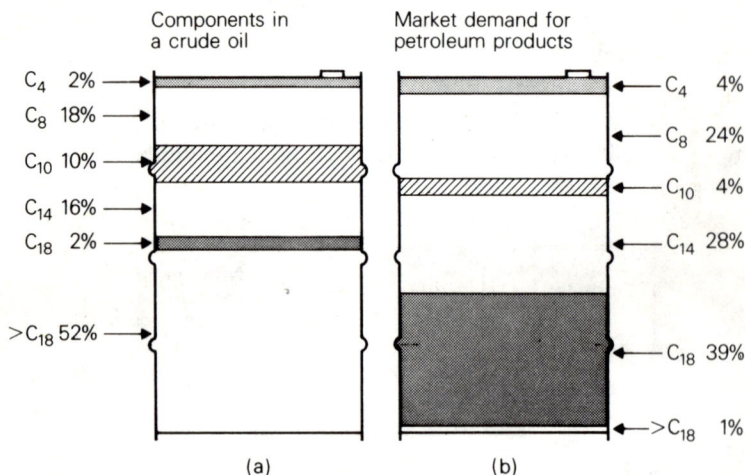

Components in a crude oil

Market demand for petroleum products

C_4 2%
C_8 18%
C_{10} 10%
C_{14} 16%
C_{18} 2%
$>C_{18}$ 52%

C_4 4%
C_8 24%
C_{10} 4%
C_{14} 28%
C_{18} 39%
$>C_{18}$ 1%

(a)   (b)

Figure 5.6

One way is to 'stick together' molecules of short-chained hydrocarbon gases to give a product containing about eight carbon atoms per molecule.

A reaction in which a number of small molecules combine to form a larger molecule is called a **polymerization** reaction (*poly* = many; *meros* = part).

More of the heavier oils are obtained from the first distillation of crude oil than are actually needed. This prompted chemists to experiment in another way in order to produce more petrol.

They tried to 'crack' larger molecules, which had perhaps eighteen or twenty carbon atoms in their chain, in much the same way as you have 'cracked' medicinal paraffin. Their experiments were successful.

Chemists have found that cracking can be speeded up by using certain kinds of finely powdered clay. The substances used for this purpose are called **catalysts**. This is a name given to any substances which speed up a chemical reaction—although they seem to do this without being chemically changed themselves. The way in which they are able to perform this useful task need not concern us now.

The catalytic cracker, or 'cat cracker', is an important installation in an oil refinery (Fig. 5.7).

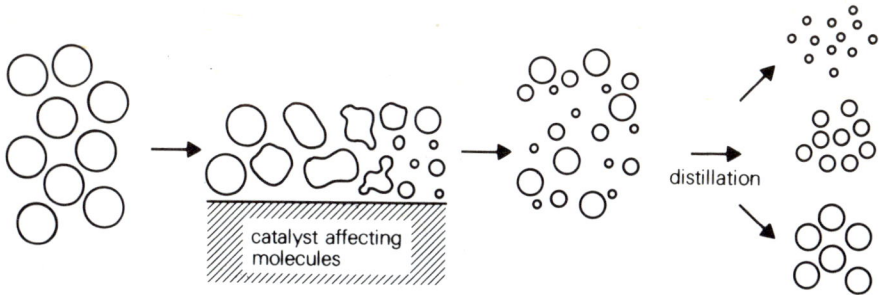

distillation

Figure 5.7

5.4 Petrochemicals

The products from the distillation of oil can also be made to react with other chemicals to form new substances, known as petrochemicals. Some of these substances will be very familiar to you and are shown in Fig. 5.8 on p. 47.

It is interesting to see how plastics such as *poly*ethene, *poly*vinylchloride, *poly*propylene, and *poly*styrene are formed.

Ethene is a product of the oil industry. It is an unsaturated hydrocarbon gas (see Section 4.6) with the molecular formula C_2H_4. Its structural formula, which has to satisfy the valency rules of both carbon and hydrogen, is

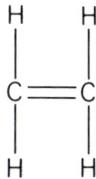

Plastics are long chain molecules. One way of obtaining long chains is to begin with short chain molecules which contain a double bond, that is, two pairs of shared electrons. If the electrons in one of these bonds in ethene can be separated, something like this would occur.

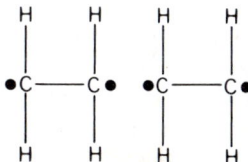

The electrons represented by the dots would no longer be making a bond. However, one electron from each molecule could form a bond between two molecules (Fig. 5.9).

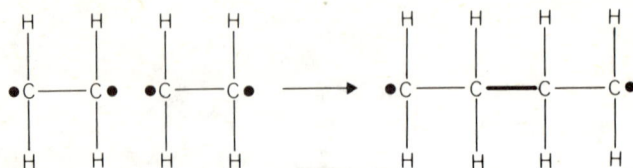

Figure 5.9

This process could be repeated many times, forming a very long chain molecule (Fig. 5.10).

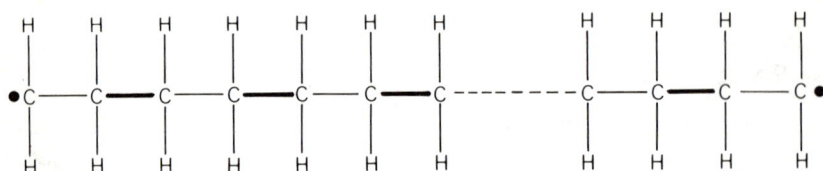

Figure 5.10

This type of linking together is called **addition**. One of the bonds in a double bond is opened and the spare electrons form bonds with neighbouring molecules.

The simple molecules which are going to be strung together are called **monomers** (= single units) while the resulting long chain molecules are called **polymers** (= many units). The 'stringing together' process is called **polymerization**.

5.5 Addition polymers

(a) Polyethene (or Polythene)

Most addition polymers are related to the simple hydrocarbon ethene, which contains one double bond in each molecule. Once this bond is broken, neighbouring molecules can join together. But how can chemists break this bond? This can be done at high temperatures and pressures in the presence of a catalyst and these conditions are used in the polymerization of ethene. In this way hundreds and even thousands of ethene molecules can be strung together to give a white, waxy, very long chain hydrocarbon called polyethene or, as it is more usually called, Polythene or polyethylene. This plastic has a large variety of uses such as insulation for underwater telephone cables, sacks for storage of fertilizers, flexible pipe for domestic water supply, kitchenware, and large unbreakable toys. By adding pigments to it before it is moulded, a range of attractive colours can be obtained in Polythene articles.

There are other ways of making this polymer, but they are rather too complex to discuss at this stage.

Figure 5.8

(b) *PVC (polyvinylchloride)*

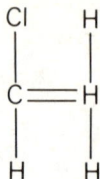

$$
\begin{array}{ccc}
Cl & & H \\
| & & | \\
C & = & H \\
| & & | \\
H & & H
\end{array}
$$

The starting material for this plastic is vinyl chloride. This has the same structure as ethene except that one atom of hydrogen has been replaced by one of chlorine. It polymerizes to give polyvinyl chloride or PVC.

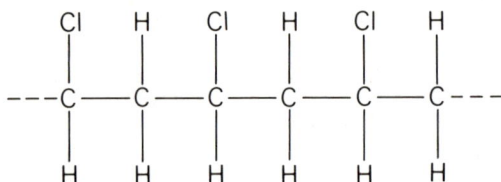

$$
\begin{array}{cccccc}
Cl & H & Cl & H & Cl & H \\
| & | & | & | & | & | \\
---C & -C & -C & -C & -C & -C--- \\
| & | & | & | & | & | \\
H & H & H & H & H & H
\end{array}
$$

PVC is used in the manufacture of bottles for oil and chemicals, rainwater goods, drainpipes, and colourful sheets for wall coverings. It can be compounded with substances called plasticizers to give a soft rubber-like material. This is used in the manufacture of 'leather cloth' to cover car seats, as insulation for electric wiring, as coated paper for wallpaper, and as floor coverings either in sheet or as tiles. Brightly coloured PVC raincoats have been popular for a number of years.

(c) *PTFE (polytetrafluoroethene)*

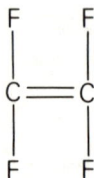

$$
\begin{array}{ccc}
F & & F \\
| & & | \\
C & = & C \\
| & & | \\
F & & F
\end{array}
$$

The name tetrafluoroethene is fairly self-explanatory (*tetra* = four; *fluoro* = of fluorine). It polymerizes like ethene to give the important non-stick plastic PTFE, sometimes called 'Teflon'. It is a hard, waxy, ivory-white plastic which is not attacked by most chemicals. It weathers and ages without breaking down and very few substances are capable of sticking to its surface.

(d) *Perspex (polymethylmethacrylate)*

Methyl methacrylate is a more complicated variation on ethene but the same pattern applies.

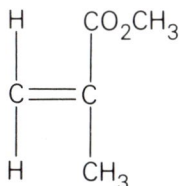

$$
\begin{array}{ccc}
H & & CO_2CH_3 \\
| & & | \\
C & = & C \\
| & & | \\
H & & CH_3 \\
\end{array}
$$

methyl methacrylate

This crystal-clear plastic has been widely used in place of glass. It has an advantage over glass in that it can be easily moulded into quite intricate shapes, but at the same time, unfortunately, it is rather more easily marked and scratched than glass is.

(e) *Polystyrene*

Once more the ethene skeleton is present.

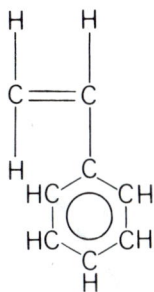

styrene

This plastic is clear, hard, and rather brittle. It is used for making toys such as constructional kits, lampshades, and flower pots. It can be blown up into a solid foam material which you may have seen moulded into beakers for keeping soup hot. The foam is also used in packages to protect fragile goods such as hi-fi equipment and cameras.

(f) *Polypropylene*

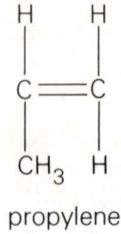

$$\underset{\underset{\displaystyle CH_3}{|}}{\overset{\overset{\displaystyle H}{|}}{C}} = \underset{\underset{\displaystyle H}{|}}{\overset{\overset{\displaystyle H}{|}}{C}}$$

propylene

The light plastic is rigid and tough. It is resistant to attack by chemicals and it withstands a higher temperature than most similar plastics. Thus polypropylene articles can be safely immersed in boiling water and, as a result, they are used as washing machine agitators and for hospital ware which requires sterilization at high temperatures.

Fibres of polypropylene can also be formed and are used for making ropes,

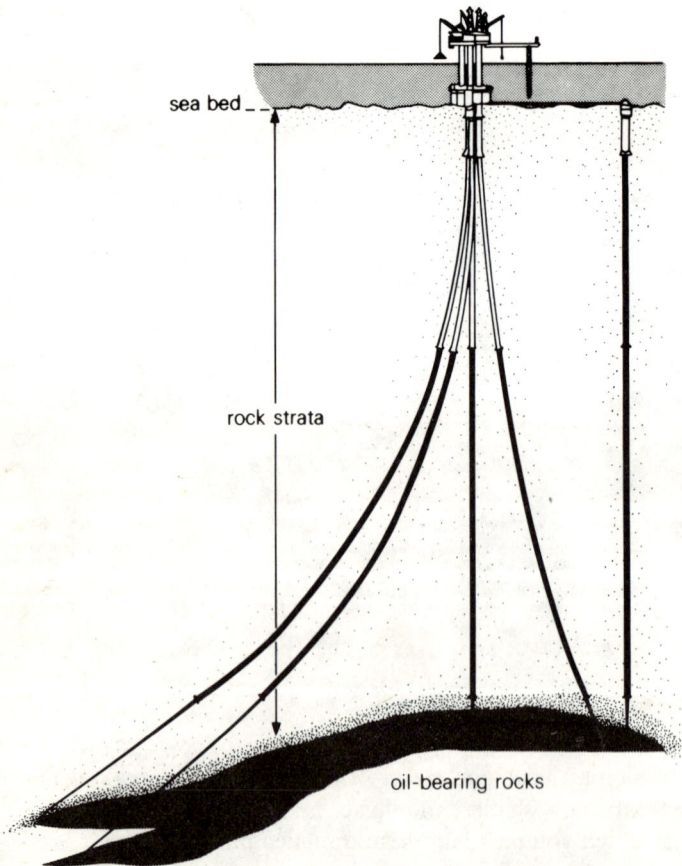

Fig. 5.11 Did you realise there was so much below the surface?

fishing nets, and brushes. When in the form of film it is transparent and has an attractive gloss.

The number of different plastics which can be produced at the present time is large and the range of their uses is endless, since plastics can be moulded into virtually any shape and given any colour. Many of the chemicals used in their manufacture come from oil. This is making us think about how we should use our scarce resources more carefully.

Clearly, oil is one of the most important chemicals for the industries of the world. Its price has increased sharply over the last few years, affecting the price of many other common materials such as plastics.

5.6

A search for oil in the northern part of the North Sea, off the coast of Britain, began in 1967. In 1972 one of the largest off-shore oilfields in the world was discovered. This was called the Brent Field. It has been estimated that this field alone could produce more than one-quarter of Britain's present oil needs for about the next twenty years, although the costs of production and transportation have proved to be enormous. Some experts have suggested that the cost of developments in the North Sea over the next ten years will exceed £20 000 million!

Oil from the Forties Field, 115 miles off Aberdeen, is already flowing and is being transported by underground pipeline from Peterhead to the refinery at Grangemouth (Fig. 5.12). Perhaps you have seen a sample of this oil in school.

5.7 Natural gas

Many oilfields have been found to contain large quantities of natural gas. Gas from the Frigg Field will meet almost one-fifth of Britain's present gas needs.

Natural gas is transported in two ways; by sea-going tanker or by underground pipeline.

Special ships called LNG (liquid natural gas) carriers are used. They contain insulated tanks (rather like giant floating thermos flasks) in which liquefied natural gas is stored. When in liquid form, about a thousand times as much 'natural gas' can be put in a given space. After the water and acid gases, such as carbon dioxide and hydrogen sulphide, have been removed, the gas is liquefied by lowering its temperature and increasing the pressure upon it. For safety reasons a compound is added to give the gas a smell.

On land, after the liquid has been allowed to turn back to gas, it is pumped along an underground steel pipeline of about one metre in diameter. This has narrower branch lines, often made of plastic, along which gas reaches local areas and eventually enters your house.

You may have seen either an oil or gas pipeline being laid. If so you will have been impressed by the efforts made to ensure that the land was returned to its original condition after the excavations had been completed.

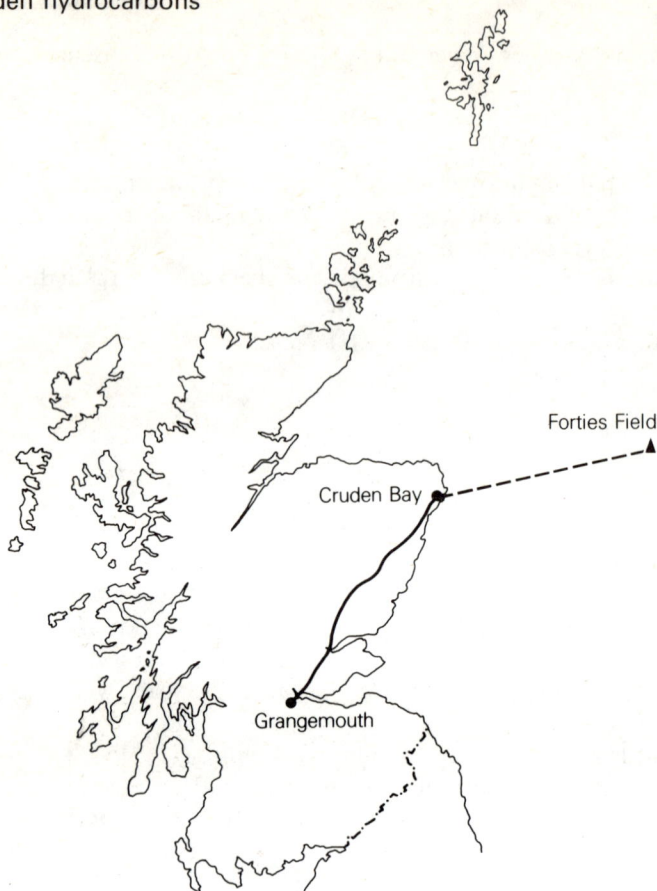

Figure 5.12

Figure 5.13 shows three stages in the laying of an oil pipeline from Cruden Bay to Grangemouth. The third picture shows the situation two years later. The tree in the centre with the hooked top is a helpful marker for comparison.

Natural gas contains about 95 % methane with small amounts of nitrogen and sulphur, plus traces of other hydrocarbons and some noble gases. The sulphur is removed before the gas is sold to the Gas Council.

At present more than 90 % of all gas used in Britain comes from natural gas. The remainder is obtained either from liquid petroleum gas or from coal. It is interesting to note that chemists are now looking to coal as a source of methane in the twenty-first century when natural gas runs out.

5.8 The effect on the environment

There are now many more large chemical manufacturing plants in the world than there were a few years ago and they have had various effects on the environment and on local communities—particularly noticeable when something goes wrong!

These new chemical plants provide employment for many people, but they

Figure 5.13

must not do this at the expense of our countryside. Industry has to keep to a minimum any escape of gases to the air and liquids to the rivers which may pollute the surrounding area.

There are various types of pollution which you might have noticed. The main ones are listed below

(a) *Pollution of the atmosphere* which may give a bad smell, damage vegetation, or be a health risk to people and animals.
(b) *Escaping liquids.* These should be treated *before* they are discharged into a river or the sea. Oil is probably the most familiar pollutant. It can spoil beaches and harm wildlife and even a thin surface film of oil on water will interfere with the normal oxygen content of the water.
(c) *Noise.* The noise level in industry must be tolerable to both employees and to people living nearby. There are, of course, laws on noise pollution which companies try hard to observe.

Society is slowly becoming more aware of the possible effects on the environment of pollution. A balance has to be found between the benefits of industry, in terms of jobs and prosperity, and the risks which an industry may bring to a town.

5.9 What of the future?

Imports of natural gas have decreased greatly since the discovery of the gas fields in the North Sea. Nevertheless, off-shore explorations must continue because wells eventually run dry. One day, although this can be postponed by using the reserves more carefully, they will all run out. What is to happen then? What can the world turn to as alternative sources of energy? Where will we be able to obtain the many tonnes of carbon-containing compounds for petrochemicals which are at present obtained from oil? Somehow the problems have to be overcome. Present predictions are that there are a number of possible sources of energy for our future requirements. These are nuclear energy; energy from waves in water; solar energy (energy directly from the Sun); energy from the wind; and geo-thermal energy (energy from the heat inside the Earth).

In addition to these we have massive coal reserves. Most of the energy sources mentioned above will not provide us with carbon compounds. These will have to be obtained from coal and plants.

Energy facts—a summary

Coal	Britain has stocks which should last for at least two hundred years. New mines which would be required to keep supplies at present levels could be opened. In Scotland there are large reserves under the Firth of Forth.
Oil	North Sea oil production will fall off at the beginning of the next century, even allowing for all new discoveries.
Gas	North Sea gas is expected to run out in just over twenty years.
Nuclear reactors	Long term prospects are good, but there are problems over the disposal of radioactive waste products.

New words you have met in this chapter

Distillation a separation process for liquids in which those with the lowest boiling point boil off first and can be recovered by cooling and condensing.

Monomers these simple molecules are the building units for larger molecules (polymers). One group of monomers is based on ethene. They link together through the double bond.

Polymers long chain molecules built from simpler repeating units called monomers.

Polymerization the process by which polymers are made from monomers.

Addition one kind of polymerization in which the monomers use their double bonds to link together.

Catalyst a substance which speeds up a chemical reaction but apparently remains chemically unchanged itself.

Chemistry in Action 2

The PVC Story

Have you ever thought what your life would be like without plastics? There would be no synthetic fibres to make carpets, curtains, or clothes; no nylon shirts and no tights; no plastic toys; no plastic light fittings; no plastic car seats; no plastic-coated electrical wires; and, of course, no 'polybags'!

Life would be very different for us all. It is worth remembering that plastics were introduced on a large scale only in the 1950s, and that their present production depends upon oil, which will be an increasingly scarce and expensive material. Let's have a look at the growth in production of one plastic in Britain.

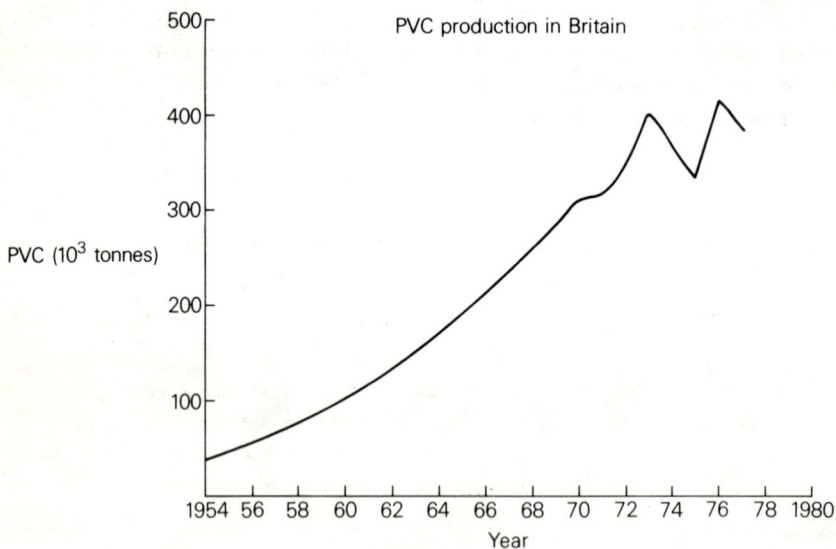

PVC production in Britain

PVC (10^3 tonnes)

Year

PVC stands for polyvinylchloride, which is a rather complicated name for a fairly simple molecule. Let us first consider the monomer, vinyl chloride. It has a simpler name—chloroethene (pronounced chloro-ethene).

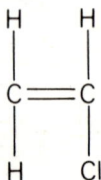

On page 47 you will have found out how alkenes can be polymerized into long chain polymers. Chloroethene polymerizes to give polychloroethene (PVC).

There are several ways to make chloroethene (vinyl chloride). It can be made either from ethene or ethyne. You have not yet met ethyne (acetylene), but this is the simplest molecule in which the two carbons are linked by a *triple* bond.

$$H\!\!-\!\!C\!\!\equiv\!\!C\!\!-\!\!H$$

You can see that carbon and hydrogen still keep their valencies of four and one.

Here are the three ways of making chloroethene industrially.

Reaction 1

natural gas $\longrightarrow$ ethyne $\longrightarrow$ chloroethene

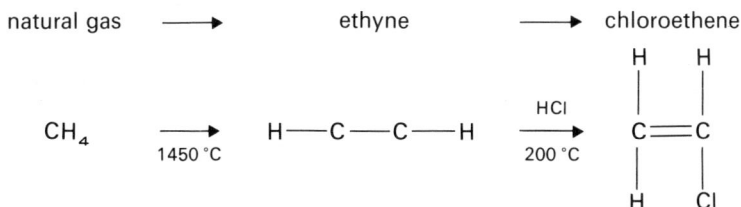

Methane is heated to around 1450 °C to form ethyne. This is mixed with hydrogen chloride gas at 200 °C and allowed to pass over a catalyst.

Reaction 2

oil $\longrightarrow$ ethene $\longrightarrow$ dichloroethane $\longrightarrow$ chloroethene

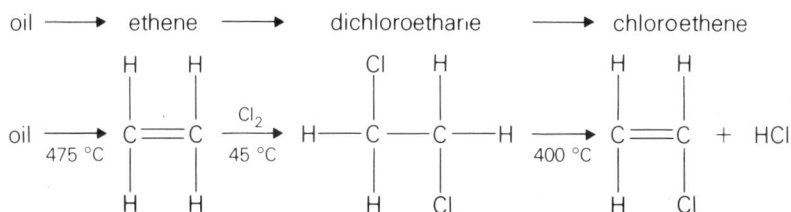

When certain fractions from crude oil are catalytically cracked, large amounts of ethene are formed. This ethene is separated, mixed with chlorine, and bubbled through a solution containing a catalyst. Dichloroethane forms and when this is heated to 400 °C chloroethene is produced.

Reaction 3

oil $\longrightarrow$ ethene $\longrightarrow$ dichloroethane $\longrightarrow$ chloroethene

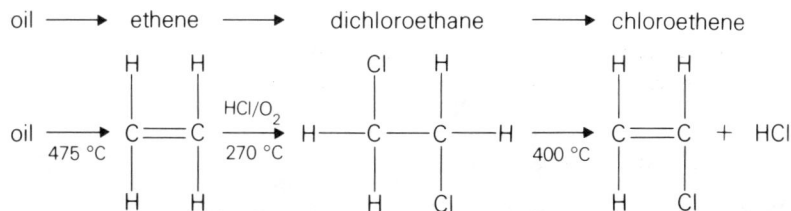

When ethene, formed from cracking crude oil, is mixed with hydrogen chloride and oxygen (from the air) and passed over a catalyst, dichloroethane is formed. This breaks up to give chloroethene when heated a little further.

Costs

The aim is to produce chloroethene as cheaply as possible, paying attention to safety and efficiency. There are two main sources of expense which you should consider:

(a) the cost of the materials which you use, e.g. oil, gas, chlorine, etc.;
(b) the cost of energy required in the processes.

You may regard oil and natural gas as similar in cost, but chlorine is about twice as expensive as hydrogen chloride. Clearly, the higher the temperature required in a reaction, the more energy is involved and the more expensive the process is likely to be.

For you to do

You should *work as a group* with two or three others from your class. Discuss possible answers to the following questions.

1 Which of the three processes would you choose to use in a new factory to keep costs as low as possible?
2 Knowing the raw materials which you will be using, suggest where in Britain you might build your factory.
3 PVC replaced leather and metal for many uses. List the advantages and disadvantages of PVC when compared with
   (a) leather,
   (b) metals.
4 Look again at the graph of PVC production. Look carefully at the dates. Try to explain the humps and troughs on the graph. Do you think that PVC production will go on growing? Explain your view.

6

The energy foods

6.1

Fuel is necessary to keep our bodies in action—but body fuels are not hydrocarbons. There would not be much pleasure in drinking a pint of oil a day!

Body fuels are compounds called **carbohydrates**. A wide variety of substances are classed as carbohydrates, although not all of them are suitable body fuels. Starch, sugar, paper, flour, cotton, and wood are some carbohydrates. They all contain the elements carbon, hydrogen, and oxygen.

The general formula for a carbohydrate can be expressed as $C_x(H_2O)_y$, where x and y can be as small as five or six, or greater than 100.

Usually the hydrogen and oxygen atoms are in the ratio of 2:1, as in water.

Some of the carbohydrates mentioned above are used as sources of energy: some are in the food we eat, while others are burnt as fuels. But how does the energy get into them in the first place?

Carbohydrates are made in plants from the raw materials carbon dioxide and water. In the building of the complicated carbohydrate molecules, energy has been supplied from the Sun (Fig. 6.1).

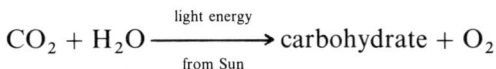

$$CO_2 + H_2O \xrightarrow[\text{from Sun}]{\text{light energy}} \text{carbohydrate} + O_2$$

The process is not nearly as simple as the equation might lead you to believe. We know that carbon dioxide and water are taken in by plants and that carbohydrates are produced, but what happens in between is not yet fully understood. Our equation is merely a summary of a large number of complicated reactions.

If carbon dioxide and water are mixed in the presence of sunlight no carbohydrate is formed. We need the presence of the living plant with its green catalyst, chlorophyll. Since something has been built up in the process by the help of light energy this reaction is called **photosynthesis** (*photo* = light; *synthesis* = putting together).

The slow reaction which produces energy from carbohydrates in our bodies is the reverse of photosynthesis. It is called **respiration**.

59

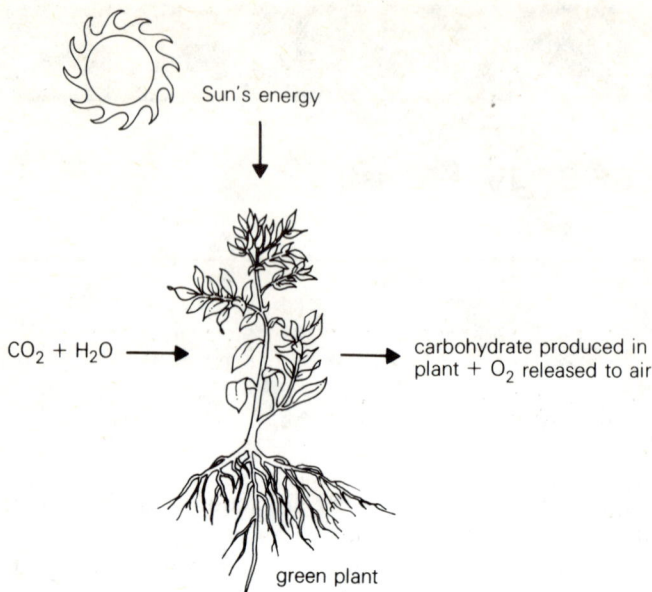

Figure 6.1

A milkman who uses an electrically driven van connects the batteries to a source of electrical energy when he is off duty. Chemical reactions take place within the batteries in which energy is stored. During the day the milkman reverses the chemical process in the batteries and this gives him the mechanical energy to run his van.

The formation and use of carbohydrates is something like that. Light energy goes in. Heat and other forms of energy come out later when required.

6.2 The common factor

To understand why all these substances are grouped under the name carbohydrate you have to learn something of how the atoms in the molecules of each are arranged.

One of the simplest carbohydrates is called glucose. It has the molecular formula $C_6(H_2O)_6$ or $C_6H_{12}O_6$. There is evidence that its structure is a ring.

Check from Fig. 6.2 that each atom in the formula shows its own expected valency: carbon—four, hydrogen—one, and oxygen—two.

There are other carbohydrates which have the same formula as glucose— $C_6H_{12}O_6$. Fructose and glucose are isomers (see Section 4.5). They are both sweet substances and dissolve easily in water.

Simple sugars like these, which contain six carbon atoms per molecule, are called **monosaccharides.**

A little more complicated are the carbohydrates known as disaccharides. They too have a sweet taste and dissolve in water, but they contain two monosaccharide (6-carbon atom) units.

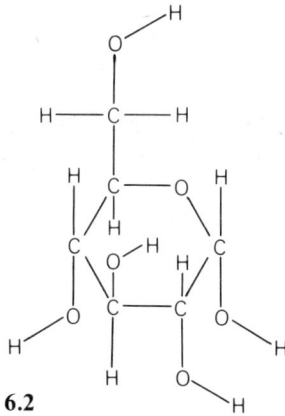

Figure 6.2

There are three common disaccharides called sucrose, maltose, and lactose (milk sugar). The formula of sucrose is $C_{12}H_{22}O_{11}$ and the atoms are arranged in two ring units, each similar to glucose, joined by an oxygen atom. Each ring 'satisfies' one of the valencies of the oxygen atom (Fig. 6.3).

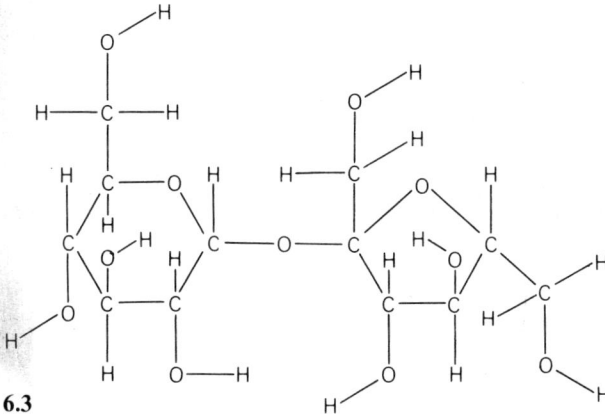

Figure 6.3

Much more complicated are the polysaccharides, substances such as cotton, starch, and wood. They are composed of a complicated network of thousands of $C_6H_{10}O_5$ units. They are not sweet to taste and, for example, starch does not form a true solution with water. These polysaccharides are really polymers made from many monosaccharide units linked together.

So the picture is shown in Table 6.1.

Table 6.1

Complicated long chain carbohydrates— **polysaccharides**	Simpler shorter chain carbohydrates— **disaccharides**	Simple, single unit carbohydrates— **monosaccharides**
Not sweet	Sweet	Sweet
Do not dissolve fully in water, e.g. starch	Dissolve in water, e.g. sucrose (ordinary sugar)	Dissolve in water, e.g. glucose

6.3

Additional evidence for including all the different substances which we have mentioned in the set 'carbohydrates' is obtained from experiments which you will have carried out in the laboratory.

You can use acid solutions to break down the more complicated carbohydrates into simpler ones. This is a process called **hydrolysis**.

Glucose and maltose can be obtained from starch and paper, while glucose and fructose can be obtained from sucrose (ordinary domestic sugar).

It is fairly easy to break down (or hydrolyse) a complicated carbohydrate and then identify some of the products by paper chromatography (Fig. 6.4).

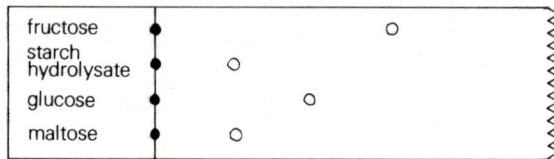

Figure 6.4

6.4 Releasing the energy

All the carbohydrates we have mentioned are sources of energy. Wood and paper will burn, releasing energy, while we get our energy from food containing starch and sugar.

Glucose is a source of heat and muscular energy: it is often used by athletes in the form of glucose tablets. Any unused glucose is converted in our bodies to a polysaccharide called glycogen. In this form it is stored in the liver and is ready to be released when sudden exercise demands it.

Plants also use polysaccharides as sources of energy. During photosynthesis plants manufacture simple water-soluble sugars. These sugary solutions are transported through the plant until they reach a suitable storage area where the plant links the monosaccharides together to form polysaccharides which are insoluble and suitable for storage. Some plants store this material in their fruits (apples), others in their stems (sugar cane), and yet others in their roots (turnips, carrots, beets).

When the plant begins to grow vigorously these polysaccharides are converted back to simple sugars and the necessary energy for growth is made available to the plant. The plant is able to call on its store of polysaccharides and to hydrolyse them to simple sugars. It is interesting to note that when old potatoes start to sprout in Spring they taste quite sweet because hydrolysis has begun.

But the hydrolysis in our bodies and in plants is achieved without the high temperature and the hydrochloric acid which is necessary in laboratory experiments. How is this done? The secret lies in very specialized catalysts called

enzymes. These enzymes are big molecules of a definite shape. Their shape and the distribution of electrons within the molecule enable them to act like spanners of a definite size, which can do one particular job. Enzymes are said to be *specific* in their action. Each can do only one job of molecule building or molecule dismantling. Both plants and ourselves have many sets of enzymes to cope with the variety of chemical tasks to be performed. These can carry out the tasks in plants or in our bodies much more efficiently than we can imitate in the laboratory.

One very efficient enzyme present in our saliva is called amylase (or ptyalin). Its specific job is to begin the digestion of starch in our food. It breaks down the complicated starch molecules in a similar way to the acid which was referred to in Section 6.3. The simpler products can be identified by chromatography.

6.5 Enzymes in industry

The monosaccharide sugars are often referred to as the 'simple' sugars, but they are really quite complicated molecules consisting of about twenty-four atoms bonded together. They can be changed into even simpler compounds.

Glucose can be converted, by an enzyme found in yeast, to a substance called ethanol. When you carry out this experiment you will observe that a lot of frothing takes place. This is because carbon dioxide gas is formed during the reaction.

The process is called fermentation. It is of great importance to distillers and brewers because ethanol is present in alcoholic drinks of various kinds.

Ethanol is commonly called 'alcohol' although it is only one member of the family of alcohols. The reaction is as follows:

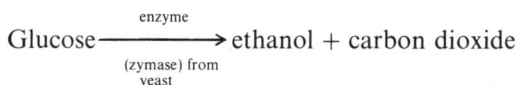

$$\text{Glucose} \xrightarrow[\substack{\text{(zymase) from} \\ \text{yeast}}]{\text{enzyme}} \text{ethanol} + \text{carbon dioxide}$$

or, using formulae:

$$C_6H_{12}O_6 \rightarrow CH_3CH_2OH + CO_2$$

Ethanol has the structural formula

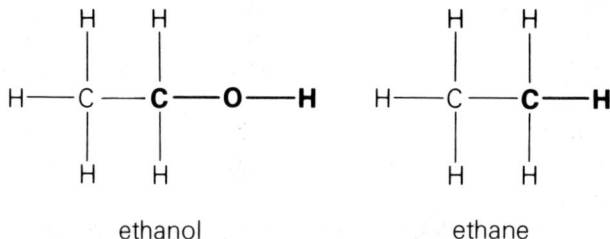

ethanol   ethane

It has the same 'skeleton' as the alkane ethane and differs from it by having a hydrogen atom removed from one of the carbon atoms and replaced by an **OH** group.

This raises the interesting possibility that for every member of the alkane series it might be possible to obtain a corresponding alcohol.

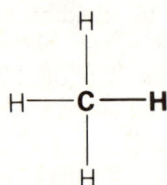

methane

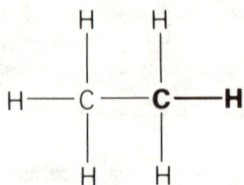

ethane

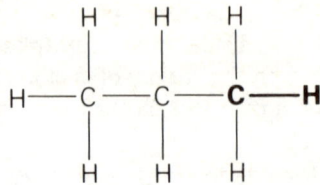

propane

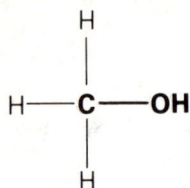

methanol

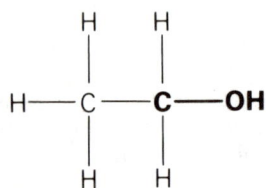

ethanol

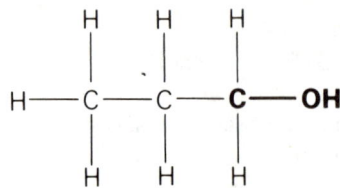

propanol

There is indeed such a series of alcohols and if you remember the name of each member of the alkane series it is easy to obtain the name of the corresponding alcohol. Each of these alcohols has an (**OH**) group called an hydroxide group attached to a **carbon atom** in the molecule.

Although a further study of the alcohol series will not be made now, you should know a little more about ethanol, the commonest member of the series.

1 It burns with a clear flame to produce carbon dioxide and water.
2 It mixes completely with water.
3 It has no effect on litmus or on pH paper.
4 When it is allowed to react with oxygen (with the right micro-organisms present) an acid called ethanoic acid (or acetic acid) is formed. This has the sour taste you associate with vinegar.

A similar reaction takes place in wine if it is not properly stored. It becomes quite sour because the ethanol in the wine is converted into ethanoic acid. Two hydrogen atoms are lost from the carbon atom attached to the OH group and both bonds then link to an atom of oxygen.

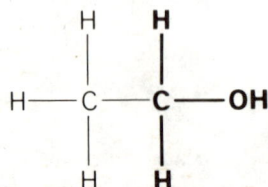

ethanol

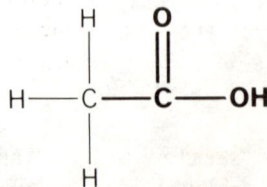

ethanoic acid

In making ethanoic acid from wine, bacteria carrying their own enzymes slowly convert the alcohol into vinegar which is a dilute solution of ethanoic acid. The vinegar is well flavoured and retains something of the richness of the wine.

Large amounts of ethanoic acid are also required for industrial purposes where the flavour does not matter. These can be made by chemical rather than by biological processes.

A look into the future

Research is in progress to find new uses for energy-rich sugar. For instance, Brazil plans to run all its cars on alcohol made from sugar. This is not a new notion. It was introduced to some extent during World War II when Brazil's oil supplies were uncertain.

Modern living depends on the chemicals which are used to manufacture the synthetic fibres in textiles, to make detergents, to make drugs to fight disease, and so on. Many of these chemicals are made from oil-based hydrocarbons (Section 5.4, p. 45).

In a recent breakthrough, however, new chemicals derived from sugar have been found which might soon replace many oil-based products. Already detergents, animal foods, a variety of plastics, and cosmetics such as lipstick have been made from this source. Some people say that sugar will become the feedstock for European chemical industries when oil runs out. At the moment the future for sugar looks bright and exciting!

6.6 The acid series

We noticed in the previous section that for each alkane there is a corresponding alcohol. Similarly, each alcohol has a corresponding acid.

The series of acids of which ethanoic acid is the second member is known as the **alkanoic acid** series. Another name for ethanoic acid is acetic acid. Its structural formula is

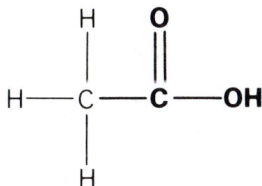

Check that the valency of each atom in the molecule is correct: carbon—four, oxygen—two, and hydrogen—one. The important group in this molecule is the carboxyl group—CO_2H or, as it is sometimes written,

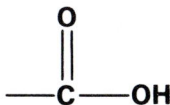

Whenever you think about the chemical behaviour of any alkanoic acid you must remember that it is the —CO_2H part which does the work. The rest of the molecule is relatively unimportant.

The acids all affect pH paper in the same way as other acids which you have met and they react with magnesium to give hydrogen gas.

This ability of certain metals to push out hydrogen when they react with acids seems to indicate that the hydrogen in an acid, or at least some of it, is loosely bound in the molecule. The structural formula of ethanoic acid,

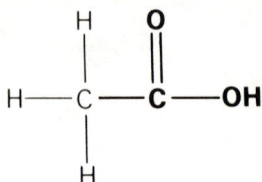

$$
\begin{array}{ccc}
\text{H} & \text{O} \\
| & || \\
\text{H} - \text{C} - \text{C} - \text{OH} \\
| \\
\text{H}
\end{array}
$$

makes it clear that the molecule contains hydrogen atoms linked to a carbon atom and a hydrogen atom which is linked to an oxygen atom. There is evidence that, when acids with this structure react with a metal, only the hydrogen which is attached *directly to an oxygen* atom is released. This seems to indicate that not all the single bonds in the molecule are identical.

6.7 Fats

No one yet seems to have discovered whether or not fats are essential in our diet. Examples of fats are butter from milk, lard from pigs, and suet from cattle. One thing we do know is that people living in cold climates eat more fat than those in warmer countries. This is because fats, when digested, release more than twice the amount of energy as the same mass of carbohydrates—although the process takes much longer.

The fats which we eat are formed by the combination of two kinds of compound, both of which we discussed earlier in the chapter. They are alcohols

(containing the **C—OH** group) and acids (containing the $-\overset{\displaystyle O}{\underset{\displaystyle OH}{C}}$ group).

Some alcohols and *some* acids combine to give fats.

The formation of fat takes place in our bodies all the time—another example of the fact that our bodies are very efficient chemical factories.

Much of the fatty material which most of us eat is not used up at once to provide energy for our bodies. It is only partly broken down. This first stage forms an alcohol and an acid.

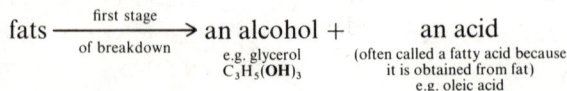

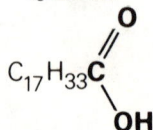

$$
\text{fats} \xrightarrow[\text{of breakdown}]{\text{first stage}} \text{an alcohol} + \text{an acid}
$$

e.g. glycerol
$C_3H_5(OH)_3$

(often called a fatty acid because it is obtained from fat)
e.g. oleic acid

$$
C_{17}H_{33}\overset{\displaystyle O}{\underset{\displaystyle OH}{C}}
$$

This alcohol contains three **C—OH** groups per molecule instead of a single one, as in the alcohols we have met so far.

These two substances, glycerol and oleic acid, are transported through the body and, if they are not broken down into simpler substances to release energy, they link together again as fat which is stored as a food reserve (Fig. 6.5).

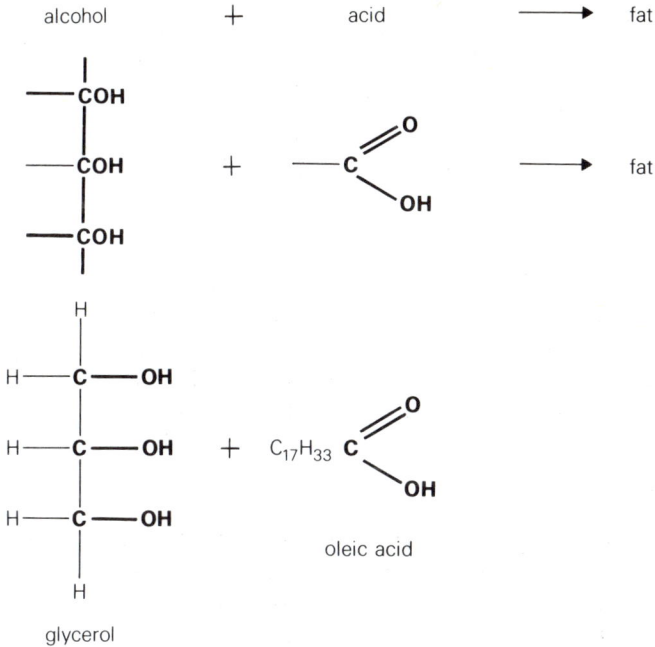

Figure 6.5

Margarine

Whale oil, coconut oil, olive oil, groundnut oil, and cottonseed oil are a few of the many oils which occur naturally in animals and plants. They are called soft oils because at ordinary temperatures they are liquid or nearly liquid. They are actually a mixture of oils and all contain a high percentage of the unsaturated compound, oleic acid, which has one double bond per molecule.

These oily substances would not be acceptable as a substitute for butter. We prefer a solid fat which looks and tastes more like butter.

Soft oils containing oleic acid can be made to solidify by treatment with hydrogen. The hydrogen is taken up by the double bonds, and this process of hydrogenation (the addition of hydrogen) is called **hardening**. A nickel catalyst is needed for this reaction. The hardening of natural oils was perfected as long ago as 1910 and is now the basis of the manufacture of margarine—a popular alternative to butter.

6.8 From fats to soap

Fats are also the starting point in the manufacture of soap. The first step is to boil them with a solution of an alkali such as sodium hydroxide. The acid from the fat reacts with the alkali to form the sodium compound of the acid. Glycerol is the second product.

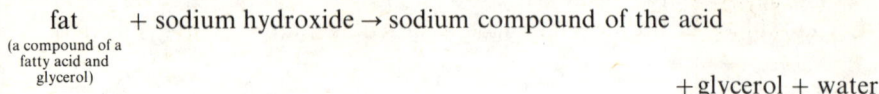

fat   + sodium hydroxide → sodium compound of the acid

(a compound of a
fatty acid and
glycerol)

+ glycerol + water

The sodium compound of the acid is a very common form of soap. 'Soap' is the potassium or sodium compound of a fatty acid which contains more than eight carbon atoms per molecule.

Stearic acid, which is common in fats, has the formula $C_{17}H_{35}CO_2H$. Its molecule consists of two parts:

(a) the long chain $C_{17}H_{35}$, and

(b) the $-C\overset{O}{\underset{OH}{\big\Vert}}$ at the end of the chain.

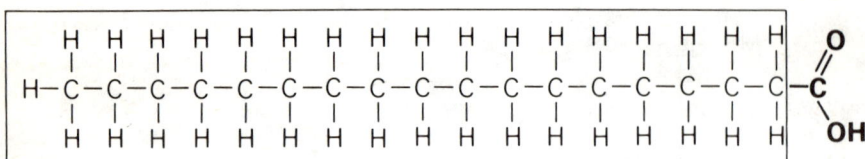

Sodium stearate (a soap) is $C_{17}H_{35}CO_2Na$. The hydrogen in the $-C\overset{O}{\underset{OH}{\big\Vert}}$

end-group has been replaced by sodium: $-C\overset{O}{\underset{ONa}{\big\Vert}}$. The sodium does not re-

place any of the hydrogen atoms in the long side chain—only the hydrogen in

the $-C\overset{O}{\underset{OH}{\big\Vert}}$ end-group (Fig. 6.6). This seems to indicate that the end

hydrogen atom is connected to the rest of the molecule in a different way from the other thirty-five hydrogen atoms. It seems to form a different kind of bond between itself and an oxygen atom. Similar evidence for this was mentioned earlier in the chapter (p. 66).

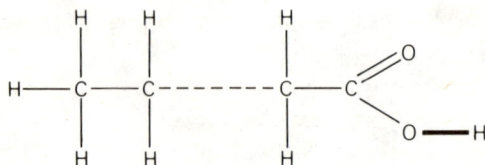

Figure 6.6

This bond could be either an easily broken bond or a different kind of bond altogether. What is certain is that this hydrogen atom is more easily detached from the molecule than are the hydrogen atoms which are joined to the carbon atoms along the chain.

We shall return to this difference in the next chapter.

6.9 Alcohols and acids

The reaction between the alcohol (glycerol) and the acid (oleic acid) is only one example of a type of reaction which can take place between alcohols and acids. All kinds of alcohols and acids can react with one another.

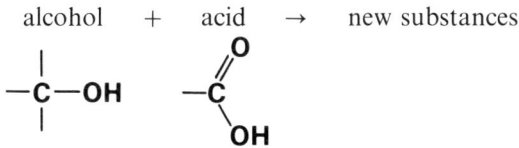

alcohol   +   acid   →   new substances

In all reactions of this type the *main parts of both molecules remain unaltered*. Only the **COH** group (or groups) in the alcohol and the $-C\overset{O}{\underset{OH}{}}$ group in the acid are affected.

There is evidence that the **H** in the **COH** group and the **OH** in the $-C\overset{O}{\underset{OH}{}}$ group combine to produce water (Fig. 6.7).

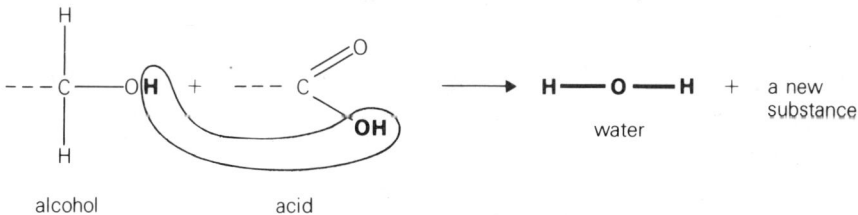

Figure 6.7

The 'new compounds' formed as a result of the other parts of the two molecules combining are called **esters**.

We have already seen that fat is formed by a reaction between an alcohol (glycerol) and oleic acid. A fat is, therefore, an ester.

A simpler example occurs when the alcohol ethanol, C_2H_5OH, reacts with the acid ethanoic acid, CH_3CO_2H.

$$\mathrm{H-\overset{\displaystyle H}{\underset{\displaystyle H}{C}}-\overset{\displaystyle H}{\underset{\displaystyle H}{C}}-OH} \quad + \quad \mathrm{\underset{HO}{\overset{O}{C}}-\overset{\displaystyle H}{\underset{\displaystyle H}{C}}-H}$$

$$\downarrow$$

$$\mathrm{H-\overset{\displaystyle H}{\underset{\displaystyle H}{C}}-\overset{\displaystyle H}{\underset{\displaystyle H}{C}}-O-\overset{O}{C}-\overset{\displaystyle H}{\underset{\displaystyle H}{C}}-H}$$

$$+$$

$$\mathbf{H_2O}$$

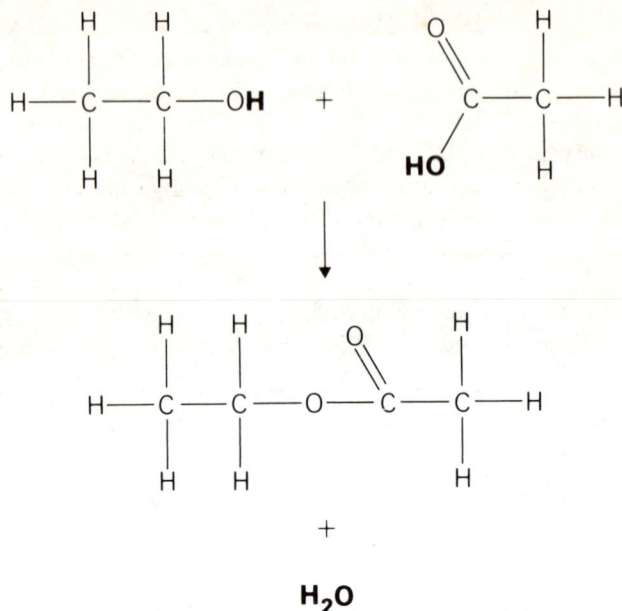

Esters are named from the alcohol and acid used to form them and have the ending **-ate** attached to the *acid* name.

For example, the ester formed from ethanol and ethanoic acid is called ethyl ethanoate (Fig. 6.8).

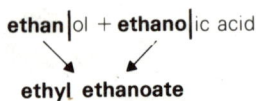

ethan|ol + **ethano**|ic acid

↘ ↙

ethyl ethanoate

Figure 6.8

The ester formed from methanol and ethanoic acid is called methyl ethanoate (Fig. 6.9).

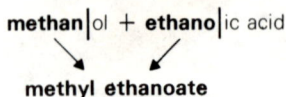

methan|ol + **ethano**|ic acid

↘ ↙

methyl ethanoate

Figure 6.9

In all these ester-forming reactions, a hydrogen atom from the **COH** group in the alcohol combines with an oxygen and hydrogen atom from the **CO₂H** group in the acid to form water. This splitting out of a small molecule between two chemicals is called a **condensation** reaction. It is a fairly common type of reaction in chemistry and we shall come across similar reactions quite often.

6.10 A reaction in reverse

When we dealt with the chemistry of fats in Section 6.7 it was mentioned that they can be broken down chemically in our bodies into simpler substances.

$$\text{fats} \rightarrow \text{an alcohol} + \text{an acid}$$

Fats are esters, and other esters can be made to react in the same way. In all cases the elements which make up water (two H atoms and one O atom) must be added to the fat in order to give back the original alcohol and acid.

This is normally done in the laboratory by warming the ester with sodium hydroxide solution in water. The breaking down of an ester by inserting hydrogen and oxygen is called **hydrolysis** (see Section 6.3). Here is an example.

$$\text{ester} + H_2O \rightarrow \text{alcohol} + \text{acid}$$

(ethyl ethanoate) (ethanol) (ethanoic acid)

Figure 6.10 shows the process diagrammatically.

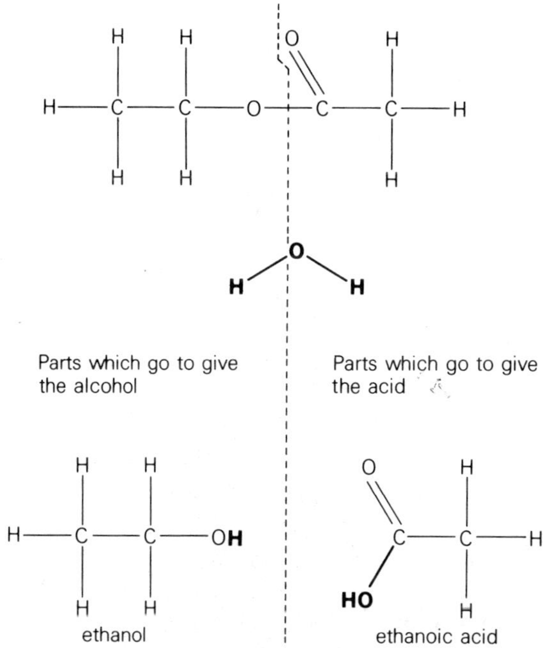

Parts which go to give the alcohol

Parts which go to give the acid

ethanol

ethanoic acid

Figure 6.10

New words you have met in this chapter

Carbohydrates compounds which contain carbon, hydrogen, and oxygen. Usually the hydrogen and oxygen are in the ratio of 2:1 (as in water). The formula for a carbohydrate can be expressed as $C_x(H_2O)_y$.

Photosynthesis the process by which green plants, in the presence of sunlight, combine carbon dioxide and water to form carbohydrates. Oxygen is released to the air during the process.

Respiration   this is the opposite of photosynthesis. During respiration carbohydrates and oxygen in the bodies of animals are slowly changed into carbon dioxide and water. Energy is released during the process.

Monosaccharides   these short chain carbohydrates have six carbon atoms per molecule. They have the formula $C_6(H_2O)_6$ or $C_6H_{12}O_6$. Examples are glucose and fructose.

Disaccharides   these are obtained when two monosaccharides are linked together and therefore have twelve carbon atoms per molecule. Examples are sucrose (ordinary sugar) and maltose.

Polysaccharides   many monosaccharide units linked together. One example is starch.

Hydrolysis   this occurs when molecules such as carbohydrates react with water to give simpler molecules.

Enzymes   big molecules of a definite shape, each of which can help to dismantle or build *one* particular molecular structure only.

Fermentation   a process by which enzymes convert carbohydrates into alcohol. Energy and carbon dioxide are released during the reactions.

Alcohols   the simplest homologous series has the general formula, $C_nH_{2n+1}OH$. All its members contain one **COH** group per molecule and all their names end in -anol. The first member of the series is methanol (CH_3OH) and the commonest alcohol is ethanol (C_2H_5OH). (Alcohols with more than one **COH** group per molecule are also possible.)

Alkanoic acids   an homologous series having the general formula $C_nH_{2n+1}CO_2H$, although the simplest member, methanoic acid, is HCOOH (i.e. $n = 0$). All the homologues contain one **CO_2H** (or COOH) group per molecule and all their names end in -anoic acid. Ethanoic acid is CH_3COOH.

Hydrogenation   a process in which liquid oils containing oleic acid can be solidified or *hardened* by reaction with hydrogen.

Esterification   the reaction between an alcohol and an acid in which an ester and water are formed.

Condensation   the coupling of two organic molecules together with the removal of a simple molecule such as water. Esterification is one example of condensation.

Revision section for Chapters 4–6

Answers to this section will be found on page 240.

1 Choose from the grid all the examples of:
(a) hydrocarbons, (b) alkanes, (c) carbohydrates, (d) alcohols, (e) alkanoic acids, (f) esters.

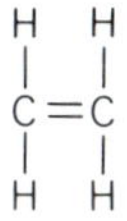 1	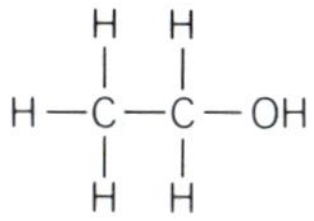 2	$C_{12}H_{22}O_{11}$ 3
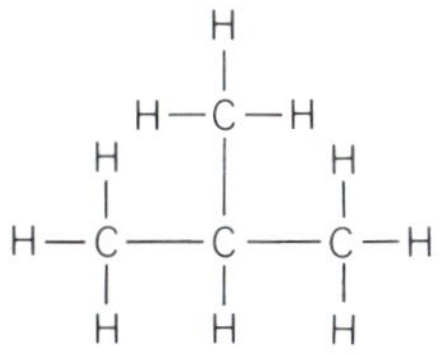 4	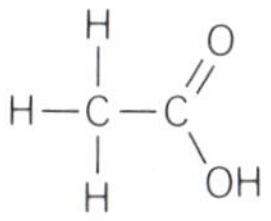 5	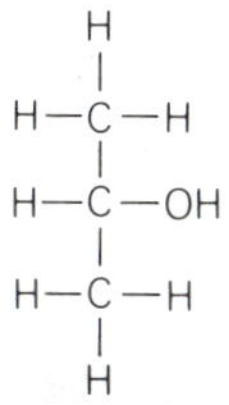 6
$C_6H_{12}O_6$ 7	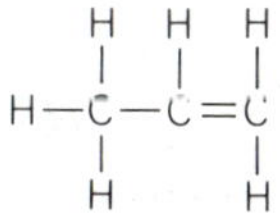 8	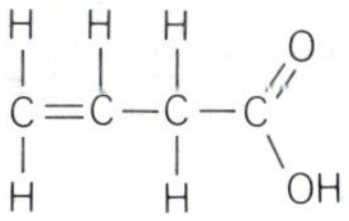 9
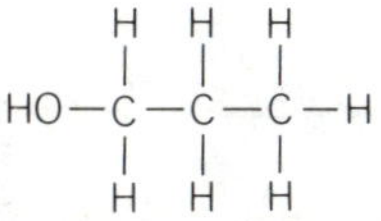 10	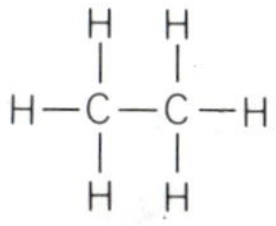 11	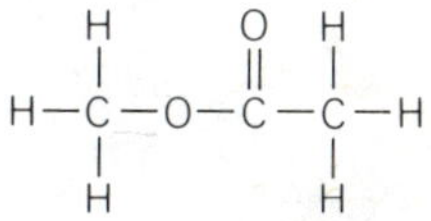 12

2 Can you explain the chemistry behind the following newspaper extract?

Fumes killed couple

Fumes from the dying embers of an all-night stove poured from hidden cracks in a chimney into a bedroom at the point where a couple had placed the head of their bed, an inquest was told yesterday. Verdict of death by misadventure due to carbon monoxide poisoning was recorded.

3 When an oil was burned in a lamp, carbon dioxide and water vapour were formed. How does this experiment help to confirm the name 'hydrocarbon' for the oil?

4 Write the formulae for the sixth and the eighth members of the alkane homologous series.

5 Write the formulae of the three isomers of pentane.

6 How would you demonstrate that an organic liquid was saturated?

7 Explain the chemistry involved in the following statements.
   (a) Ethene can be made to polymerize to give polyethene.
   (b) When starch is mixed with saliva and kept warm for a time, it no longer behaves like starch.
   (c) Polysaccharides are polymers.

8 Make a list of materials which you have used today which you think were made from petrochemicals.

9 When fat is overheated in a frying pan, the fumes do not condense back to liquid fat but remain as an unsaturated gas. Suggest an explanation for this behaviour.

10 Water is sometimes referred to as 'the simplest alcohol'. In what respect can water be considered like this? (Think about the structure of a water molecule.)

11 Starch has been broken down in two ways and the products separated on chromatograms. Examine the results below and decide what the products are from each experiment.

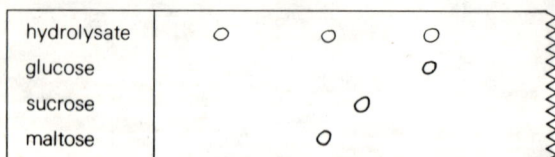

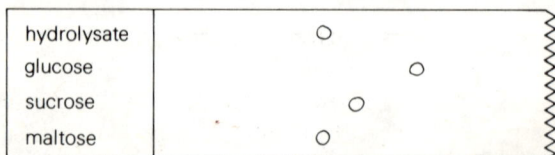

hydrolysate	○	○	○
glucose			○
sucrose		○	
maltose		○	

hydrolysate	○		
glucose		○	
sucrose	○		
maltose	○		

12 When ethanoic acid is warmed with some propanol and a few drops of concentrated sulphuric acid, a sweet smelling ester is formed. What is its name?

Chemistry in Action 3

Energy—past, present, and future

(Before you start this, you will need graph paper, a pencil, and a ruler.)

We need energy to power our cars and trains, to heat our homes, and to power our industry. Today, our energy comes mainly from coal, oil, and natural gas, with a small amount coming from hydro-electric power and nuclear power. We tend to use a lot of energy. In Britain in 1980 we used energy equivalent to the efficient burning of about 350 million tonnes of coal!

There are about 56 million of us living in Britain and so, on average, each of us uses roughly the equivalent of $6\frac{1}{4}$ tonnes of coal each year! It is difficult to imagine $6\frac{1}{4}$ tonnes, but it is *125 sacks of coal*, enough to make one complete layer of sacks on a large coal lorry. On average, each person in the world uses the equivalent of just over 2 tonnes of coal each year, but some countries are much poorer and use less. In India, for example, each person uses, on average, the equivalent of only about 0.2 tonnes. By contrast, people in the USA use the equivalent of over 11 tonnes per person each year.

Although there are many sources of energy, coal has been chosen to define a unit of energy. The unit which Government planners often use is the 'million tonne coal equivalent'. It is very useful because it gives numbers which are easy to handle. One million tonne coal equivalent is the energy released when one million tonnes of coal are burned efficiently. It has the symbol 'mtce'. (1 mtce is equivalent to 2.64×10^{16} joules).

It is easy to plot a graph showing how our use of energy in Britain has increased during the past twenty years. It is not so easy to predict what will happen in the next thirty years. However, Government advisers have to make intelligent guesses about the future, so that planning can take place for new coal mines, new power stations, and new oil wells. The following graph is accurate up to 1979, but guesswork from then on, although the guessing has not been entirely blind.

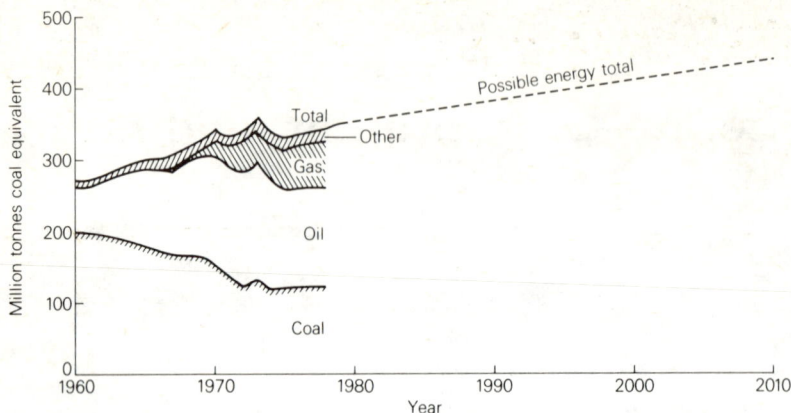

Have a close look at the earlier part of the graph. The proportion of our energy from various sources (such as coal, oil, and gas) is shown. Look at 1960. We used just under 280 mtce of energy in total, of which nearly 200 came from coal. Look at 1970. How much energy did we use in total? How much came from oil? How much came from 'Other'? 'Other' includes hydro-electric power and nuclear power.

Now *form a group* with two or three of your class and discuss the following questions. One of your group can write down the answers.

1 When, roughly, did North Sea gas start to come into production?
2 Can you account for the 'dip' in coal production in 1974?
3 What percentage of our energy came from 'Other' in 1978?

Start by copying out the graph on to your own paper. You are now required to complete the graph by filling in what you think will be the proportions of coal, gas, oil, other, etc., up to the year 2010. It will need intelligent guesswork on your group's part! Here is some information to help you.

(a) Britain has large reserves of coal. Increasing coal production is possible, although it is unlikely that production will get anything near 200 mtce by the year 2010.
(b) North Sea oil production will grow slightly in the early 1980s, remain constant for several years, and then decrease steadily.
(c) North Sea gas will grow only a little more. It is likely to remain steady for several years, then steadily decrease.
(d) In the 'Other' group, hydro-electric power contributes only about 2 mtce and cannot be developed much more. Nuclear power completes this group at the moment. Nuclear energy could be expanded by building many nuclear power stations, but the total nuclear output is unlikely to reach 100 mtce much before the year 2010, even if there is an enormous building programme.
(e) There are other sources of energy such as wave power, tidal power, wind power, solar energy, and geothermal energy, which have yet to be developed. However, it is unlikely that all of these together would contribute more than 10 mtce by the year 2000.

7

Giving or sharing?

7.1

In Chapter 1 we spent some time considering the mass of atoms. This mass is measured in very small units (called atomic mass units) because a gram would be far too large a unit. A hydrogen atom, for instance, weighs about 0.000 000 000 000 000 000 000 002 g. These tiny specks of material not only have a mass but they also have a volume. Just as we can think about their masses without knowing the actual value in grams, we can also think about their volumes, not in cm^3, but in comparison to each other.

Look at column 1 of the Periodic Table (Fig. 7.1). This begins with hydrogen and then continues with lithium, sodium, potassium, rubidium, caesium, and francium. As you look down the column you can see that each atom has one electron on its outside layer and that each atom has one layer of electrons more than the one above it.

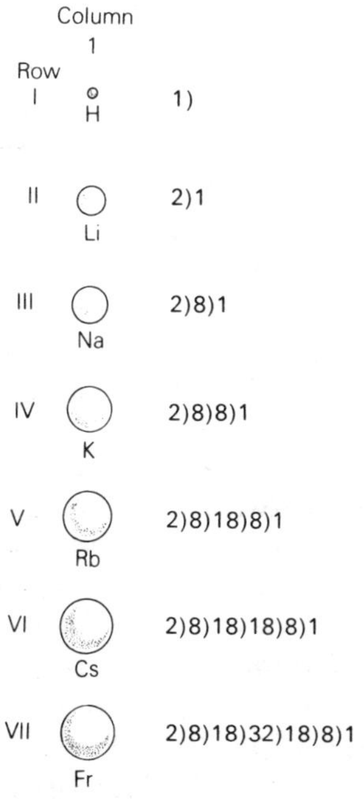

	Column 1	
Row		
I	⊙ H	1)
II	◯ Li	2)1
III	◯ Na	2)8)1
IV	◯ K	2)8)8)1
V	◯ Rb	2)8)18)8)1
VI	◯ Cs	2)8)18)18)8)1
VII	◯ Fr	2)8)18)32)18)8)1

Figure 7.1

Hydrogen must be the smallest atom and francium the largest.

A similar pattern must apply to all of the columns: small atoms at the top and large ones at the bottom.

How do they compare in size as we go from left to right across the table? Look at the row which begins with lithium and goes across to fluorine. The electron arrangement is:

Li	Be	B	C	N	O	F
2)1	2)2	2)3	2)4	2)5	2)6	2)7

The nuclei of these atoms must contain as many protons as there are electrons and so the proton pattern is:

Li	Be	B	C	N	O	F
3	4	5	6	7	8	9

The charge on a proton is positive and so the nucleus of these elements is becoming more positive as we go from left to right. This will have the effect of pulling the negatively charged electrons closer to the nucleus and reducing the size of the atoms (Fig. 7.2).

Column

	1	2	3	4	5	6	7
Row II							
	Li	Be	B	C	N	O	F

Figure 7.2

This will apply to any of the rows in the Table giving the pattern with larger atoms on the left, smaller atoms on the right.

If we now look at the whole Table (Fig. 7.3) we can see these two patterns together. The noble gases in Column 8 are a special case which need not concern us at present.

7.2

These differences in volume have an effect upon the way atoms join together. In Chapter 3 we saw that atoms join by sharing pairs of electrons.

If the volume of the two joining atoms is the same and if they have the same nuclear charge, the shared electrons will be attracted equally by the nucleus of each atom. Although the electrons are always moving about they will tend to spend most of their time evenly between the two atoms which they are holding together (Fig. 7.4). This kind of bond, in which the electrons are shared equally, is called a **covalent bond**. A chlorine molecule has two identical atoms and so the bond between them will be **covalent**. A perfect covalent bond like this normally exists only between atoms of the same element.

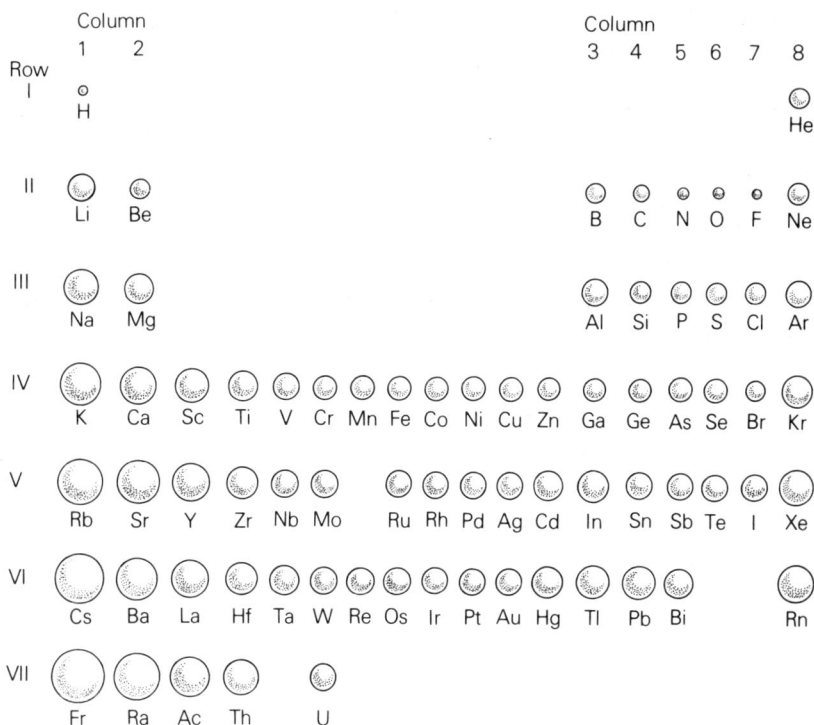

Figure 7.3

If the volume of the two atoms being joined is slightly different, usually the smaller atom will tend to pull the shared electrons nearer to itself because its positive nucleus is nearer the outside surface of the atom. The electrons are, of course, always moving but they will tend to spend more of their time nearer the smaller atom (Fig. 7.5). An example of this is the bond between a carbon and a fluorine atom.

This uneven sharing has the effect of making the bond slightly more negative at one end than the other. This slight charge is shown by the small letter delta (δ). This kind of bond is called **polar covalent**.

$$\overset{\delta+}{C}-\overset{\delta-}{F}$$

It is by far the most common type of bond because most molecules are made up of atoms of different kinds joined together. Since the small atoms are at the

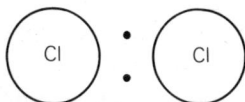

Figure 7.4

Figure 7.5

right of the Periodic Table and the larger atoms at the left, atoms at the right are the electron attractors.

There is a third possibility.

If the atoms being joined together are very different in size the smaller atom may pull the shared electrons so strongly that they leave the bigger atom altogether (Fig. 7.6). A good example of this would be the bond between lithium and fluorine.

Figure 7.6

	Lithium atom	Fluorine atom
electrons	2)1	2)7
protons	3	9
overall charge	0	0

Lithium will share its one outer electron with the single electron still unpaired in the fluorine atom. If the fluorine atom captures the shared pair for itself, the lithium atom will now be short of an electron and the fluorine atom will have an extra electron:

	Lithium ion	Fluorine ion
electrons	2)	2)8
protons	3	9
overall charge	1 positive unit	1 negative unit

The lithium atom minus its electron is written as Li^+. The positive sign shows that it has lost one electron and now has one proton (positive) which is not being balanced by an electron.

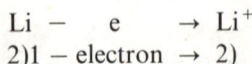

$$Li - e \rightarrow Li^+$$
$$2)1 - electron \rightarrow 2)$$

The fluorine atom plus the extra electron is written as F^-. The negative sign shows that it has gained one electron and now has one electron (negative) which is not being balanced by a proton.

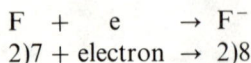

$$F + e \rightarrow F^-$$
$$2)7 + electron \rightarrow 2)8$$

These charged atoms are called **ions**. They are held together, not by sharing a pair of electrons, but by the attraction of the positive charge on one ion for the negative charge on the other ion. This kind of bonding is called **ionic**. It is the most common kind of bonding between atoms on the far left and the far right of the Periodic Table because these differ most in size. In Sections 6.6 and 6.8 we noticed that, in organic acids, one of the bonds was different from the rest. It is an ionic bond while all the others are covalent or polar covalent.

Summing up so far

1 Two identical atoms share electrons equally, forming a **covalent bond**.
2 Two atoms which are of slightly different size share electrons unequally, forming a **polar covalent bond**.
3 Atoms of a very different size do not share electrons, but the smaller atom attracts electrons completely away from the larger atom, forming charged atoms called **ions**.

  The ions are held together by the attraction of the positive ion for the negative ion. This is called **ionic bonding**.

7.3

You have met many examples of compounds in which the bonds have been covalent or polar covalent. These include the hydrocarbons, carbohydrates, fats, and esters which you studied in Chapters 4, 5, and 6.

  The next few chapters will be spent looking at compounds which have ionic bonding.

  What experimental evidence do we have for these different kinds of bonds?

7.4

If you allow a fine stream of water to run from a tap and bring the barrel of your pen up to it, nothing happens. If you then rub the pen on your sleeve to charge it and then bring it up to the stream of water, the water is attracted to the pen (Fig. 7.7).

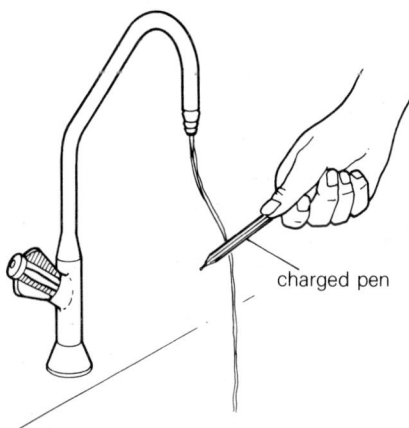

charged pen

Figure 7.7

Figure 7.8

How does this fact fit our theory? Hydrogen and oxygen are fairly far apart in the Periodic Table and so the H—O bonds will be polar covalent. In this case the electrons are attracted to the oxygen end of the bonds, making the oxygen end more negative than the hydrogen end (Fig. 7.8).

In the water stream passing the charged rod something like Fig. 7.9 must be happening. If the rod is positively charged the negative ends of the molecules will move round to point towards it, causing attraction between the rod and the water.

Many other liquids behave in this way when they pass the charged rod and our theory helps us to explain each of them. Their bonding is polar covalent. However, there are many liquids, like the hydrocarbon fuels, which are not affected by a charged rod and so their bonding must be purely covalent (or very nearly so).

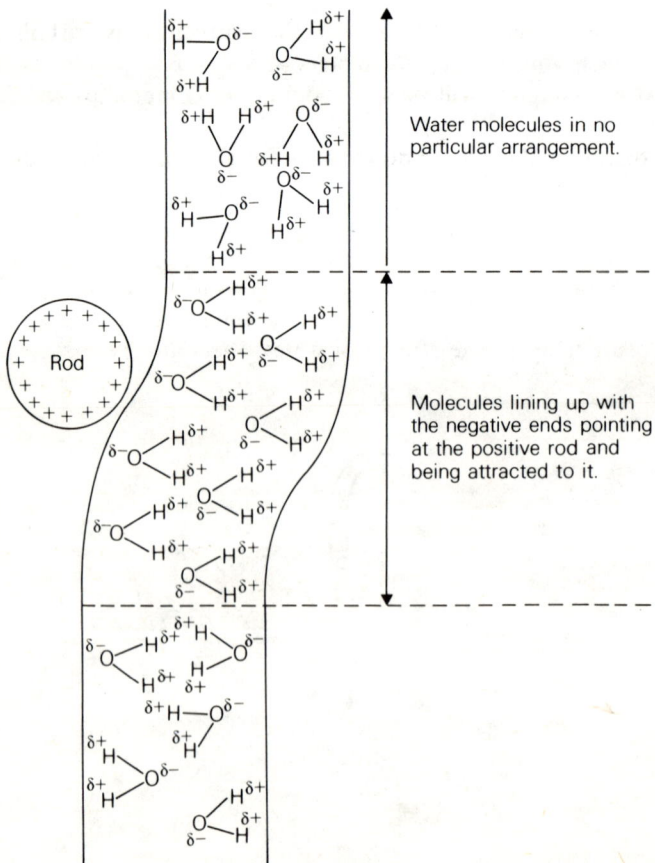

Water molecules in no particular arrangement.

Molecules lining up with the negative ends pointing at the positive rod and being attracted to it.

Figure 7.9

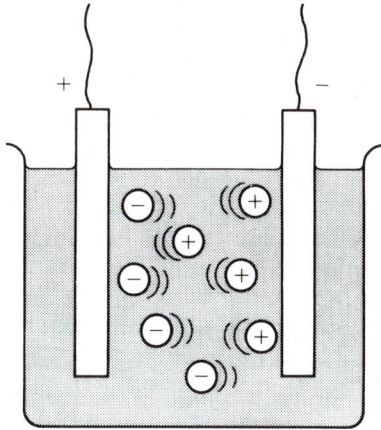

Figure 7.10

7.5

If we were going to look for evidence for electrically charged ionic substances some electrical method would be most likely to succeed.

We could put two wires into the ionic substance and attach one wire to the positive end of a battery and the other to the negative end of the battery (Fig. 7.10). It would be reasonable to expect the positive ions to be attracted and move to the negative wire and similarly we might expect the negative ions to move to the positive wire. Since the ions are so very small, we could never hope to see them moving, so how could we detect their movement? A movement of electrically charged particles is really an electric current and so, if the ions were to move, a current would flow. Electric currents can be detected by the fact that they cause bulbs to light up. The simple circuit shown in Fig. 7.11 should be able to detect ions if they exist. If a current flows, the bulb should light up.

It was suggested in Section 7.2 that compounds made from elements at opposite sides of the Periodic Table were most likely to be ionic. One such

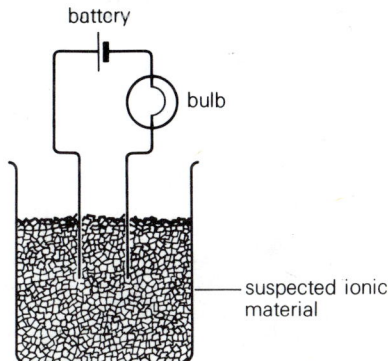

Figure 7.11

compound is lithium chloride which is a crystalline substance at room temperature.

If some solid lithium chloride is placed in the apparatus shown in Fig. 7.11 the *bulb does not glow*—so much for our idea! But let us think again. It may be that the attraction of the negative and positive ions for each other in the solid is so great that they cannot move freely to give a current. How could they be freed from each other? We could try to melt the solid.

If the solid lithium chloride is heated until it just begins to *melt*, the *bulb starts to glow*. Our ideas were not so wrong after all. If the heat source is removed, the glow in the bulb begins to fade and, as the liquid solidifies, the bulb goes out because the ions are once more locked in a solid.

The bonds which hold these ions together in the solid must be quite strong. As the liquid solidifies each positive ion must try to keep away from other positive ions and surround itself with negative ones. In the same way, the negative ions will be repelled from each other and attracted to the positive ones. This should produce a three-dimensional pattern (Fig. 7.12) in which there are alternately positive and negative ions.

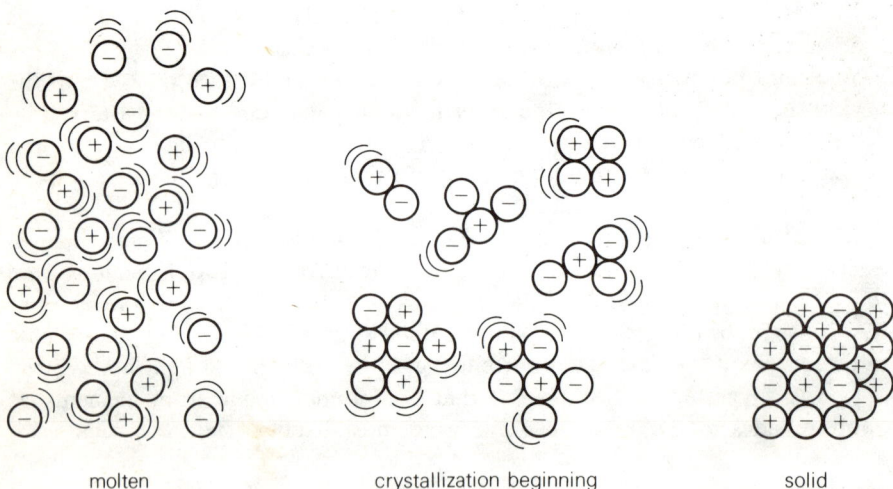

molten   crystallization beginning   solid

Figure 7.12

When the lithium chloride has solidified and cooled to room temperature, it is interesting to add some water to the tube. As soon as some of the solid *dissolves* in the water the *bulb lights up again*.

Here is another way to set the ions free so that they can carry an electric current.

7.6

We now have good evidence for the existence of ions. With our ion detecting apparatus (Fig. 7.11) we are in a position to examine the materials in the laboratory to see if their bonding is ionic. We could melt a variety of substances and insert the pair of wires into them or, more easily, we could dissolve the substances in water and then test the solutions.

However, we are not being very scientific. Perhaps water itself has ionic bonding. In this case the addition of water to other materials to give a conducting solution would not prove that the dissolved material was ionic. We must test pure water first to see if it conducts an electric current and allows the bulb to glow. When we do so, we find that pure water does not conduct enough to allow the bulb to glow. Water itself is not an ionic substance although it is polar covalent.

If water itself does not conduct electricity, but if a solution of a substance in water does conduct electricity (Fig. 7.13), then the dissolved material must have released ions as it dissolved in the water (Fig. 7.14).

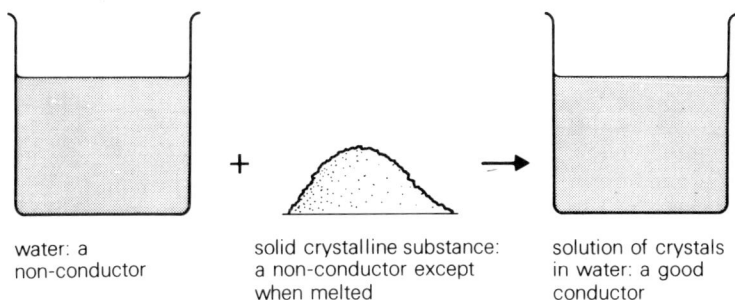

water: a
non-conductor

solid crystalline substance:
a non-conductor except
when melted

solution of crystals
in water: a good
conductor

Figure 7.13

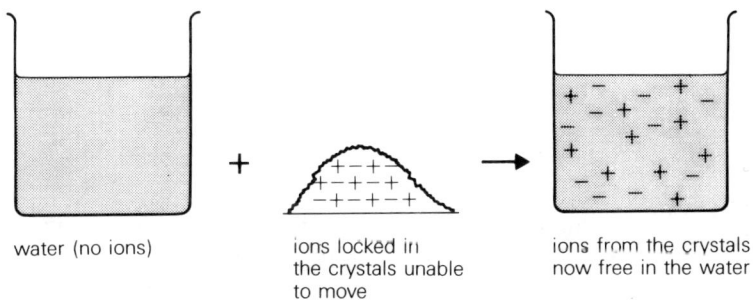

water (no ions)

ions locked in
the crystals unable
to move

ions from the crystals
now free in the water

Figure 7.14

If a whole range of substances is dissolved in water and tested in this way we get the results in Table 7.1. Some substances are already liquids at room temperature and so do not need to be dissolved in water.

We now have two groups, the ionic substances and the rest which may be covalent or polar covalent. Among the list of non-conductors are many of the substances you met in Chapters 4, 5, and 6. They are all carbon compounds (organic) although there are many other covalent compounds which do not contain carbon.

The 'ionic substances' list contains acids, alkalis (such as potassium hydroxide) and salts (such as sodium chloride, copper sulphate, and sodium carbonate). Notice that ethanoic acid (an organic substance) is a conductor because *one* of the bonds in the CO_2H part is ionic.

Table 7.1

Conducts electricity	Does not conduct electricity
Sodium chloride	Sugar
Potassium hydroxide	Glycerine (glycerol)
Ethanoic acid	Alcohol (ethanol)
Hydrochloric acid	Methanol
Copper sulphate	Hexane (pure liquid not dissolved in water)
Sodium hydrogencarbonate	Toluene (pure liquid not dissolved in water)
Sodium carbonate	Oils (pure liquids not dissolved in water)
Sulphuric acid	

Summary

1 Compounds made between elements *far apart* in the Periodic Table usually contain *ions*.

2 Compounds made between elements *close together* in the Periodic Table usually *do not* contain ions.

7.7

The formulae for ionic substances are also written according to the rules we met in Chapter 3.

Potassium bromide

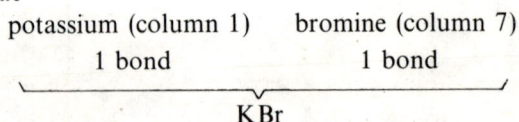

potassium (column 1)   bromine (column 7)

1 bond   1 bond

KBr

Sometimes ionic formulae are written showing the charges on the ions.

In the K—Br bond, the pair of electrons go completely over to the bromine atom. This makes the potassium atom short of one electron while the bromine atom gains an extra electron.

K   Br
2)8)8)1   2)8)18)7
no charge   no charge

K^+ Br^-
2)8)8   2)8)18)8

Potassium bromide can therefore be written K^+Br^-. This *ionic formula* is sometimes useful and we shall employ it now and again for special purposes. Otherwise we shall use the simpler KBr formula.

Here are two other examples.

Calcium oxide is usually written as CaO, calcium having two electrons for bonding and oxygen forming two bonds. If the calcium electrons are given completely to the oxygen atom, the calcium will lose two electrons giving Ca^{2+} and the oxygen will gain two electrons giving O^{2-}. Put together, the formula for calcium oxide will be $Ca^{2+}O^{2-}$ or simply CaO.

Magnesium chloride

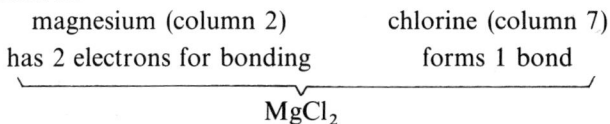

| magnesium (column 2) | chlorine (column 7) |
| has 2 electrons for bonding | forms 1 bond |

$$MgCl_2$$

If the magnesium loses its share of the two pairs of electrons it will become the magnesium ion, Mg^{2+}. Each of the chlorine atoms will gain an electron from the magnesium atom, giving two Cl^- ions. Putting these together will give

$$Mg^{2+}(Cl^-)_2$$

Remember that the small $_2$ multiplies only the Cl^- in the brackets.

New words you have met in this chapter

Covalent bond this is a link between two atoms in which a pair of electrons is shared equally between them. The atoms are usually identical.

Polar covalent bond in this bond the pair of electrons is not shared equally between the atoms. Usually the smaller atom pulls the electrons towards itself making the bond very slightly positive at one end and very slightly negative at the other.

Ionic bond one of the atoms in the bond pulls the electrons so strongly that it takes over the electrons completely. It gains a negative charge and the other atom gains a positive charge. The atoms are held together by the attraction of the positive for the negative.

Ion this is an atom which has either lost or gained electrons so that it now has either a positive or negative charge. Metals on the *left* of the Periodic Table tend to *lose* electrons and become positive ions. Non-metals on the *right* of the Table tend to *gain* electrons and become negative ions.

8

More about ions

8.1

You may have wondered how the word **ion** came to be applied to the charged particles we were talking about in the last chapter. It is a Greek word meaning 'wanderer'. We have seen some evidence for their wandering as they move carrying an electric current.

There is another way in which we can *see* this wandering more directly.

Look at Table 8.1 which gives information about the colour of ionic substances. If we do some careful detective work we can find out the colour of various ions.

Table 8.1

Solid substance	Colour
Potassium chloride	White
Copper chloride	Blue/green
Sodium chloride	White
Copper sulphate	Blue
Sodium sulphate	White
Nickel sulphate	Green
Nickel chloride	Green
Potassium dichromate	Orange
Sodium dichromate	Orange
Copper dichromate	Greenish brown

Look at the white substances in the list first. If they are white we can take it that neither ion has any colour. The colourless ions must therefore be the potassium ion, the sodium ion, the chloride ion, and the sulphate ion.

Now look at the colour of copper chloride and copper sulphate. Both are blue. Since the chloride ion and the sulphate ion are colourless, the blue colour must come from the copper ion. Similarly we can see that the green of nickel compounds must come from the nickel ion.

Potassium and sodium dichromates are orange. We have already decided that potassium and sodium ions are colourless and so the orange colour must come from the dichromate ion.

The last substance on the list, copper dichromate, must have a colour which is a blend of the blue of the copper ion and the orange of the dichromate ion, making it a greenish brown.

Summary

Table 8.2

Ion	Colour
Sodium	Colourless
Potassium	Colourless
Chloride	Colourless
Sulphate	Colourless
Copper	Blue
Nickel	Green
Dichromate	Orange

If we choose coloured ions for our experiments we should be able to see them 'wandering'. Once these ions are released into solution they move freely by diffusion. We can see blue copper ions moving to meet orange dichromate ions if we set up the apparatus shown in Fig. 8.1.

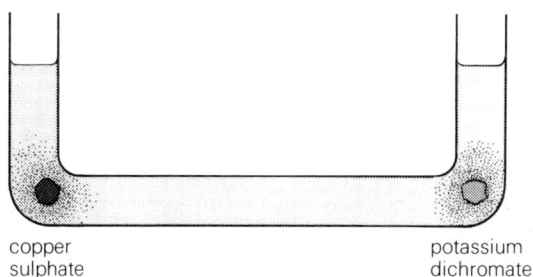

copper
sulphate

potassium
dichromate

Figure 8.1

The other ions are also moving but we cannot see them. Diffusion is a movement in all directions. It should be possible to get all the ions of one kind to move in the same direction because they all have the same charge. If we set up a U-tube with a concentrated solution of copper dichromate at the bottom and insert wires as shown in Fig. 8.2 we find that a blue band comes out of the copper dichromate solution and moves slowly to the negative wire.

At the same time an orange band moves up the other arm of the U-tube towards the positive wire. This shows that the copper ions must have a positive charge and the dichromate ions must have a negative charge.

This time the wandering has been controlled by the effect of an electric charge applied by a battery.

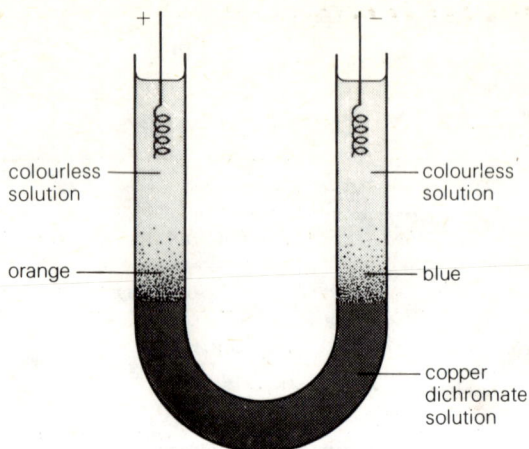

Figure 8.2

8.2

By a series of experiments like this it is possible to see if some ions move more quickly than others. It has been found that most ions move through water at about the same speed when a fixed electric charge is applied to them. But there are two exceptional ions which move much faster than all the others. If we were to have an 'ion race' the finishing situation would look something like Fig. 8.3.

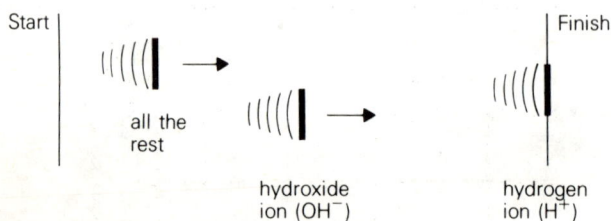

Figure 8.3

When the hydrogen ion had reached the tape the hydroxide ion would be half-way along the course and all the rest would be only about one-fifth of the way along. This difference in speed will be useful to us later in our work (Chapter 18, p. 191).

8.3

You will have noticed that the positively charged ions are those which come from elements in the left portion of the Periodic Table, while the negatively charged ions come from elements to the right of the Table (Fig. 8.4). Those on the left are metals while those on the right are non-metals such as sulphur, oxygen, and chlorine.

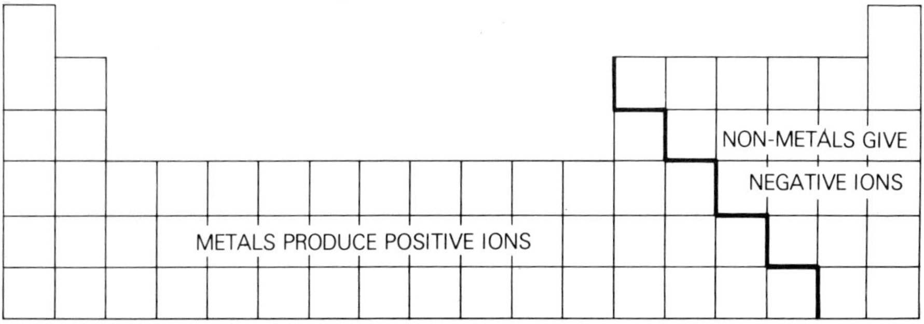

Figure 8.4

Saying that metals lose electrons to give positive ions is really just another way of saying that metals rust or corrode. We know from experience that not all metals rust equally easily.

If we can understand what is going on when metals rust we shall be in a better position to decide how to control rusting. We shall spend the rest of the chapter investigating this problem and seeing if our ideas about electrons and ions are helpful.

8.4 Metals and water

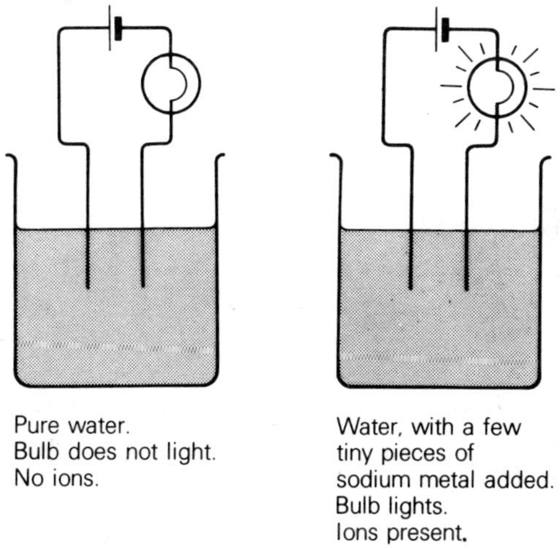

Pure water.
Bulb does not light.
No ions.

Water, with a few
tiny pieces of
sodium metal added.
Bulb lights.
Ions present.

Figure 8.5

In Section 7.6 we found that pure water was almost a non-conductor of electricity showing that it had few ions, if any. If some *tiny* pieces of sodium are added to water, the solution conducts current, showing that ions are now present (Fig. 8.5). The sodium metal has reacted quite fiercely with the water causing bubbles to be released and the metal has rusted or corroded away very rapidly to produce sodium ions.

$$Na \rightarrow Na^+$$
$$\text{metal} \quad \text{ion}$$

In doing so, it must have lost electrons:

$$Na - electron \rightarrow Na^+$$

What has happened to the electrons which the sodium atoms have given up?

The bubbles given off when the metal was reacting with the water are bubbles of hydrogen which catch fire very easily. Another clue is to be found when we add an indicator to the solution. It is now an alkali. All alkalis contain the hydroxide ion (OH^-) (Chapter 18). How can we piece the evidence together?

In Section 7.4 we noticed that the electrons in water were not equally shared in the bonds and tended to spend most of their time near the oxygen atom (Fig. 8.6).

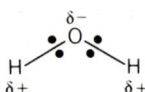

Figure 8.6

If another electron becomes available from a sodium atom, it can be attracted to one of the slightly positive hydrogen atoms in the water. This hydrogen atom, if it accepts the electron, will give up its share of the electron pair in the bond and so the oxygen will take both electrons (Fig. 8.7).

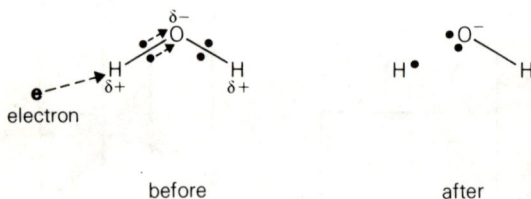

before   after

Figure 8.7

This now gives us a single atom of hydrogen and a negatively charged OH^- ion. When the single atom of hydrogen meets another single, they will tend to share their electrons to make a covalent bond between them giving an H_2 molecule.

$$H\cdot + \cdot H \rightarrow H—H$$

Hydrogen is a gas and will bubble to the surface of the water.

The positive Na^+ ions will be balanced by the negative OH^- ions giving an alkaline solution of sodium hydroxide.

sodium + water   will give   sodium ions + hydroxide ions + hydrogen

We can represent this in chemical symbols as follows:

$$Na + H_2O \rightarrow Na^+ + OH^- + H$$

But we need two atoms of hydrogen to give us H_2 molecules to make the gas. If we double everything we shall have:

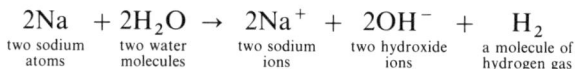

$$2Na + 2H_2O \rightarrow 2Na^+ + 2OH^- + H_2$$

two sodium atoms	two water molecules	two sodium ions	two hydroxide ions	a molecule of hydrogen gas

Notice that big numbers coming *before* a chemical formula multiply *everything* in the formula. We shall look at this more carefully in Chapter 12.

8.5

Do all metals behave like this with water and do they all react equally quickly?

With cold water, only a very few metals react quickly. In order of speed they are:

slower ↓
| Potassium
| Sodium
| Calcium
| Magnesium (takes a day or two)

Other metals do react, but usually quite slowly.

When the four fast metals react with water they give off hydrogen and an alkali is left in solution.

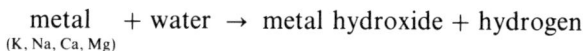

metal + water → metal hydroxide + hydrogen
(K, Na, Ca, Mg)

You will have noticed earlier in your study of science that heating often speeds up a chemical reaction. With the slower metals it might be worth finding out if they react more rapidly with hot water or even with steam. This can be done quite easily in the apparatus shown in Fig. 8.8.

The metal is heated and enough heat spreads along the tube to turn some of the water in the plug into steam. As the steam passes over the hot metal there is a chance that they will react together.

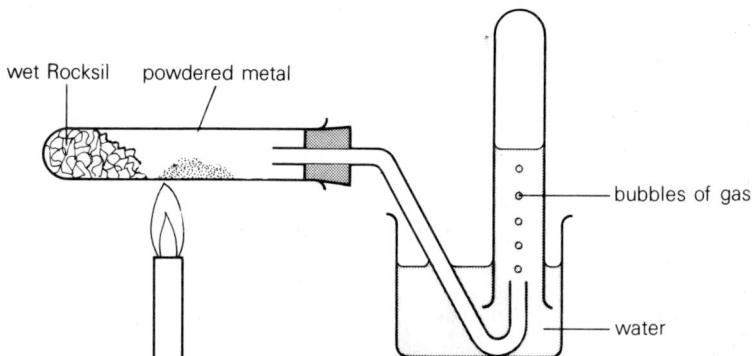

Figure 8.8

The metals which do react with steam are magnesium, aluminium, zinc, iron, and, to a slight extent, tin and lead.

At these high temperatures the metal oxides rather than the hydroxides are made.

$$metal + steam \rightarrow metal\ oxide + hydrogen$$
$$Ca + H_2O \rightarrow CaO + H_2$$

The metals which do not react are those which we use for coins or for jewellery because they react only very slowly or not at all. They are copper, silver, gold, and platinum.

Summary

Table 8.3

Potassium Sodium Calcium Magnesium	React with cold water to give hydrogen and a metal hydroxide	Metals on the far left of the Periodic Table
Aluminium Zinc Iron Tin Lead	React with steam to give hydrogen and metal oxide	Metals from the middle section of the Periodic Table
Copper Mercury Silver Gold Platinum	Hardly corrode at all	

8.6

Water is not the only liquid in which metals corrode. Acids attack some metals quite fiercely.

If we place samples of metals into hydrochloric acid we find that a pattern emerges quite similar to that which we saw for water and steam (Table 8.4).

Table 8.4

Metal	Conditions required for metal to push hydrogen easily from the acid
Magnesium (Mg)	Cold dilute acid
Aluminium (Al)	Cold dilute acid after a time lag
Zinc (Zn)	Moderately concentrated acid
Iron (Fe)	Moderately concentrated acid
Tin (Sn)	Hot concentrated acid
Copper (Cu) Mercury (Hg) Silver (Ag) Gold (Au) Platinum (Pt)	No effect

When these metals react with hydro**chloric** acid (HCl) they push out the hydrogen and form metal **chlorides**.

$$\text{metal} + \text{hydrochloric acid} \rightarrow \text{hydrogen} + \text{metal chloride}$$

In hydrochloric acid there are hydrogen ions (H^+) and chloride ions (Cl^-). The metal exchanges some of its electrons with the hydrogen ions to make hydrogen atoms and hydrogen molecules.

$$Mg - 2 \text{ electrons} \rightarrow Mg^{2+}$$
$$2)8)2 \qquad\qquad 2)8$$

$$2 \text{ electrons} + \begin{Bmatrix} H^+ \\ H^+ \end{Bmatrix} \rightarrow H + H \rightarrow H_2$$
$$1) \quad 1)$$

or

$$Mg + \begin{Bmatrix} H^+ + Cl^- \\ H^+ + Cl^- \end{Bmatrix} \rightarrow Mg^{2+} + \begin{Bmatrix} Cl^- \\ Cl^- \end{Bmatrix} + H_2$$

or

$$Mg + 2HCl \rightarrow MgCl_2 + H_2$$

Summary

The common metals fall into two groups:

(a) those which can push hydrogen out of acids and water (or steam) and give metal ions;

(b) those which cannot push hydrogen out of acids, water, or steam.

8.7

What happens when we put together metals which corrode easily and others which do not? This is often mistakenly done in practice. Copper strips are sometimes nailed on with iron nails. Aluminium valves are sometimes fitted to copper pipes.

This is easily investigated with some simple apparatus. Take a piece of copper as an example of a metal which does not corrode easily and bring it into contact with a metal which corrodes easily. To imitate corrosion conditions we can place a piece of wet filter paper between them giving a 'sandwich' of the kind shown in Fig. 8.9.

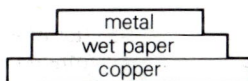

Figure 8.9

If the upper metal is corroding, it should be giving off electrons and turning into metal ions. Electrons should collect on the upper plate. If we join the upper and lower plates by a voltmeter and wires we should get some measure of the amount of extra electrons on the upper plate (Fig. 8.10).

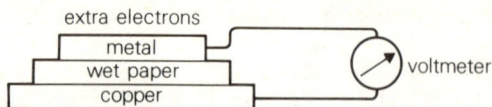

Figure 8.10

When we set this up we do, in fact, get a reading on the voltmeter. Among the common metals the highest reading is obtained from magnesium, showing that it is corroding easily. The other metals give lower readings than magnesium in the order given in Table 8.5, showing that the metals tend to corrode less easily as we go down the list.

Table 8.5

Metal	Meter reading
Magnesium	High reading—'good' corroder
Zinc	
Iron	
Tin	
Lead	Low reading—'poor' corroder

If the upper and lower metals are both pure copper there should be no reading at all on the meter.

It can be shown that if any two metals are in contact with each other, the one higher up the list on Table 8.3 will corrode faster than usual and the one lower on the list will corrode slower than usual. In other words, the higher metal protects the lower metal from corroding by sacrificing itself.

Imagine the following situation. The two metals are placed in water. Both metals will be giving ions off into solution and leaving electrons behind on the metals (Fig. 8.11). The 'better' corroder, giving off more ions, will have more electrons left on it than on the 'poorer' corroder.

If the two metals are joined by a wire, the electrons will flow from the 'good' to the 'poor' corroder.

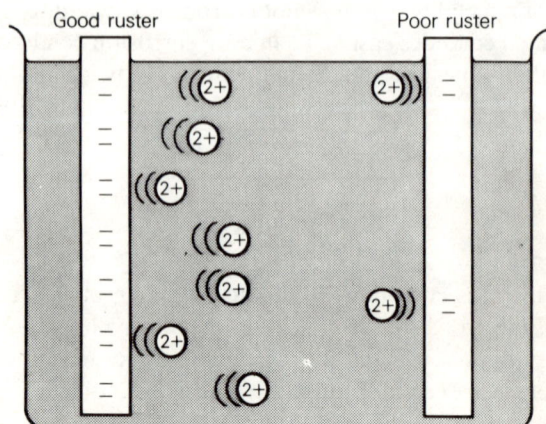

Figure 8.11

More ions will come off the 'good' corroder, leaving behind more free electrons. However, the 'poor' corroder has received many extra electrons from its neighbour and so it will be hard for it to lose any more positive ions. It will stop corroding as long as it is attached to the 'good' corroder (Fig. 8.12).

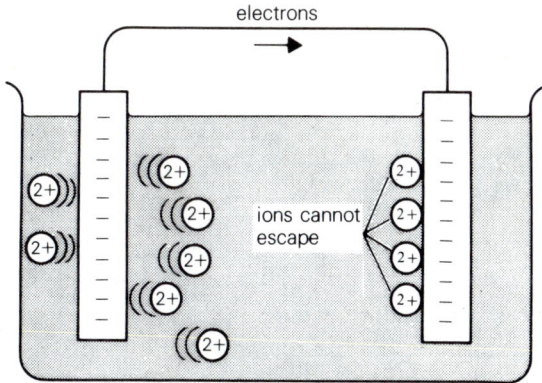

Figure 8.12

We have now found one way of preventing corrosion or rusting. We have also seen that it is stupid to put two different metals in contact with each other in a building or similar situation. The more reactive metal will corrode very quickly. Sometimes this is done intentionally to keep the less reactive metal from corroding while sacrificing the more reactive one.

8.8

Table 8.6 lists metals in order of their chemical reactiveness. This list is called the Reactivity Series. Let us sum up so far and see how the pattern is fitting together.

Summary
Table 8.6

Potassium	Left-hand columns of Periodic Table	Push hydrogen out of cold water	Corrode very rapidly. Kept under oil.
Sodium			
Calcium			
Magnesium			Corrode easily
Aluminium		Push hydrogen out of steam and acids	
Zinc			
Iron			
Tin			
Lead	Middle of the Periodic Table		Corrode slowly
*Hydrogen			
Copper		Cannot push hydrogen out of steam or acids	Corrode very little, if at all
Mercury			
Silver			
Gold			
Platinum			

 * Hydrogen is not a metal but it is put in to show the point at which metals can push it out of solution.

8.9

One last piece of evidence for electrons and ions and the Reactivity Series can be seen in the following reactions.

If we take a metal which forms ions in solution quite readily and place it in a solution in which there are ions of a metal further down the Reactivity Series we might expect to get something like this.

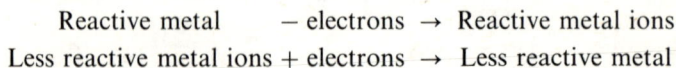

Reactive metal   − electrons → Reactive metal ions

Less reactive metal ions + electrons → Less reactive metal

Here is a real example. If zinc metal is dropped into a solution containing blue copper ions we get the following:

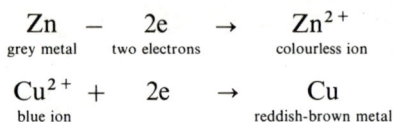

$$Zn \quad - \quad 2e \quad \rightarrow \quad Zn^{2+}$$

grey metal   two electrons   colourless ion

$$Cu^{2+} \quad + \quad 2e \quad \rightarrow \quad Cu$$

blue ion   reddish-brown metal

We say that zinc (a more reactive metal) **displaces** copper (a less reactive metal) from one of its compounds.

The same applies to any pair of metals we choose in the Reactivity Series. The upper metal will displace (push out) the lower metal from its compounds. This has a lot of practical importance as we shall see in the next chapter.

New words you have met in this chapter

Reactivity Series   a list of metals in a particular order. Those at the top of the list can push hydrogen out of acids and steam and push metals below them out of their compounds. They corrode easily. Those at the bottom of the list do not push hydrogen out of acids or steam and do not corrode to any extent.

Displacement   the ability of one metal to push other metals (or hydrogen) out of their compounds.

Corrosion   a metal corrodes when it gives off electrons and turns into positively charged metal ions. Metals do not all corrode at the same rate.

The reactivity series in use

9.1 Why metals have different reactivities

We have been talking in the last two chapters as if metals were anxious to give up electrons, but this is not so. Energy has to be found to pull the negatively charged electrons away from the positive nucleus. This cannot happen of its own accord unless something else happens which 'makes up' for the energy used. This 'something else' involves water. You may remember that water molecules have slightly charged ends:

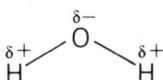

$$\overset{\delta-}{O}$$
$$\underset{H}{\delta+} \qquad \underset{H}{\delta+}$$

When an ion is placed in water, the water molecules arrange themselves round the ion (Fig. 9.1) and this process *gives out* energy.

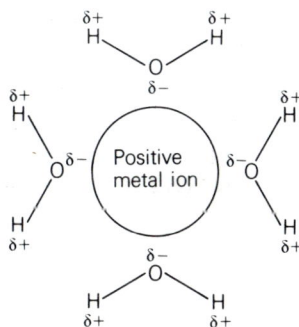

Figure 9.1

For each metal the energy required to pull off its electrons is different and the energy given back by the water molecules clustering round the ions is different. Both of these energy values are related to the size of the atoms and the ions. We therefore have a complicated relationship in which no two metals need the same amount of energy, and so we have a series of metals ranging from the very reactive to the very unreactive.

9.2

Some of the ideas we have been looking at in the previous chapter may appear to have been very theoretical. However, they have many applications in everyday life: in the home and in industry, in cars and bridges, in ships and oil rigs. Even our history has been shaped by metals and their discovery. It is this practical reality which we have tried to explain by the theory of ions and electrons.

When the Reactivity Series is ignored, there are serious consequences.

(a) In the days of wooden warships, the growth of barnacles on the hull slowed the ships down and they had to go into port frequently to have the barnacles scraped off. Then someone noticed that barnacles did not grow on copper and so the hulls were covered with sheets of copper held on by iron nails. All was well for a short time until the ships began to lose their expensive copper coating. The reactive iron of the nails was rusting faster than usual since it was in contact with a less reactive metal (copper). The nail heads were lost and so also was the copper sheath.

(b) In a large laboratory there was a vacuum system for drawing air out of various pieces of apparatus. The piping was of copper but the valves were of aluminium. After a few months the vacuum system was no longer operating. The copper pipes were found to be choked with a white powder—aluminium oxide. The reactive aluminium was corroding more rapidly than usual to give the white oxide which was then sucked into the copper pipes, blocking them.

(c) Incendiary bombs contain magnesium metal. Attempts to put them out with water cause even bigger fires. The reactive magnesium displaces hydrogen from the steam, and hydrogen is an excellent fuel!

9.3 The Reactivity Series used

Our ancestors used the Reactivity Series without knowing it. To begin with the only material they used for tools was stone because they had as yet not discovered metals which were strong enough to use for tools.

Gold was known from very early times because, since it does not corrode, it is found in the ground as the metal. No extraction was necessary but it was too soft for making tools and weapons.

The first usable metal was a mixture of copper and tin (bronze), both metals in the bottom half of the Reactivity Series. These were fairly easy to extract. By heating their ores (oxides) with carbon, the carbon was able to compete with the metals for the oxygen.

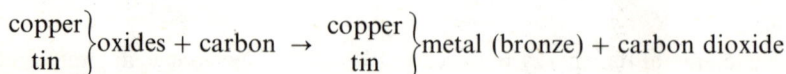

$$\left.\begin{array}{c}\text{copper}\\ \text{tin}\end{array}\right\}\text{oxides} + \text{carbon} \rightarrow \left.\begin{array}{c}\text{copper}\\ \text{tin}\end{array}\right\}\text{metal (bronze)} + \text{carbon dioxide}$$

When the carbon dioxide gas had gone, the metals were left. This discovery led to the Bronze Age. There is evidence that it happened in Eastern Europe about 8500 years ago, even before it occurred in Egypt or Troy.

The next metal that early man learned to extract was iron. This was more difficult to get because of the higher reactivity of the iron. Again carbon was used to compete for the oxygen, but higher temperatures were needed to make the extraction successful. Temperatures approaching 1000 °C were made possible by channelling the wind into the primitive furnaces to blow up the fire. We are still in the Iron Age since iron is our main constructional metal for almost every structure requiring high strength.

Metals such as aluminium, sodium, and magnesium are historical newcomers when compared with copper and iron. Their large scale production had to wait for the arrival of electricity on an industrial scale.

Even newer metals such as titanium and vanadium are now in industrial use; for example titanium is one of the main metals used in the construction of Concorde. It is a metal of medium reactivity and is extracted from its oxide, or more often from its chloride, by heating it with either magnesium or sodium. The more reactive magnesium or sodium competes for the oxygen (or chlorine) and releases the titanium.

The natural behaviour of metals is to corrode, that is to combine with other elements. To get metals back from their ores we have to supply energy to reverse their natural direction of change.

9.4 Corrosion and its prevention

An experiment to detect corrosion

There is a detector which is very sensitive to iron ions. If it turns blue in the presence of iron it shows that the iron is rusting. The detector can be used in this experiment.

Four similar iron nails are thoroughly cleaned with emery paper. Three of them are attached to strips of other metals. Each nail is placed in a test-tube, and each tube is filled with a hot solution of gelatine and the detector. This is rapidly cooled to make the jelly set and fix the nails in place, and then set aside for a day or so. The results are shown in Fig. 9.2. In two cases the nail does not rust; in the fourth case the nail rusts even more than it does in the third tube.

When the iron nail is attached to a metal above it in the Reactivity Series, it is protected from rusting, but if it is attached to a metal below it in the Series it rusts even faster than usual. This has a number of very practical applications

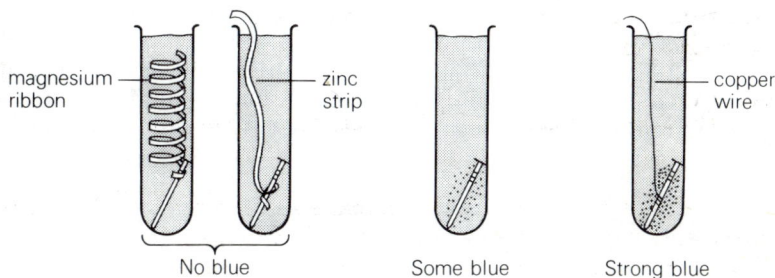

Figure 9.2

Rusting in pipelines

It costs many thousands of pounds to lay a mile of pipeline to carry oil or gas. The oil and gas are slightly damp and the pipe is buried in wet soil and so the conditions are right for the steel pipes to rust even if they are cased in tar and other wrappings. The cost of digging up and renewing a pipe is very high indeed. Instead the pipe is linked to a metal higher than iron in the Reactivity Series (Fig. 9.3). This reactive metal corrodes, passes electrons on to the pipe, and so makes it difficult for iron ions to escape and for rust to set in.

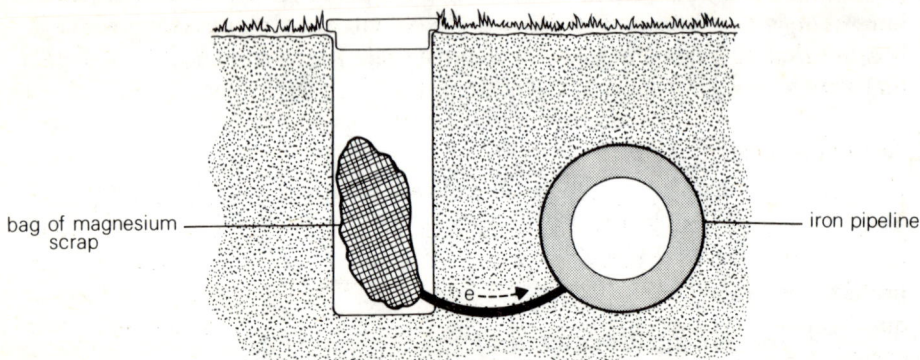

Figure 9.3

The metal usually employed is magnesium, which is placed in bags connected by a wire to the pipe. The bags which sit in holes alongside the pipe can be inspected regularly and replaced when necessary. In this case the magnesium is sacrificed to protect the iron. The process is called **sacrificial protection**.

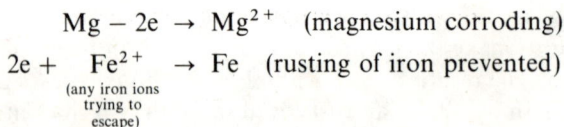

$$Mg - 2e \rightarrow Mg^{2+} \quad \text{(magnesium corroding)}$$

$$2e + Fe^{2+} \rightarrow Fe \quad \text{(rusting of iron prevented)}$$

(any iron ions trying to escape)

Galvanized iron

Another example of sacrificial protection is seen in the house and in the garden. Iron is often coated with zinc (galvanized) so that the zinc can protect the iron. This is not a very good-looking plating and so is used for rough work such as plating dustbins, garage doors, roofing nails, and pails.

Zinc has an extra advantage. Not only does it protect the iron if the plating is chipped, but zinc rust (zinc oxide) forms a water- and air-proof layer on the zinc itself which keeps it from rusting further (Fig. 9.4).

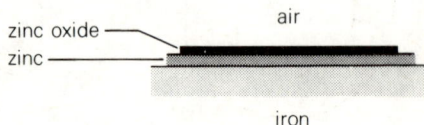

Figure 9.4

Anti-rust paint

Zinc is also the basis of some car touch-up preparations. If the paint on a car is chipped, the metal is cleaned and then treated with a zinc paint before it is sprayed with touch-up paint which matches the colour of the car.

Plating iron

There are other metals, such as chromium, which are used to plate iron and give a shiny finish. This is found on the 'bright work' on cars—on bumpers, radiator grilles, headlamp cowlings, and wheel trims. Chromium protects the iron well as long as it is not scratched or broken. However, when it breaks, rust sets in because iron and chromium are so close to each other in the Reactivity Series that the chromium is no longer able to protect the iron.

Tin plating

If the iron is to be used in contact with foodstuffs, as in cans, zinc plating is no good. It is easily attacked by the acids in foods and fruit juices and so another, less reactive metal is required for plating. The metal commonly used is tin. This protects the iron if the tin layer is unbroken, but if the layer breaks, rust sets in quite rapidly because tin is *below* iron in the Reactivity Series and so it encourages iron to rust. The real advantage of tin is that, like zinc, it has its own protective layer of tin oxide which keeps the plating in good condition.

9.5

We noticed above that iron is kept from rusting because electrons are given to it from the more reactive metal. There is another obvious source of electrons, the negative terminal of a battery. If our theory is correct, an electric battery could be used to stop corrosion. An experiment to prove this can be done using the apparatus in Fig. 9.5.

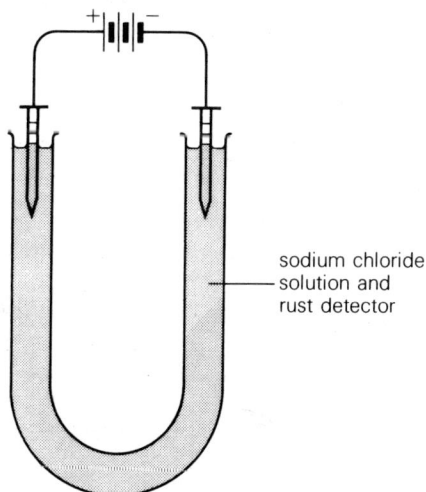

Figure 9.5

In a few minutes the nail attached to the positive end of the battery is surrounded by blue, while the other nail attached to the negative end of the battery has no blue colour round it. Electrons from the battery have been protecting one nail. The positive end of the battery has been pulling electrons from the other nail and encouraging it to rust.

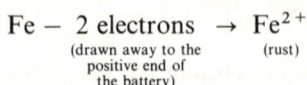

$$Fe - 2 \text{ electrons} \rightarrow Fe^{2+}$$
$$\text{(drawn away to the} \qquad \text{(rust)}$$
$$\text{positive end of}$$
$$\text{the battery)}$$

This fact has also found practical use in industry. Modern cars now have a 'negative earth', that is the negative end of the battery is attached to the car body. This is supposed to reduce rusting!

Ships in harbour are sometimes attached to a negative electric terminal. Steel pipelines and steel piling are protected in the same way. This is an alternative to the method described on p. 102.

Since the metal is protected by being attached to the negative end of a battery the process is sometimes called **cathodic protection**.

New words you have met in this chapter

Corrosion (or rusting) occurs when a metal gives off electrons and turns into positively charged metal ions.

Sacrificial protection this occurs when a less reactive metal is protected from corroding by attaching it to a more reactive metal. The more reactive metal rusts rapidly (is sacrificed) to protect the less reactive one.

Cathodic protection in this method of protection the metal is attached to the negative terminal (cathode) of a battery which supplies electrons.

Galvanizing a form of rust protection in which the iron is coated with zinc. This is achieved by dipping the iron object into molten zinc.

Chemistry in Action 4

Metals at work

Have you ever thought about the kinds of materials of which most things are made? We make our homes of stone or brick, wood, and various metals, together with a wide range of plastic materials. Cars, trains, and planes are made of metal, while tools and electrical wires are also made of metal. However, different metals are used for different purposes. This is because different metals behave in different ways. For example, a metal like silver is shiny, melts at around 960 °C and conducts electricity very well. A small amount of silver is quite heavy for its size, that is to say silver has a *high density*. Silver could have several uses, including electrical wiring. Unfortunately, silver is rare and therefore too expensive to use in this way.

On the following page is a table which shows how several metals behave.

From the list of metals in the table, can you choose the right metal for the job?

Here is how to start. Work *as a group* and list the kind of behaviour which is required of a metal for *each* of the following jobs. Set out your answers in a table as shown below.

(a) Main structure and body of an aeroplane.
(b) Wires for the electrical wiring of a house.
(c) Main structure and body of a car.
(d) Solder for filling cracks in water pipes.
(e) Filament for a light bulb.

Job to be done	What the metal should be like	Possible metals
(a) Plane structure	The metals should be strong, have a low density, and not react with water or air.	
(b) Wires for electricity		
(c) Car structure		
(d) Solder for water pipes		
(e) Filament for light bulb		

Once you have agreed on the kind of behaviour which is required for each job, look at the table of metals on the following page and see if you can find the best choice for each job. You are looking for a metal for *each* of the jobs. No one metal will be able to be used for all five jobs. You may also be able to make a good second choice for each job.

What metal would you use for these jobs?

(a) Main structure and body of an aeroplane.
(b) Wires for the electrical wiring of a house.
(c) Main structure and body of a car.
(d) Solder for filling cracks in water pipes.
(e) Filament for a light bulb.

Metal	Melting point (°C)	Boiling point (°C)	Density (g cm⁻³)	Conductivity* (microhm⁻¹ cm⁻¹)	Reaction with			Strength†	% in Earth's crust
					cold water	acid	damp air		
A	660	2467	2.70	0.38	nil	slow	nil	medium	7.5
B	839	1484	1.55	0.22	fast	fast	slow	low	3.4
C	1083	2567	8.96	0.59	nil	nil	nil	high	0.01
D	1064	2807	19.30	0.42	nil	nil	nil	high	5×10^{-7}
E	1535	2750	7.87	0.10	nil	slow	slight	very high	4.7
F	328	1740	11.35	0.05	nil	slight	nil	low	2×10^{-3}
G	649	1090	1.74	0.22	slow	fast	slow	medium	1.94
H	64	774	0.86	0.14	fast	fast	fast	very low	2.40
I	232	2270	7.31	0.09	nil	slow	nil	low	6×10^{-4}
J	1660	3287	4.54	0.02	nil	slight	nil	high	0.58
K	3410	5660	19.30	0.18	nil	nil	nil	very high	6×10^{-3}

* The higher the value, the better the electrical conduction.
† Based on bending and stretching behaviour.
'Nil' means 'No obvious reaction can be seen occurring'.

10

Taking ionic compounds apart

10.1 Corrosion in reverse

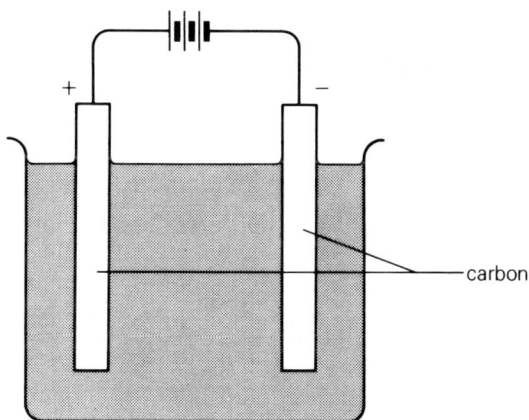

Figure 10.1

If we set up the apparatus shown in Fig. 10.1 we shall have both a negatively charged and a positively charged stick of carbon. If these are dipped into a solution containing ions we know that a current will flow round the circuit (Chapter 7, p. 85). The two pieces of carbon are called **electrodes**—the positive one is called the **anode** and the negative one the **cathode**. When we did this experiment before, we were concerned about whether or not a current was going to flow. This time we shall concentrate upon what is happening at the electrodes. To begin with, let us put copper chloride solution in the beaker and insert the electrodes. You should notice fairly quickly that the surface of the cathode (the negative electrode) is changing colour to a reddish-brown. At the other electrode streams of gas bubbles are coming off and the gas has an unpleasant, choking smell. How can we account for this?

According to our earlier reasoning, copper chloride solution should contain copper ions (Cu^{2+}) and chloride ions (Cl^-) surrounded by water molecules. The cathode is negative and so must be attracting the positive copper ions towards it.

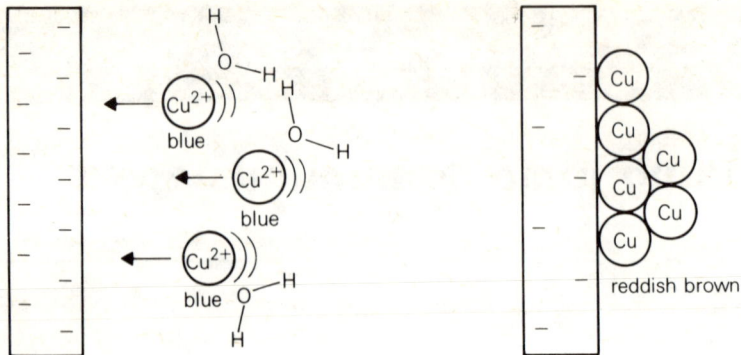

Figure 10.2

When these ions arrive at the cathode they will pick up two electrons and once more become atoms of copper metal. This will steadily coat the electrode with a reddish-brown layer (Fig. 10.2).

At the anode there is a shortage of electrons (this electrode has a positive charge). The negative chloride ions will move towards it, each carrying its extra electron (Fig. 10.3). When a chloride ion arrives it will give up its extra electron and once more become a chlorine atom.

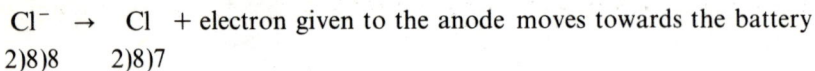

$$Cl^- \rightarrow \quad Cl \ + electron \ given \ to \ the \ anode \ moves \ towards \ the \ battery$$
$$2)8)8 \qquad 2)8)7$$

As we saw in Chapter 7, page 79, chlorine atoms pair up to form molecules of chlorine gas. The unpleasant smelling bubbles which we noticed must have been chlorine.

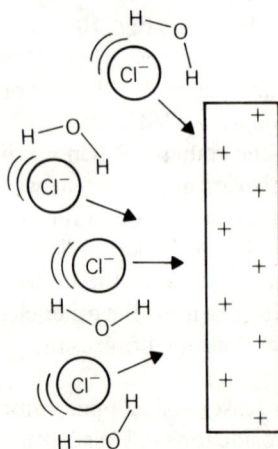

$$Cl + Cl \rightarrow Cl_2$$

Figure 10.3

We have used electricity to turn an ionic compound back into the elements from which it was made.

$$CuCl_2 \rightarrow Cu + Cl_2$$

The metal on the cathode has been remade from its ions. This is the opposite of corroding.

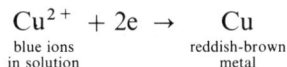

$$Cu^{2+} + 2e \rightarrow Cu$$

blue ions
in solution

reddish-brown
metal

Remember that the natural direction of change (even for a fairly unreactive metal such as copper) is from metal to ion. To get it to go in the opposite (unnatural) direction we have to supply energy from our battery.

The process of using electricity to dismantle an ionic compound is called **electrolysis**.

10.2

We must not base too much theory on one experiment. If we repeat the experiment using a number of ionic substances in solution we get the results shown in Table 10.1. These give enough examples to help us find the pattern in electrolysis.

Table 10.1

Substance	Cathode result	Anode result	Left in solution
Hydrogen chloride (hydrochloric acid)	Hydrogen	Chlorine	Water
Sodium bromide	Hydrogen	Bromine	Sodium hydroxide
Silver nitrate	Silver	Oxygen	Hydrogen nitrate (nitric acid)
Copper sulphate	Copper	Oxygen	Hydrogen sulphate (sulphuric acid)
Magnesium chloride	Hydrogen	Chlorine	Magnesium hydroxide
Potassium nitrate	Hydrogen	Oxygen	Potassium nitrate
Sodium fluoride	Hydrogen	Oxygen	Sodium fluoride
Mercury nitrate	Mercury	Oxygen	Hydrogen nitrate (nitric acid)

To begin with look at the cathode column. Hydrogen is the commonest element appearing in it. The metals which do appear are those which come *below* hydrogen in the Reactivity Series. Table 10.2 lists the Series again as a reminder. Even though there are metal ions present in most of the solutions, the metals above hydrogen in the Reactivity Series do not appear at the cathode. In their place hydrogen is released.

Table 10.2 The Reactivity Series

Most reactive	Potassium
	Sodium
	Calcium
	Magnesium
	Aluminium
	Zinc
	Iron
	Tin
	Lead
	Hydrogen
	Copper
	Mercury
	Silver
	Gold
Least reactive	Platinum

The only possible source of the hydrogen is the water in which the substances are dissolved.

This is fairly easy to understand if you think of it in the following way. Imagine a hillside with hollows in it. Imagine a boulder sitting in each hollow (Fig. 10.4). The highest boulder represents a very reactive metal such as potassium. The middle boulder represents hydrogen and the lowest one represents an unreactive metal such as silver.

When these boulders tumble down to the plain (become ions in solution) they give out energy. Potassium, coming from the highest level, gives out most energy, hydrogen gives out less, and silver gives out least.

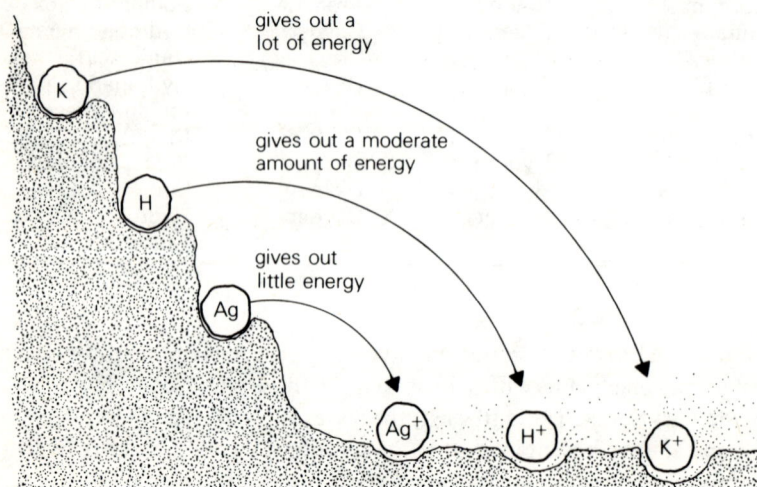

gives out a lot of energy

gives out a moderate amount of energy

gives out little energy

Figure 10.4

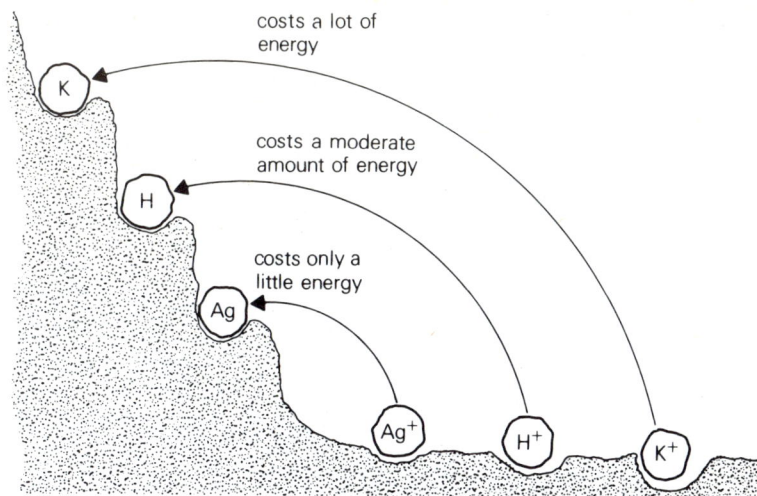

Figure 10.5

Electrolysis is the opposite of this process. It lifts the ions out of solution and turns them back to atoms. This lifting process *requires* energy. It is easier to lift a silver ion back to the silver metal level than it is to lift a hydrogen ion back to the hydrogen level. The most difficult job of all is to lift a potassium ion back to the level of potassium metal (Fig. 10.5).

Suppose we have a solution containing a mixture of positive ions. These will all arrive at the cathode trying to 'catch' an electron. The ion which requires *least* energy to turn it back to an atom will succeed. The others will be left in solution. There is a similar pattern in the anode column of Table 10.1. The commonest element appearing here is oxygen. Once again this comes from the water. The only elements which appear instead of oxygen are chlorine and bromine. These must require less energy than oxygen does to release them.

The other ions (mostly ending in **-ate**) are more difficult than oxygen to discharge (see Table 10.3). This raises a problem because in water there are no oxygen ions, just hydrogen ions (H^+) and hydroxide ions (OH^-).

The oxygen must come from the hydroxide ions:

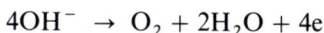

$$4OH^- \rightarrow O_2 + 2H_2O + 4e$$

We can now use these ideas to predict what will happen during an electrolysis.

Table 10.3

-**ate** ions	Difficult to electrolyse
Fluoride	
Hydroxide (giving oxygen)	
Chloride	
Bromide	
Iodide	Easy to electrolyse

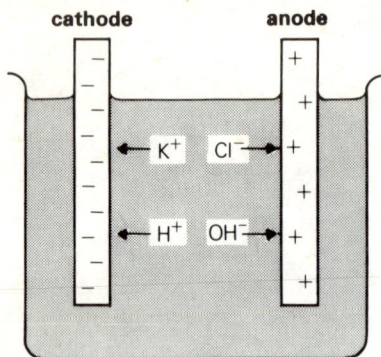

Figure 10.6

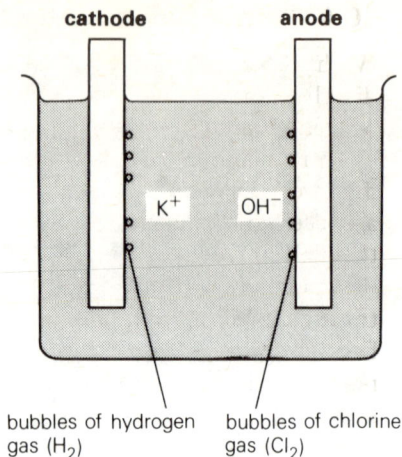

bubbles of hydrogen gas (H_2)   bubbles of chlorine gas (Cl_2)

Figure 10.7

Suppose we have a solution of potassium chloride to electrolyse. What will be the result? There are four ions; two positive ions competing at the cathode and two negative ions competing at the anode (Fig. 10.6). At the cathode the hydrogen ions need least energy to turn them into atoms. They will become hydrogen gas and the potassium ions will be left behind in solution.

At the anode the chloride ions need less energy than hydroxide ions and so chlorine gas will appear at the anode. The hydroxide ions will be left in solution (Fig. 10.7).

The solution of potassium chloride will gradually become a solution of potassium hydroxide as the hydrogen and chlorine escape.

10.3 Electrolysis without water

We learned in Chapter 7, page 84, that not only did electricity pass through solutions of ionic substances in water, it also passed through molten ionic substances.

When this is done there will be no question of ions competing at the electrodes because only one kind of ion will turn up at each electrode. When molten potassium chloride is electrolysed *potassium* and *chlorine* will be released at the electrodes.

It is by the electrolysis of molten ionic substances that many of the very reactive metals are made industrially. These include the metals in columns 1 and 2 of the Periodic Table, plus aluminium. Before electricity became available many of these metals were unknown. Some of them could be made only by very expensive methods and so they were regarded as very precious. It is said that Napoleon used to eat off aluminium plates while his guests used less expensive gold ones! Nowadays electrolysis has made aluminium a cheap and common metal.

10.4 Metals and electricity

We have noticed that when an electric current is passed through a molten or dissolved ionic compound, the compound comes apart (decomposes) into its original elements.

There is another family of substances which conduct electricity *without* being dissolved in water or melted. The other remarkable thing about them is that they are chemically unaffected by the current. These substances are the *metals* themselves.

A piece of copper wire is still a piece of copper wire after a current has passed through it. What holds the copper atoms together? It cannot be normal covalent bonding because covalent bonds do not allow electricity to pass. It cannot be normal ionic bonding because the metal might then be expected to break up in some way.

A special type of bonding, called **metallic bonding** has been suggested. It has to explain why the metal conducts electricity without being broken up. The metal atoms are thought to be packed together in a neat geometrical pattern (Fig. 10.8).

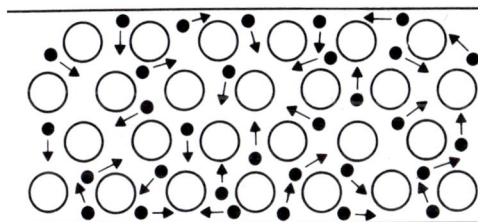

Figure 10.8

Their outer layer of electrons is free to move from atom to atom so that no particular atom 'owns' any particular group of outer electrons, although all of them have a share in enough electrons to balance the positive charge on their nucleii. We have a collection of metal atoms held together by a 'glue' of moving electrons.

If the metal is in the form of a wire and it is attached across the terminals of a battery, the positive end of the battery will attract electrons out of that end of the wire. But at the negative end of the wire electrons are being fed in so that the total number of electrons in the wire remains the same. The passage of current is the flow of electrons in the same direction through the wire (Fig. 10.9). When the battery is

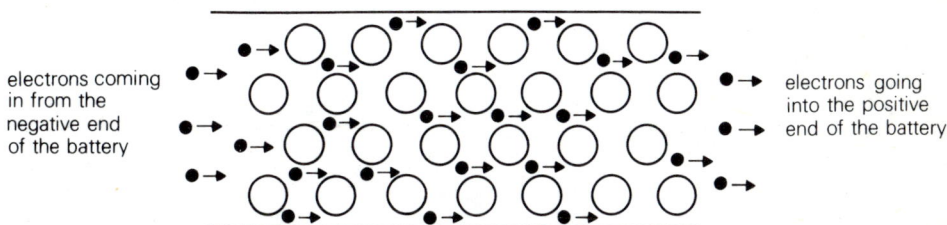

electrons coming in from the negative end of the battery

electrons going into the positive end of the battery

current on

Figure 10.9

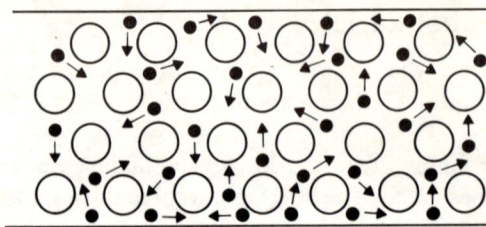

current off
Figure 10.10

removed we have the same wire with the same number of electrons as before. These are moving, in no particular direction, among the metal atoms (Fig. 10.10).

Summary of bonding

Table 10.4

	Covalent	*Polar covalent*	*Ionic*	*Metallic*
	Between atoms which attract electrons equally	Between atoms which attract electrons unequally	Between atoms which attract electrons very differently	Between atoms of metals
	Cl$\overset{\bullet}{\underset{\bullet}{}}$Cl	$\overset{\delta+}{H}\overset{\delta-}{\underset{\bullet}{\overset{\bullet}{}}Cl}$	Na$^+$ Cl$^-$	
When solid	Do not conduct electricity	Do not conduct electricity	Do not conduct electricity	Conduct electricity well
When molten	Do not conduct electricity	Do not conduct electricity	Conduct electricity and break up into elements	Conduct electricity well and do not break up
When in solution in water	Do not conduct electricity	Sometimes conduct electricity	Conduct electricity and break up into elements	Do not dissolve in water

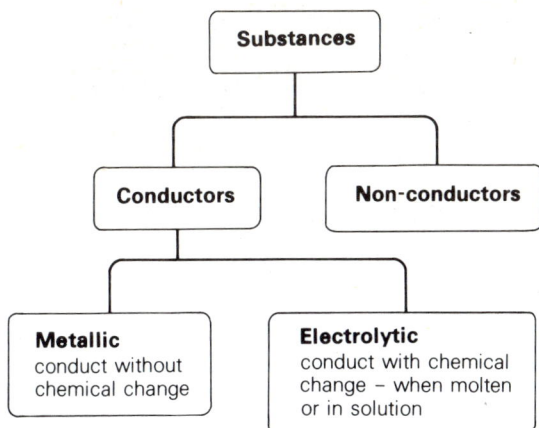

Figure 10.11

New words you have met in this chapter

Electrode   an object at which electrons enter or leave a solution or a molten substance.

Anode   an electrode attached to the *positive* end of a battery. It is short of electrons and so it attracts negative ions which are carrying extra electrons. These ions are often non-metals.

Cathode   an electrode attached to the *negative* end of a battery. It has extra electrons and so it attracts positive ions which are short of electrons. These ions are usually metals or hydrogen.

Electrolysis   the process by which ionic substances can be taken apart using electricity.

Decompose   when a chemical compound breaks up into simpler parts it is said to decompose.

Answers to this section will be found on page 241.

1 With the help of Fig. 7.3 on page 79 decide what kind of bonding you would expect between the following pairs of atoms. The rules are to be found on page 81.
(a) potassium and fluorine; (b) silicon and oxygen; (c) calcium and bromine; (d) magnesium and sulphur; (e) barium and chlorine; (f) bromine and bromine; (g) boron and oxygen.

2 Write the formulae of the compounds formed in (a), (b), (c), (d), (e), and (g) in question 1.

3 Divide the following elements into two groups:
(a) those which will give positive ions, and
(b) those which will give negative ions.

(If in difficulty, refer back to Section 8.3, p. 90.)

   zinc, copper, caesium, oxygen, sulphur, aluminium, strontium, iodine.

4 With the help of the Reactivity Series in Section 8.8, page 97, answer the following questions.
(a) Why does a knife blade dipped into copper sulphate solution become reddish-brown?
(b) A boy was stupid enough to try to steal a drop of mercury and keep it in an aluminium box. The box in his pocket became hot and turned into a pile of white powder. Why?
(c) Why is potassium metal usually kept in a bottle of oil?
(d) Iron nails, which are to be used for outdoor purposes such as roofing, are often coated in zinc (galvanized). Why?

(e)

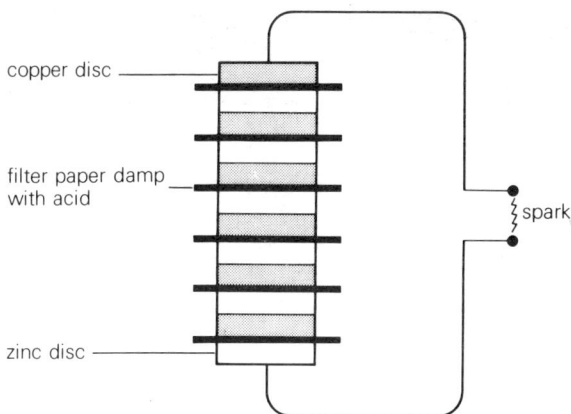

If a pile of copper and zinc discs are set up, as in the diagram, with filter paper moistened with acid between them, a small electric spark can be seen to jump between the ends of the wire when they are brought close together.

Explain how this electric current is made.

5 (a)

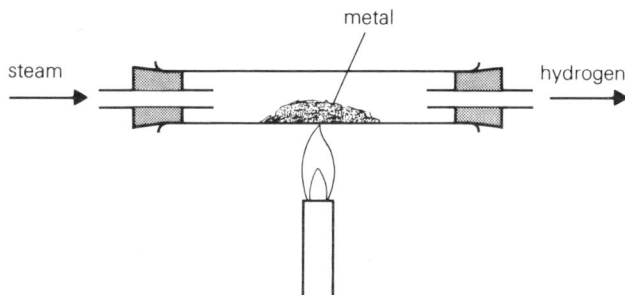

List three metals which would behave in this way.

(b) If the arrows are reversed and a metal oxide is placed in the tube it is sometimes possible to obtain the metal from the oxide.

From which oxide could you be *sure* of obtaining the metal by this method? Are there any other metals which you think might be extracted this way? If so, which?

6 A pupil has been trying in vain to obtain lithium metal from lithium chloride by passing an electric current through a solution of the compound in water.

(a) Explain to him why he is having no success.

(b) Suggest a method by which he could extract the metal.

7 The brown stains on the prongs of a silver fork, after it has been used for eating eggs, are caused by an ionic silver compound (silver sulphide).

The stains can be removed by dipping the fork into an alkaline solution and touching a piece of aluminium foil. Try to explain this. (Do not worry about the alkaline solution in your explanation.)

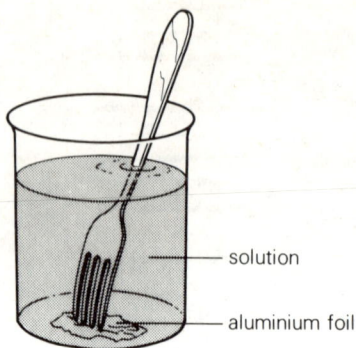

8 Let us assume for the moment that there are only three types of bonding:

covalent, ionic, and metallic.

Here are descriptions of the behaviour of three different substances. From these descriptions decide upon the bonding in each substance. (If you need help, look at Table 10.4.)

Substance A
White solid which does not conduct electricity. When it is melted or dissolved in water it carries current quite well.

Substance B
White solid which does not conduct electricity even when melted or when in solution.

Substance C
Conducts current when solid or when molten. Does not dissolve in water.

Chemistry in Action 5

Polar or ionic?

Bob: What d'you get for number 3?
Mary: M'mm..... ionic..... d'you agree?

Bob: I'm not sure..... let's ask Joe.....

Bob: Joe ..... what kind of bonding is present in aluminium chloride?
Joe: Polar.

Bob: Why? It's metal and non-metal! Mr McLeod said that was ionic.
Joe: You don't believe him, do you? Half the time he's wrong........!

Mary: Why polar, though?
Joe: Well ..... aluminium's sort of odd, isn't it?

Mary: That's no reason..... what........
Bob: Shhh..... here he comes........

Mr. McLeod started to go over their answers. When he reached question 3, he found a lot of confusion in the class; some thought aluminium chloride contained ionic bonds, some thought polar, but most pupils were not sure. Bob asked Mr. McLeod which was correct and confessed he did not understand how to get the answer. To his surprise, Mr. McLeod said, 'I'm not going to tell you. Let's see if we can find out. . . .' Mary heard Joe muttering under his breath, 'I told you—he doesn't know himself!' But Mr. McLeod continued, 'How could we find the answer?' There was a moment's pause; then Bob suggested, 'Let's look it up in a book.' Mr. McLeod gave out several rather large books, but no one could find any mention of the kind of bonding present in aluminium chloride.

Not willing to give up his idea, Bob suggested trying more advanced books, '. . . written by professors and folk like that . . .' he suggested.

What do you think? Do you reckon that looking up books is a good idea? And, what about asking a professor?

Discuss this.

Now turn to page 125.

11

Quantities in chemistry

11.1

The formulae which you have learned to write in chemistry are more than just a kind of chemical shorthand. They tell us which elements have combined to form a compound and they also give us information about the *quantities* of the elements which have combined.

For example, the formula for water (hydrogen oxide) is H_2O. This formula tells us that water is made by the combination of the elements hydrogen and oxygen. The formula is also one way of representing one molecule of water and it shows that the molecule consists of two atoms of hydrogen bonded to one atom of oxygen. (Where no small number appears after an atom it means that there is only one atom present.)

Another common way of representing this molecule is $H\diagup^{O}\diagdown_H$.

As you learned in Chapter 2, atoms have a mass. On the atomic mass scale, $^{12}_6C = 12$, the hydrogen atom has a mass of one atomic mass unit (amu) and the oxygen atom has a mass of 16 amu.

A little bit of arithmetic will tell us that the mass of a water molecule is $(2 \times 1) + 16 = 18$ amu.

*This is known as the **formula mass** of water.* This is the strictly correct name, but chemists tend to use the term **formula weight**.

We say that the formula weight of water is 18. When we are dealing with quantities measured in grams, then the *gram formula weight* of water would be 18 g. We can even apply this idea to tonnes. The *tonne formula weight* of water would be 18 tonnes.

Therefore, we can write that

2 g hydrogen will combine with 16 g oxygen to make 18 g water
or 1 g hydrogen will combine with 8 g oxygen to make 9 g water
or 1 tonne hydrogen will combine with 8 tonnes oxygen to make 9 tonnes water.

Let us apply the same treatment to another compound, calcium chloride. The formula for the compound is $CaCl_2$. This tells us that one atom of the element calcium combines with two atoms of the element chlorine.

After consulting the Periodic Table, we can write that

40 amu calcium will combine with 2 × 35.5 amu chlorine
or 40 amu calcium will combine with 71 amu   chlorine
or 40 g   calcium will combine with 71 g   chlorine.

So   the formula weight of calcium chloride = (40 + 71) amu
                                          = 111 amu
or   gram formula weight of calcium chloride = 111 g

The gram formula weight of a substance is simply the formula weight expressed in the unit grams.

Try the following examples for yourself. You will find the answers on page 127.

What are the gram formula weights of

(a) magnesium oxide;   (b) sodium bromide;   (c) aluminium sulphide;
(d) carbon monoxide;   (e) ethanol;   (f) methane?

11.2 Formulae from experiments

So far you have been able to write the formula for a compound when you know the symbols for the elements which combine together and the valency of each. However, before the discovery of the Periodic Table, formulae had to be obtained by experiments involving accurate weighing. Even today the formulae of all new compounds are obtained by methods involving weighing.

Finding the formula for magnesium oxide

You will already have burned the element magnesium in oxygen and obtained the white ash, magnesium oxide. It is possible to weigh the magnesium at the beginning of the experiment and to weigh the white ash formed. It sounds simple, but your teacher will have to guide you if your results are to be sufficiently accurate to be used in a calculation.

If a number of people in the class each weigh a different piece of magnesium and then weigh the magnesium oxide formed, each person can find the weight of the oxygen used by subtraction.

Now plot all the results in the class of the weight of magnesium against the weight of oxygen.

This should give a graph of a straight line which passes through the origin. This indicates that the amount of oxygen required is always in the same proportion to the amount of magnesium burned. You can get a wide range of results if you extend the graph upwards as shown in Fig. 11.1.

Inspection shows that every 1 g oxygen reacts with 1.5 g magnesium.

Now read off the amount of oxygen which combines with 2.4 g magnesium.

2.4 g   Mg have combined with 1.6 g   oxygen.
24 g   Mg will combine with   16 g   oxygen.
24 amu Mg will combine with   16 amu oxygen.

The weight of 1 atom of Mg will combine with the weight of 1 atom of oxygen.
The simplest formula for magnesium oxide is MgO. But the graph also shows that

4.8 g Mg combine with 3.2 g oxygen.
48 g Mg will combine with 32 g oxygen.
48 amu Mg will combine with 32 amu oxygen.

The weight of 2 atoms of Mg will combine with the weight of 2 atoms of oxygen.
This gives a formula Mg_2O_2.

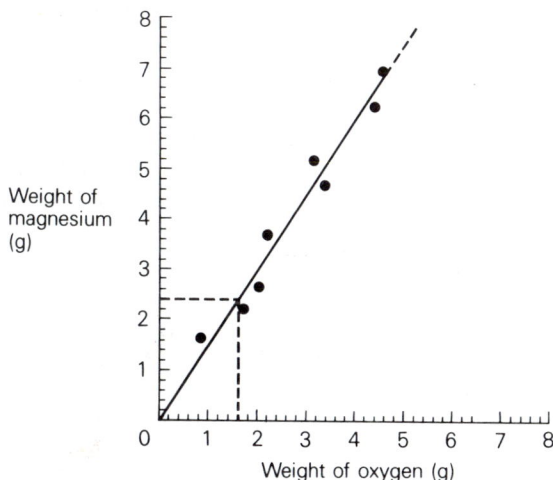

Weight of magnesium (g)

Weight of oxygen (g)

Figure 11.1

From the graph we also see that

7.2 g Mg combine with 4.8 g oxygen.

A similar calculation will give us a formula Mg_3O_3.
A whole series of formulae for magnesium oxide can be arrived at, but it is common for us to use the simplest of these (MgO) as the formula for the compound.

11.3

Another experiment which you can do is to form the yellow powder, lead iodide, starting with a known weight of the element lead. The experimental details will be explained to you by your teacher.
Let us suppose that, from a class graph of weight of lead against weight of iodine, you decide that

2.00 g lead produce 4.45 g lead iodide.

Can you arrive at the simplest formula for lead iodide? The answer is worked out for you on page 127.

11.4 An unusual term

The formula weight of a substance—element or compound—is often used in chemistry and it is given the special name of a **mole** (not to be confused with a little furry animal).

The formula weight in grams, or the gram formula weight, is referred to as the **gram mole**. How do we work out what a gram mole of an element, such as zinc, is?

From the Periodic Table you find that the atomic weight of zinc is 65 and so the gram atomic weight of the element zinc is 65 g. Expressed in another way, 1 mole of zinc atoms weighs 65 g.

Normally metallic elements are thought of as single atoms, but in the case of elements which are gases, we have to be a bit more careful when we calculate the weight of a gram mole of them. Only the noble gases (column 8 of Periodic Table) exist as single atoms.

So, 1 mole of helium atoms would weigh 4 g and 1 mole of argon atoms would weigh 40 g—information easily obtained from the Periodic Table.

But gases like oxygen, hydrogen, and nitrogen exist as molecules which contain *two* atoms combined. Therefore a molecule of oxygen is written O_2; that of hydrogen, H_2; and that of nitrogen, N_2. The $_2$ indicates two combined atoms of the gas.

So 1 mole of oxygen gas will weigh $(2 \times 16) \, g = 32 \, g$. You will be able to calculate the weight of 1 mole of hydrogen molecules and of nitrogen molecules in the same way.

See if you can match up the following lists before you look at the answer table on page 127. The first one is done for you.

1 mole of carbon (C) atoms	63.5 g
1 mole of copper (Cu) atoms	12 g
1 mole of chlorine (Cl_2) molecules	28 g
1 mole of nitrogen (N_2) molecules	71 g
1 mole of neon (Ne) atoms	20 g

11.5

To find the weight of 1 gram mole of a *compound*, the rule is simply to write the correct formula for the compound and then, using the Periodic Table, calculate its formula weight. The formula weight, expressed in grams, is the gram formula weight or the weight of 1 gram mole of the compound.

Take the compound sodium oxide. The valency of sodium is 1 and that of oxygen 2. Therefore the formula for the compound is Na_2O. From the Periodic Table the atomic weight of sodium is 23 and of oxygen 16.

The formula weight will be, therefore,

$$Na_2 \quad O$$
$$(2 \times 23) + 16 = 62$$

Therefore the gram formula weight of sodium oxide is 62 g.

We can do similar arithmetic for ethanoic acid. Its formula is CH_3COOH.

Knowing the atomic weight of C (12), H (1), and O (16), we can calculate the formula weight:

$$C \ H_3 \ C \ O \ O \ H$$
$$12 + (3 \times 1) + 12 + 16 + 16 + 1 = 60$$

The gram formula weight of ethanoic acid is 60 g.
That is, 1 gram mole of the compound weighs 60 g.

Try to match up the following lists, before checking your answers on page 127. Make sure that you start with the correct formula!

1 gram mole of sodium chloride	102 g
1 gram mole of aluminium oxide	30 g
1 gram mole of calcium sulphide	32 g
1 gram mole of ethane	72 g
1 gram mole of methanol	58.5 g

Let us do the first one together. The formula for sodium chloride is NaCl.

$$Na \ Cl$$
$$23 + 35.5 = 58.5$$

So 1 gram mole of sodium chloride will weigh 58.5 g.

Now try the others. We shall return to this important idea of a mole of substance in Chapter 19.

Chemistry in Action 5 (*continued from p. 120*)

Books *are* useful sources of information and usually we can rely on them. Sometimes, however, there can be mistakes: for example, the author might not check that his facts were correct, but just copy them from an older book. Even very clever people can get things all wrong.

Yes, by all means, look up books and ask others who are 'experts', but let us remember that we might find a wrong answer!

What else could the class have done?

Discuss an answer to this question.

Now turn to page 134.

New words you have met in this chapter

Simplest formula
This is the simplest whole number ratio of the numbers of atoms of the different elements in a compound, which agrees with the experimental composition of the compound

The simplest formula for magnesium oxide is MgO and not Mg_2O_2, Mg_3O_3, Mg_4O_4, ..., etc.

The simplest formula for aluminium chloride is $AlCl_3$, not Al_2Cl_6, Al_4Cl_{12}, ..., etc.

Formula weight
this is obtained by adding the atomic weights of all the atoms in a chemical formula. The formula weight of sodium sulphate (Na_2SO_4) would be (2 × atomic weight of sodium) + (atomic weight of sulphur) + (4 × atomic weight of oxygen) = (2 × 23) + (32) + (4 × 16) = 142.

Gram formula weight
this is the formula weight expressed in grams. The gram formula weight of sodium sulphate would be 142 g.

The gram mole
the gram mole is just another way of saying the gram formula weight. One gram mole of sodium sulphate = 142 g.

Mole
A mole of a substance is that amount of it which contains as many particles as there are atoms of carbon in 12 g of $^{12}_6C$ (see Chapter 2, p. 12).

The actual number of particles in a mole is huge— 600 000 000 000 000 000 000 000   (6×10^{23}). This colossal number is sometimes called Avogadro's number.

ANSWERS TO QUESTIONS IN CHAPTER 11

Page 122.

Formula	Gram formula weight
(a) MgO	40
(b) NaBr	103
(c) Al_2S_3	150
(d) CO	28
(e) C_2H_5OH	46
(f) CH_4	16

Page 123.

The simplest formula for lead iodide

From the graph,

2.00 g Pb combine with iodine to give 4.45 g lead iodide.
2.00 g Pb combine with 2.45 g iodine (that is, 4.45 − 2.00 g).
The atomic weight of lead is 207.

207 g Pb will combine with $\dfrac{207 \times 2.45}{2.00}$ g iodine

$$= 253.6 \text{ g iodine}$$

But the atomic weight of iodine is 127 and, remembering that only whole numbers of atoms combine with one another, the weight of 1 atom of lead combines with the weight of 2 atoms of iodine.
  The simplest formula is PbI_2.
  This is the formula which we normally use for lead iodide.

Page 124.

Gram moles of elements

Carbon	12 g	Nitrogen	28 g
Copper	63.5 g	Neon	20 g
Chlorine	71 g		

Page 125.

Gram moles of compounds

Aluminium oxide, Al_2O_3	102 g
Calcium sulphide, CaS	72 g
Ethane, C_2H_6	30 g
Methanol, CH_3OH	32 g

12

Striking a balance

12.1

You have already had some practice in writing 'word equations' to summarize reactions which you have carried out in the laboratory. The starting materials (the **reactants**) are always written on the left-hand side of the equation and the new substances formed (the **products**) appear on the right.

For example, when carbon monoxide gas was used to convert iron oxide to the metal iron and the gas carbon dioxide, we summarized the reaction in the following way.

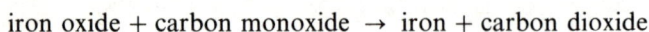

iron oxide + carbon monoxide → iron + carbon dioxide

The arrow means 'gives'. When lead ions gained two electrons to form lead metal we wrote

lead ions + 2 electrons → lead   (metal)

This is another example of a chemical equation.

We can summarize the reaction which takes place when hydrogen gas and oxygen gas are made to react to form water (hydrogen oxide) in a similar way.

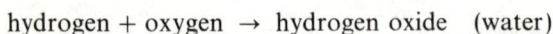

hydrogen + oxygen → hydrogen oxide   (water)

It is fairly easy to replace the names of the substances in a reaction with formulae, now that you have learned how to work out the formula for a substance.

For instance, instead of the first equation we could write

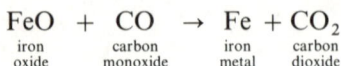

$$\underset{\substack{\text{iron} \\ \text{oxide}}}{FeO} + \underset{\substack{\text{carbon} \\ \text{monoxide}}}{CO} \rightarrow \underset{\substack{\text{iron} \\ \text{metal}}}{Fe} + \underset{\substack{\text{carbon} \\ \text{dioxide}}}{CO_2}$$

The second example is no more difficult.

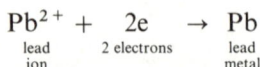

$$\underset{\substack{\text{lead} \\ \text{ion}}}{Pb^{2+}} + \underset{\substack{\text{2 electrons}}}{2e} \rightarrow \underset{\substack{\text{lead} \\ \text{metal}}}{Pb}$$

The third example is a little more difficult.
Using symbols and formulae we would write

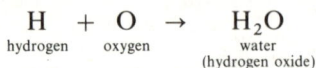

$$\underset{\text{hydrogen}}{H} + \underset{\text{oxygen}}{O} \rightarrow \underset{\substack{\text{water} \\ \text{(hydrogen oxide)}}}{H_2O}$$

This would certainly tell a reader that the element hydrogen and the element oxygen can be made to combine in some way to form the compound water. The formula for water is certainly H_2O, but we learned in the previous chapter (Section 11.4, p. 124) that most of the common gases do not exist as single atoms, but as molecules, composed of clusters of two atoms, covalently linked together. This being so, it might be better to write the equation like this.

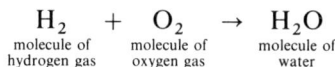

$$\underset{\substack{\text{molecule of} \\ \text{hydrogen gas}}}{H_2} + \underset{\substack{\text{molecule of} \\ \text{oxygen gas}}}{O_2} \rightarrow \underset{\substack{\text{molecule of} \\ \text{water}}}{H_2O}$$

We could write this equation in another way showing the bonds.

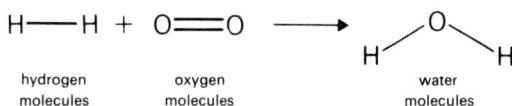

$$\underset{\substack{\text{hydrogen} \\ \text{molecules}}}{H-H} + \underset{\substack{\text{oxygen} \\ \text{molecules}}}{O=O} \longrightarrow \underset{\substack{\text{water} \\ \text{molecules}}}{H\diagup^{O}\diagdown H}$$

To sum up, chemical equations, whether written as word equations or using molecular formulae, are useful ways of summarizing what happens in a reaction. They should only be used to represent a reaction which you *know* can take place.

12.2 Calculations from equations

In Section 8.4 the idea of 'balancing' a chemical equation was introduced. To understand why this operation is sometimes necessary, we shall have to discover how equations are used to calculate the quantities of substances in a reaction.

In Section 8.6 we discussed what happens when metals were added to hydrochloric acid. If you were asked to give a shorthand description of this reaction, you could write the following equation.

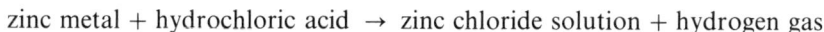

zinc metal + hydrochloric acid → zinc chloride solution + hydrogen gas

If you wanted to show that you knew something about symbols and formulae, you might write

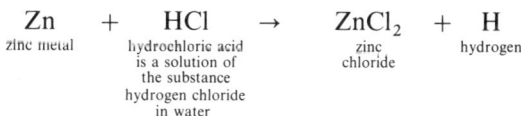

$$\underset{\text{zinc metal}}{Zn} + \underset{\substack{\text{hydrochloric acid} \\ \text{is a solution of} \\ \text{the substance} \\ \text{hydrogen chloride} \\ \text{in water}}}{HCl} \rightarrow \underset{\substack{\text{zinc} \\ \text{chloride}}}{ZnCl_2} + \underset{\text{hydrogen}}{H}$$

This equation could be 'improved' if you remembered that most common gases, including hydrogen, did not exist as single atoms, but as molecules containing two atoms. We could then write

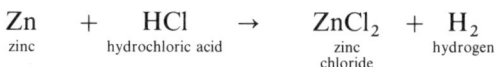

$$\underset{\text{zinc}}{Zn} + \underset{\text{hydrochloric acid}}{HCl} \rightarrow \underset{\substack{\text{zinc} \\ \text{chloride}}}{ZnCl_2} + \underset{\text{hydrogen}}{H_2}$$

But what does this equation tell us about quantities? To find this out, we have to apply the ideas we discussed in the previous chapter.

During a chemical reaction, the bonds present in the reacting substances are broken. New bonds are made which produce different substances.

The atoms present to begin with are just rearranged during the reaction. No atoms are lost and no new atoms are gained. This means that the weight of the substances on the left-hand side of the equation (the reacting substances) should equal the weight of the substances on the right-hand side (the products of the reaction).

In the example given above, the quantities on the two sides of the equation are not equal. They do not balance. The left-hand side is 'short' of 36.5 g (or 1 mole) of hydrochloric acid (Fig. 12.1).

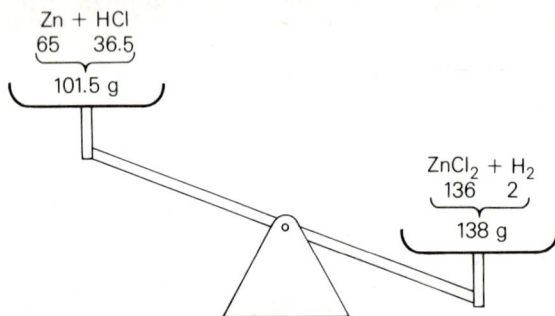

Zn + HCl
65   36.5
101.5 g

$ZnCl_2 + H_2$
136   2
138 g

Figure 12.1

A balanced equation which represented this reaction would have to include two moles of hydrochloric acid on the left-hand side (Fig. 12.2). This is written as 2 HCl and so the fully balanced equation would read

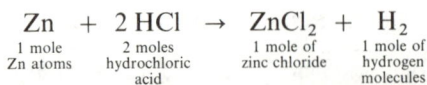

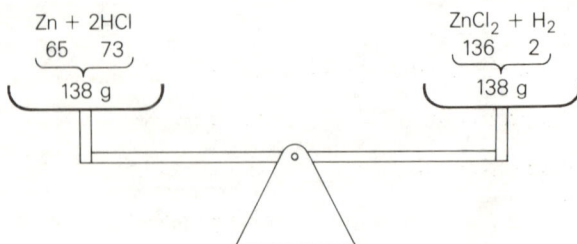

$$Zn + 2\,HCl \rightarrow ZnCl_2 + H_2$$

1 mole   2 moles   1 mole of   1 mole of
Zn atoms   hydrochloric   zinc chloride   hydrogen
                  acid   molecules

Zn + 2HCl
65   73
138 g

$ZnCl_2 + H_2$
136   2
138 g

Figure 12.2

It is not necessary to fill in formula weights to check if an equation is balanced. An atom has the same weight whether it is on the left or right of an equation. If we check that the number and kinds of atoms on both sides are the same, then the equation is balanced.

Left-hand side   Right-hand side
$Zn + 2HCl$ $ZnCl_2 + H_2$

1 zinc atom   1 zinc atom
2 hydrogen atoms   2 chlorine atoms
2 chlorine atoms   2 hydrogen atoms

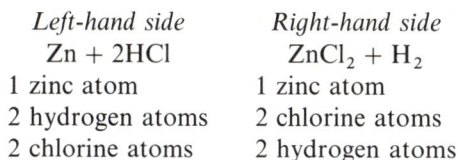

Both sides are the same and so the equation is balanced.

Balanced equations, in addition to indicating the starting materials and the products of a reaction, also tell us *how much* of each substance is involved. You need to write a balanced equation only if you are asked to carry out a calculation concerning the *quantities* of any of the substances involved.

For example, if you were asked to calculate how much copper would be obtained when 53 g of copper(II) oxide had reacted completely with carbon, you would have to follow these steps.

(a) Write (and check) a balanced equation for the reaction.

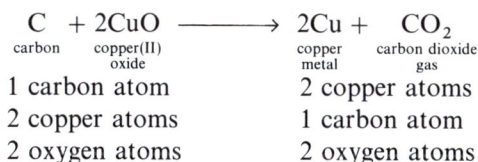

$$C + 2CuO \longrightarrow 2Cu + CO_2$$
carbon copper(II)   copper carbon dioxide
        oxide   metal   gas

1 carbon atom   2 copper atoms
2 copper atoms   1 carbon atom
2 oxygen atoms   2 oxygen atoms

Both sides are the same, therefore the equation is balanced.

(b) Calculate the mass of the substances involved.

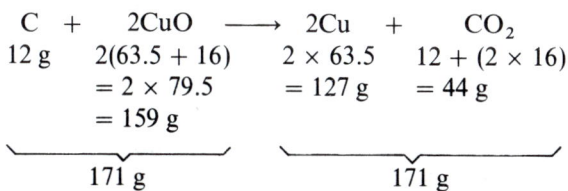

$$C + 2CuO \longrightarrow 2Cu + CO_2$$

12 g $2(63.5 + 16)$ 2×63.5 $12 + (2 \times 16)$
        $= 2 \times 79.5$ $= 127$ g $= 44$ g
        $= 159$ g

171 g   171 g

(c) Carry out a little arithmetic.
    From the balanced equation you can tell that

159 g copper(II) oxide give   127 g copper

53 g copper(II) oxide give $\dfrac{127 \times 53}{159}$ g copper

$= 42.3$ g copper

One thing which makes chemical equations different from equations in algebra, is that chemical equations do not *always* have to be balanced. For many purposes

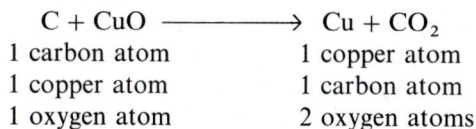

$$C + CuO \longrightarrow Cu + CO_2$$

1 carbon atom   1 copper atom
1 copper atom   1 carbon atom
1 oxygen atom   2 oxygen atoms

tells us all that we want to know. Only when we want to make any calculations involving quantities do we need a balanced equation.

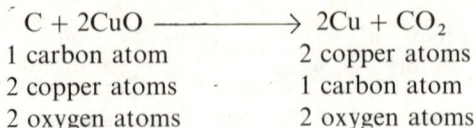

$$C + 2CuO \longrightarrow 2Cu + CO_2$$

1 carbon atom	2 copper atoms
2 copper atoms	1 carbon atom
2 oxygen atoms	2 oxygen atoms

Summary

You will meet the following types of equations in chemistry.

(a) *Word equations*, such as

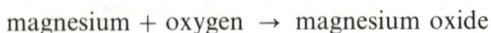

$$\text{magnesium} + \text{oxygen} \rightarrow \text{magnesium oxide}$$

and

$$\text{hydrogen} + \text{oxygen} \rightarrow \text{hydrogen oxide (water)}$$

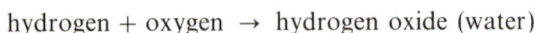

(b) *Equations which use symbols and formulae*, each substance being represented by its molecular formula. For example,

$$Cu^{2+} + 2e \rightarrow Cu$$

and

$$Zn + HCl \rightarrow ZnCl_2 + H_2$$

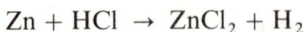

If you are asked to write a chemical equation it is better to be able to build the formulae as required. You should *not* have to rely on your memory.

(c) *Balanced equations*, which are necessary only when an equation is to be used for calculating the weights of chemicals which react with one another.

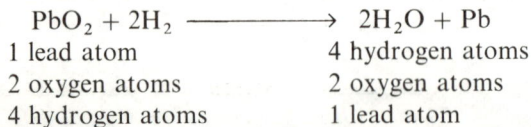

$$PbO_2 + 2H_2 \longrightarrow 2H_2O + Pb$$

1 lead atom	4 hydrogen atoms
2 oxygen atoms	2 oxygen atoms
4 hydrogen atoms	1 lead atom

However, now that you have learnt to balance equations you might like to practise your skill by going back and balancing equations which you wrote earlier in your course.

12.3 A warning!

Just because you read something which someone has been writing you do not necessarily have to believe it. You have probably used your own imagination when writing an essay at school and written something which has not actually taken place. The point is, that the mere *writing* of something does not necessarily mean that it is true.

Because you can write a chemical equation and even make it balance does not mean that the reaction *will* take place. An equation is simply an attempt to represent what *has actually happened* in an experiment. No more should be taken from an equation than what it actually says.

Equations have other limitations. Equations which we have met so far do not tell us everything about chemical reactions. They do not tell us

(a) whether the reaction is fast or slow;
(b) whether heat is required to make the reaction go;
(c) whether the substances concerned are solids, liquids, or gases;
(d) whether the substances are in solution or not;
(e) whether the reaction takes place in one stage or in more than one stage;

there may be other substances made which, later in the reaction, disappear again.

As you become familiar with more chemistry, you will certainly remember some of the facts which the equation does not actually state. For example, whenever you see H_2 or O_2 you can safely assume that hydrogen and oxygen will be gases. Zn and Fe will represent the metallic solids zinc and iron. Most reactions which involve acids will be carried out dissolved in water. This is called an aqueous solution (Latin *aqua* = water).

If there is any doubt about the form (or state) a substance is in, it is helpful to write letters such as l, s, g, or aq, in brackets, after the formula. The letter 'l' stands for liquid, 's' for solid, 'g' for gas, and 'aq' for a solution in water. For example,

Hg(l) stands for mercury liquid.
Cl_2(g) stands for chlorine gas.
NaCl(s) stands for solid (crystalline) sodium chloride.
NaCl(aq) stands for a solution of sodium chloride in water.

New words you have met in this chapter

Reactants   the chemical substances which are put together to bring about a reaction.

Products   the new substances made as a result of a chemical reaction.

Balanced equation   in this type of equation the numbers of the different kinds of atom in the reactants must be equal to those which appear in the products. Balanced equations are essential for calculating quantities in a reaction.

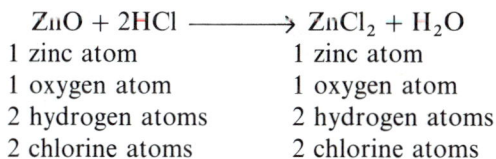

$$ZnO + 2HCl \longrightarrow ZnCl_2 + H_2O$$

1 zinc atom	1 zinc atom
1 oxygen atom	1 oxygen atom
2 hydrogen atoms	2 hydrogen atoms
2 chlorine atoms	2 chlorine atoms

Aqueous solution   a solution in water.

State   when applied to substances, state means solid, liquid, or gas.

Chemistry in Action 5 (*continued from p. 125*)

Back in the laboratory, Bob, Mary, and Joe were still thinking about their problem.

'What about an experiment?' asked Joe, in an inspired flash.

'Yes . . .', said Mr. McLeod, 'but which experiment?' Joe sat quietly, not really knowing what to say next.

'Let's see if it conducts electricity—that'll give us the answer!' Mary announced triumphantly.

'Good idea', said Mr. McLeod while Bob looked at Mary admiringly. Joe scowled. So they set up the apparatus, dissolved some aluminium chloride in water, and tried to find the conductivity of the solution. The meter needle flicked up across the scale. . . .

'There!' exclaimed Mary, 'What did I tell you at the beginning? It conducts— it *must* be ionic.'

Do you agree?

Ionic bonds give rise to ions. If these ions are free to move, the substance will conduct electricity.
So, did the experiment give the answer?

Discuss this as a group.

Now turn to page 142.

Answers to this section will be found on page 244.

1 Calculate the formula weight of the following compounds:
  (a) SnO_2 (b) P_2O_5 (c) $MgBr_2$ (d) $C_2H_5CO_2H$ (e) $(CH_3)_2O$

2 Write the formulae and then calculate the formula weights of the following compounds. (Use the Periodic Table to help you.)
  (a) magnesium sulphide (b) bismuth chloride (c) strontium bromide
  (d) sodium nitride   (e) butane

3 Calculate the mass of a gram mole of 1(a), 1(d), 2(b), and 2(e) above.

4 Examine each of the equations below and check whether they are balanced or not. If you decide that one is not balanced, rewrite it in a balanced form.
  (a) $PbO + H_2 \rightarrow Pb + H_2O$
  (b) $FeO + C \rightarrow Fe + CO_2$
  (c) $Al + HCl \rightarrow AlCl_3 + H_2$
  (d) $MgO + 2HCl \rightarrow MgCl_2 + H_2O$

5 Use equation 4(a) (balanced if necessary) to calculate the number of grams of lead which could be obtained from 4.46 g lead ore (PbO).

6 When mercury oxide (HgO) is heated, mercury metal and oxygen are released. Write and balance the equation for the reaction. Calculate the weight of oxygen which could be obtained from 10.85 g mercury oxide.

7 In a number of experiments different weights of zinc were allowed to combine with sulphur and the weight of the zinc sulphide was found in each case. In the graph below the weights of zinc are plotted against the weights of sulphur required.
    Calculate the formula of zinc sulphide.

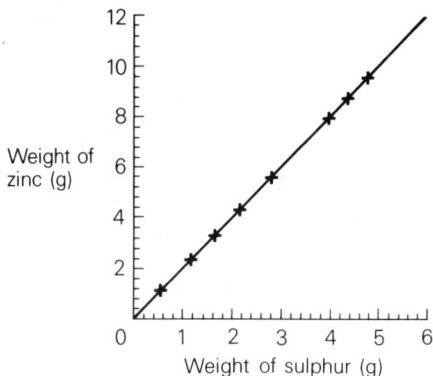

Chemistry in Action 6

From visible to invisible

During the late eighteenth century chemists noticed that, when they were carrying out reactions with gases, the volumes of the gases involved were all related to each other in a simple way. In 1808 a French chemist called Gay-Lussac summarized this when he said that the volumes of the gases were always related to each other by simple whole numbers. Let us look at a few examples of what he meant.

(a) When water is split up using electricity, for every 10 ml of oxygen formed, we always obtain 20 ml of hydrogen.
(b) When ammonia gas is split up, for every 20 ml of ammonia gas at the start, we end up with 10 ml of nitrogen and 30 ml of hydrogen.
(c) When hydrogen reacts with chlorine, hydrogen chloride gas is formed. For every 10 ml of hydrogen, we need 10 ml of chlorine and we obtain 20 ml of hydrogen chloride.

Look again at example (a) above. Chemists of the day thought something like this:
Suppose we were making water from oxygen and hydrogen gas.

For　　10 ml of oxygen gas, we would need　　20 ml of hydrogen gas.
For　　 1 ml of oxygen gas, we would need　　 2 ml of hydrogen gas.
For　0.1 ml of oxygen gas, we would need　0.2 ml of hydrogen gas.
For 0.01 ml of oxygen gas, we would need 0.02 ml of hydrogen gas.

We could imagine the volumes of oxygen and hydrogen used becoming smaller and smaller, until we end up with a very, very tiny volume of oxygen gas containing only **one** particle of oxygen. This would require twice the volume of hydrogen gas, which would contain **two** particles of hydrogen. This could be written as:

For **one** particle of oxygen, we would need **two** particles of hydrogen.

Gay-Lussac and his friends then concluded that water was made up of one particle of oxygen linked to two particles of hydrogen. They referred to these particles as atoms and wrote an equation like

$$2H + O \rightarrow H_2O$$

Let us now look at the other two examples.

For ammonia, the early chemists concluded by saying that:

2 particles of ammonia give **1** particle of nitrogen plus **3** particles of hydrogen.

$$2NH_3 \rightarrow N + 3H$$

Look at this equation carefully. Can you see what is wrong with it?

For the reaction involving hydrogen chloride, they concluded by saying that:

1 particle of hydrogen plus **1** particle of chlorine gives **2** particles of hydrogen chloride.

$$H + Cl \rightarrow 2HCl$$

Look at this equation carefully. What is wrong with it?

Now *form a group* with two or three other members of your class.

You are now living a long time after Gay-Lussac and you know much more about atoms and molecules than he did. Imagine for a moment that you, with your knowledge, could go back in time and talk to Gay-Lussac. *You* could help him with his difficulty in understanding these reactions. Do it in the following way.

1 As a group try to work out exactly what was the difficulty which faced Gay-Lussac and his fellow chemists. Why did the equations not fit the experimental information about volumes? Write down (in a few sentences) what their problem was.

2 As a group, work out a way to show Gay-Lussac why his equations were wrong. How could he correct his ideas? Write this down in a few sentences.

3 One member of your group should then tell the rest of the class how they would help Gay-Lussac to understand these gas reactions. You may need to use a blackboard or overhead projector.

An extra problem
You may like to try this problem in your group, or do it at home.

Ozone is a gas which occurs in the upper atmosphere and is very important for us all. It absorbs harmful radiation from the Sun, protecting us on the Earth's surface. In a series of experiments it can be shown that, for every 20 ml of ozone which breaks up, 30 ml of oxygen is formed. No other element is involved.

This can be written:

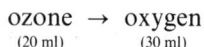

$$\text{ozone} \rightarrow \text{oxygen}$$
$$\text{(20 ml)} \qquad \text{(30 ml)}$$

Can you work out a formula for ozone?

Ozone has been at the centre of many arguments in recent years. Strangely, the arguments are connected to our use of aerosols, such as hair sprays and paint sprays. Try to find out what aerosols have to do with the ozone miles above the surface of the Earth.

13

First contact with sulphur

H							He
Li	Be	B	C	N	O	F	Ne
Na	Mg	Al	Si	P	$^{32}_{16}\mathbf{S}$	Cl	Ar

Figure 13.1

13.1

Sulphur is a yellow, non-metallic element. In normal, everyday life you are unlikely to meet sulphur or sulphuric acid (its most important compound). Yet vast amounts of the element are used annually in the world, especially in industrially advanced countries.

First of all we shall find out where it comes from and then what it is used for.

13.2 Sources of sulphur

In certain parts of the world, sulphur is found as the uncombined element. Volcanoes have deposits of sulphur on their slopes and, at one time, Italy exported sulphur which had been taken from volcanic regions. In parts of the USA veins of sulphur exist in beds, about 200 metres underground, mixed with calcite rock. This is very difficult to mine by normal methods because in places it is covered with quicksand, and elsewhere it is under the sea.

Sulphur compounds are quite common in the Earth's crust. Some examples are iron pyrites (iron sulphide), zinc blende (zinc sulphide), galena (lead sulphide), gypsum and anhydrite (calcium sulphate), and barytes (barium sulphate).

Sulphur compounds are found in oil and sometimes in natural gas. France gets all her supplies of sulphur from her own gas wells. The gas from the North Sea, however, is almost sulphur-free and so Britain has to import the sulphur she requires, mainly from the USA, Canada, and Poland.

13.3 Behaviour of sulphur

(a) Sulphur exists in two solid crystalline forms. The normal one at room temperature is rhombic sulphur, which has crystals of the kind shown in Fig. 13.2. Above 96 °C and up to its melting point of 119 °C another crystalline form takes over. It is called monoclinic sulphur (Fig. 13.3).

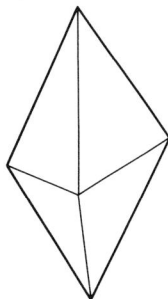

Figure 13.2

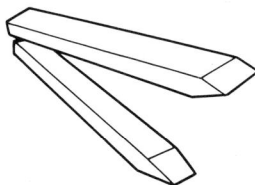

Figure 13.3

(b) Another important thing about sulphur is that it burns to give a choking, colourless gas with a 'dry' taste, called sulphur dioxide (SO_2). This is one of the most common air pollutants. It has been estimated that millions of tonnes of this gas escape into the air over Britain every year. It comes not so much from burning the sulphur itself as from burning coal and oil which contain sulphur compounds.

For example, some coals contain golden streaks of a sulphide of iron (FeS_2) and during the burning of the coal this sulphide reacts as shown below.

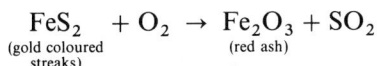

$$\underset{\substack{\text{(gold coloured}\\\text{streaks)}}}{FeS_2} + O_2 \rightarrow \underset{\text{(red ash)}}{Fe_2O_3} + SO_2$$

Ordinary domestic fires and central heating systems are responsible for much of the SO_2 in the air. More sulphur (as sulphur dioxide) escapes from power station chimneys each year than is used to make all of Britain's sulphuric acid.

13.4 Behaviour of sulphur dioxide

This gas has several interesting properties of its own, but by far the most important is that it can combine with more oxygen to give sulphur trioxide (SO_3) from which sulphuric acid is made (see Chapter 14). Before we look at this in detail we shall examine some of the other things which sulphur dioxide can do.

The difference in time between parts (a) and (b) of Fig. 13.4 is only a few seconds after the stopper has been removed. The solution which is made is

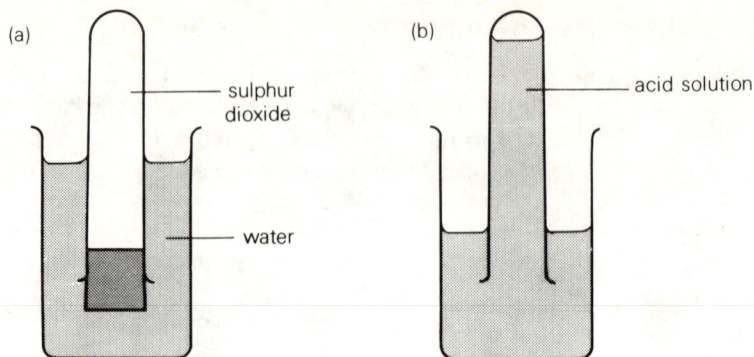

(a) sulphur dioxide

water

(b) acid solution

Figure 13.4

shown, by pH paper, to be acid, but this is *not* sulphuric acid. It is another acid called sulphur*ous* acid.

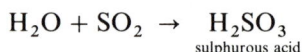

$$H_2O + SO_2 \rightarrow H_2SO_3$$
sulphurous acid

Like all acids, sulphurous acid releases hydrogen ions. A solution of it conducts electricity but it does not conduct very well. Acids which are poor conductors are said to be **weak**. Acids (like sulphur*ic* acid) which are good conductors are said to be **strong**. This has nothing to do with their concentration. If both acids are equally concentrated, sulphuric acid conducts well and sulphurous acid not so well. This is because sulphuric acid molecules let their hydrogen ions go free easily, while sulphurous acid molecules release hydrogen ions with difficulty.

If sulphurous acid releases H^+ ions, a negative ion must be left in solution. It is the sulph*ite* ion, SO_3^{2-}.

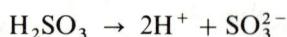

$$H_2SO_3 \rightarrow 2H^+ + SO_3^{2-}$$

This is the first time we have met an ion which contains more than one element. The sulphite ion has a pyramid shape (Fig. 13.5) and carries a double negative charge.

This charge was brought from the water by the oxygen which was carrying two extra electrons. This whole ion remains together in the pyramid cluster and behaves like any other more simple ion you have met. The double negative charge is spread out over the ion and is balanced by two hydrogen ions (H^+) to give H_2SO_3.

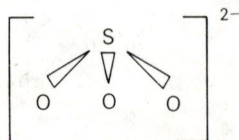

Figure 13.5

Tests for sulphite ions

(a) Sulphite ions are colourless, but they can be detected as follows. If a little barium chloride solution is added to a solution of a suspected sulphite, the barium ions and the sulphite ions team up to form a white solid (barium sulphite) and settle out to the bottom of the test-tube (Fig. 13.6). This solid dissolves again if a little dilute hydrochloric acid is added. Any soluble sulphite behaves like this and so we have a special test for sulphite ions.

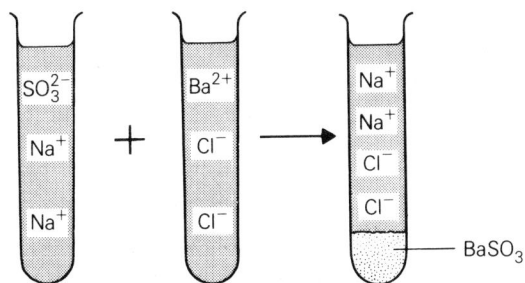

Figure 13.6

(b) In the test above it was noted that the $BaSO_3$ dissolved when hydrochloric acid was added to it. What actually happened was this.

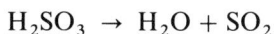

$$2HCl + BaSO_3 \rightarrow BaCl_2 + H_2SO_3$$
$$H_2SO_3 \rightarrow H_2O + SO_2$$

This also happens to all other sulphites. If hydrochloric acid is added to any sulphite and if it is warmed a little, the choking gas, SO_2, is given off. (It can be detected because it turns orange dichromate paper green.) This is not only a test for sulphites but is also a convenient way of making SO_2 in small quantities in the laboratory.

Usually sodium sulphite crystals are warmed with dilute hydrochloric acid and this gives a good stream of the gas.

13.5 Sulphur dioxide solution (sulphurous acid) and electron acceptors

In Section 7.2, page 79, we noticed that elements on the right of the Periodic Table were likely to be electron acceptors. Chlorine, bromine, and iodine are examples of these elements.

If a U-tube is set up as shown in Fig. 13.7, there is a meter reading showing that electrons are flowing from the sulphite solution to the chlorine, bromine, or iodine solution. When these elements accept electrons they become chloride ions, bromide ions, or iodide ions.

$$Cl_2 + 2e \rightarrow 2Cl^-$$
$$Br_2 + 2e \rightarrow 2Br^-$$
$$I_2 + 2e \rightarrow 2I^-$$

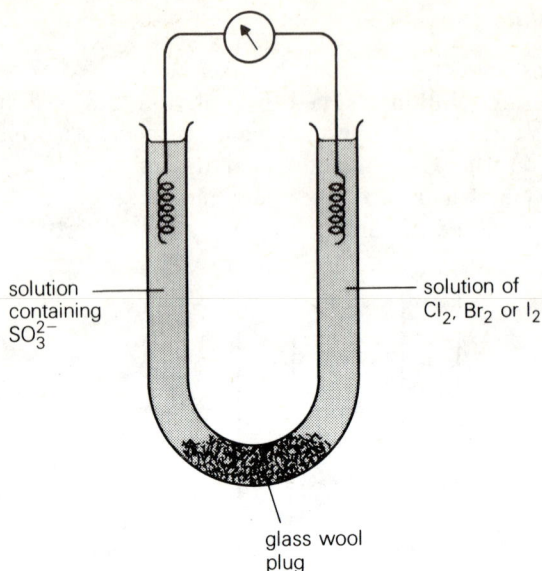

solution containing SO_3^{2-}

solution of Cl_2, Br_2 or I_2

glass wool plug

Figure 13.7

But what happens to the sulphite ions? They (or the water in which they are dissolved) must be losing electrons.

To speed this process up, we can add some sulphite solution to some bromine solution in water until the bromine just loses its brown colour.

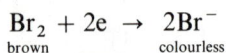

$$Br_2 + 2e \rightarrow 2Br^-$$

brown   colourless

If we now test the solution with barium chloride solution (Section 13.4, page 141) a white solid settles to the bottom of the container. It seems that the sulphite is unchanged, but there is one part of the test which we have missed out.

Chemistry in Action 5 (*continued from p. 134*)

Mary was still smiling triumphantly: after all *she* had said it was ionic from the start! Then Mr. McLeod spoke softly, 'It wasn't *pure* aluminium chloride we used . . .'

'Of course!' interrupted Joe, 'It must be the water that was conducting . . . not the aluminium chloride.'

'Don't be daft!' retorted Bob. 'Water doesn't conduct!'

There was a long silence while Bob and Joe eyed each other coldly. Then Mr. McLeod spoke. 'Well, water *does* conduct . . . but very badly.'

'So it *must* have been the aluminium chloride,' insisted Mary, 'because we got a good conductivity reading.'

Do you agree with Mary?

Discuss this and then turn to page 147.

We must add dilute hydrochloric acid to see whether the solid disappears. When we do this the solid does *not* dissolve and so we can no longer have sulphite ions present. Something new has been made. This is a new ion called the **sulphate** ion and has the formula SO_4^{2-}. We now have a test for this new sulphate ion. Add barium chloride solution to the substance you want to test. If a white solid forms which does *not* dissolve in dilute hydrochloric acid, we have identified a sulphate ion.

Something like Fig. 13.8 must have happened.

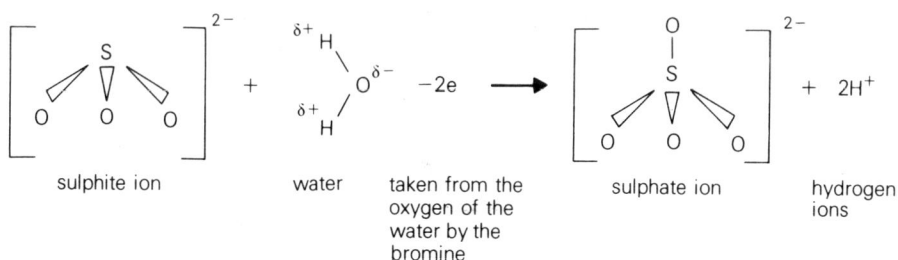

| sulphite ion | water | taken from the oxygen of the water by the bromine | sulphate ion | hydrogen ions |

Figure 13.8

This sulphate ion has the oxygen atoms arranged tetrahedrally around the sulphur atom and the double negative charge is spread round the ion. This cluster of atoms in the sulphate ion behaves just like any of the simpler ions you met earlier.

Summing up so far

Sulphur dioxide
(a) is a colourless gas with an unpleasant choking smell and a dry taste.
(b) dissolves well in water giving the weak acid, sulphurous acid (H_2SO_3).
(c) in solution can give electrons to good electron acceptors such as chlorine, bromine, or iodine. When it loses electrons it becomes the new sulphate ion (SO_4^{2-}).

Useful tests

1 Add $BaCl_2$ solution to the solution suspected of containing sulphite or sulphate ions } → white solid ⟶ dissolves in dilute HCl → sulphite ions present
⟶ does not dissolve in dilute HCl → sulphate ions present

2 If a gas with a choking smell is mixed with a solution of bromine or iodine and their brown colour disappears, the gas is likely to be sulphur dioxide.
3 If burning magnesium is dropped into a gas and yellow pieces of sulphur are left, the gas is sulphur dioxide.

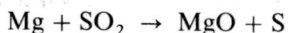

$$Mg + SO_2 \rightarrow MgO + S$$

A similar reaction occurs with CO_2 in which black specks of carbon are left.

13.6 Industrial uses

Sulphur dioxide gas or sulphite solutions have some other uses:

(a) as a mould or bacteria killer;
(b) as a food preservative;
(c) as a bleach for wool and paper.

Vats in which cheese or beer are made are regularly treated with sulphur dioxide to kill off undesirable moulds which would otherwise spoil the products. Packets of dried fruit are often marked 'treated with sulphur dioxide'. This is done to stop moulds growing on the fruit.

Wood pulp, from which paper is made, is naturally yellow and it has to be bleached to make it white. Some bleaches are so harsh that they do not only bleach the pulp but also destroy it. Sulphur dioxide or sulphite solutions are gentle bleaches which can be used without fear of damaging the fibres. There is a snag, however. You will have noticed that, as books and newspapers get old, they become yellow again. The bleach has not lasted for long. Why should this be so? As they react with electron acceptors we found that sulphites become sulphates, that is, they accepted oxygen.

sulphite + material being bleached → sulphate + bleached material

The wood pulp must be giving up oxygen to the sulphite as it is being bleached. When the bleached material is left exposed to the air for some time, the paper picks up oxygen from the air and slowly regains its yellow colour.

You will have seen the same effect with white woollen pullovers which slowly become yellow with age. Sulphite bleaches have been used for the wool and the air slowly reverses the bleaching process.

13.7 Sulphuric acid

By far the most important use of sulphur dioxide is in the manufacture of sulphuric acid.

We have seen in the previous sections that sulphur dioxide solution in water (sulphurous acid) can become sulphuric acid if there is an electron acceptor such as chlorine present. Water molecules are split between the chlorine and the acid.

$$Cl_2 + H_2|O + H_2SO_3 \rightarrow 2HCl + H_2SO_4$$

This works very well, but there is a problem in that the result is a mixture of hydrochloric and sulphuric acids. These are difficult to separate and the acids are both very dilute. How much cleaner and easier it would be if we could persuade either sulphur dioxide or sulphurous acid to combine rapidly and directly with oxygen gas.

Sulphur dioxide does combine directly with oxygen, but at room temperatures this is a very slow business indeed.

$$2SO_2 + O_2 \rightleftharpoons 2SO_3$$

If we have plenty of time to wait (several years) much of the sulphur dioxide will become sulphur trioxide. However, the reaction is **reversible**, which explains why *two* arrows are shown in the equation. That means that some of the SO_3 is turning back to SO_2 and O_2 at the same time as SO_2 and O_2 are combining to give SO_3. This is something like the crazy situation shown in Fig. 13.9.

At the beginning we have only SO_2 and O_2 and the man on the left of the

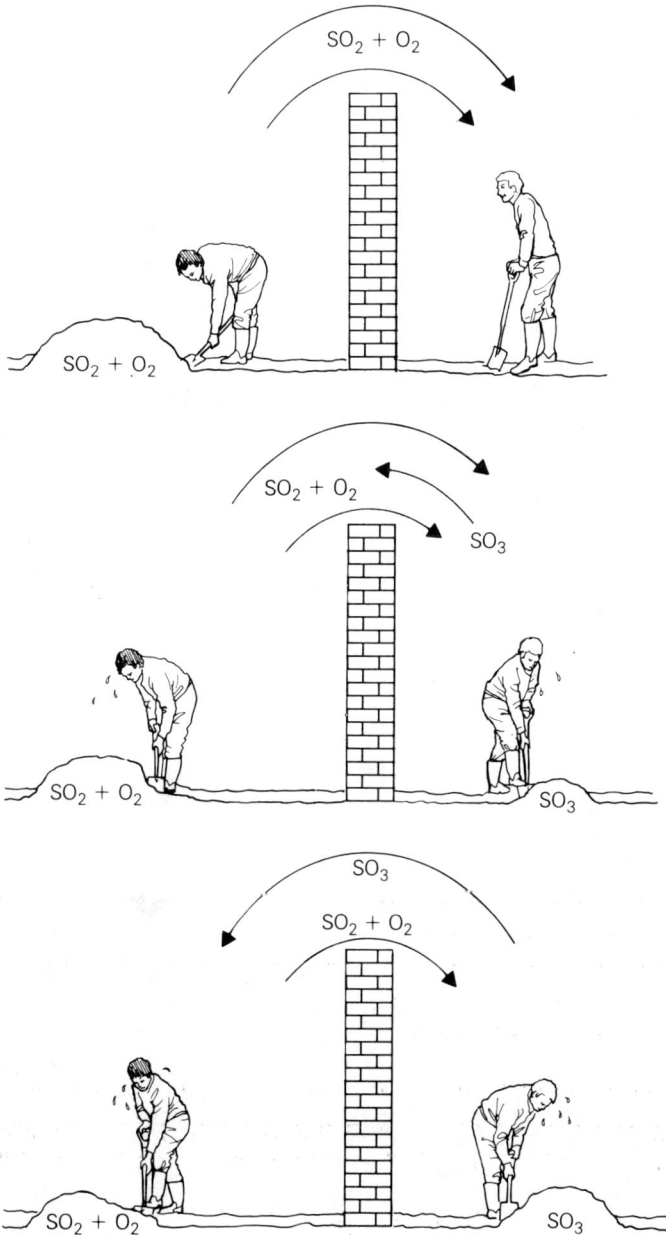

Figure 13.9

three-metre wall can shovel material over it. However, as time passes, the man on the SO_3 side has a big enough pile to start shovelling back over the wall. There will come a time when there is a balance between the sides and the rate of SO_2 and O_2 combining will equal the rate of SO_3 turning back to SO_2 and O_2.

To get any SO_3 at all we have to settle for this balanced situation, but there is a way of getting to the balance more quickly (Fig. 13.10).

If it were possible to lower the wall to one metre the men would achieve the same balance more quickly.

In chemical reactions there *are* barriers between reactants and products, but these can be lowered by means of substances called **catalysts**. These are substances which allow molecules to meet on their surface and react more easily.

Figure 13.10

For this particular reaction, a small amount of finely powdered platinum is able to lower the barrier. The balance between the reactants and products is achieved quickly enough to make the process worthwhile. The best temperature for the reaction has been found to be about 450 °C. The interesting thing about a catalyst is that it is not used up and can be used over and over again.

This process for making sulphur trioxide is called the **Contact Process**. Industrially the catalyst used is not expensive platinum metal, but pellets of a compound called vanadium pentoxide (V_2O_5).

So far so good; but we have not yet reached our goal of making sulphuric acid. Now that we have seen how sulphur trioxide is made, the last step, at least on paper, seems easy. We just have to add water.

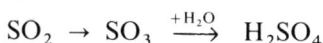

$$SO_2 \rightarrow SO_3 \xrightarrow{+H_2O} H_2SO_4$$

In practice, sulphur trioxide does not dissolve very rapidly in water so, if we bubble it directly into water, much of it passes through unchanged and is lost.

The problem has been neatly overcome because it has been found that SO_3 dissolves very well in concentrated sulphuric acid.

Chemistry in Action 5 (*continued from p. 142*)

Yes, there is another possible explanation for the conductivity. Perhaps the aluminium chloride *reacted* with the water to produce the ions, giving the high conductivity reading on the meter. Mr. McLeod pointed out this possibility to the group and then asked, 'What do you suggest now . . .?'

Mary pondered for a moment: 'See if it conducts *without* any water present,' she suggested.

'Huh! That won't prove anything', Bob commented quickly. 'Ionic *solids* don't usually conduct anyway. Remember we tried it with a chunk of salt? The ions are not free to move.'

'Then we'll melt it!' cried Mary. There was a stunned silence until Bob asked, 'What temperature does it melt at?' 'Hang on', interrupted Mr. McLeod. 'Pass over that blue book on the shelf above you. We'll look it up.'

Mr. McLeod flicked through the pages, then he straightened up again, 'We've had it. It doesn't melt!'

'What!' said Mary, 'It *must*!!'

'No', replied Mr. McLeod, 'it sublimes. The solid turns directly into a gas at 178 degrees, it says'.

'Well, that's that', announced Joe with a note of resignation. 'We'll never know!' Then he half smiled, 'Tell us, sir, what *is* the answer—polar or ionic?' There was a note of triumph in his voice; would he catch Mr. McLeod out? But Mr. McLeod was not going to be caught as easily as that. He smiled, and looked directly at Joe, 'What experiment would we need to do to find the answer?' he asked.

What is your answer?

Try to agree on an answer. Then turn to page 155.

This makes a 'super concentrated' sulphuric acid which can be diluted with water to make acid of the required concentration.

The laboratory and industrial processes are shown for comparison in Figs 13.11 and 13.12.

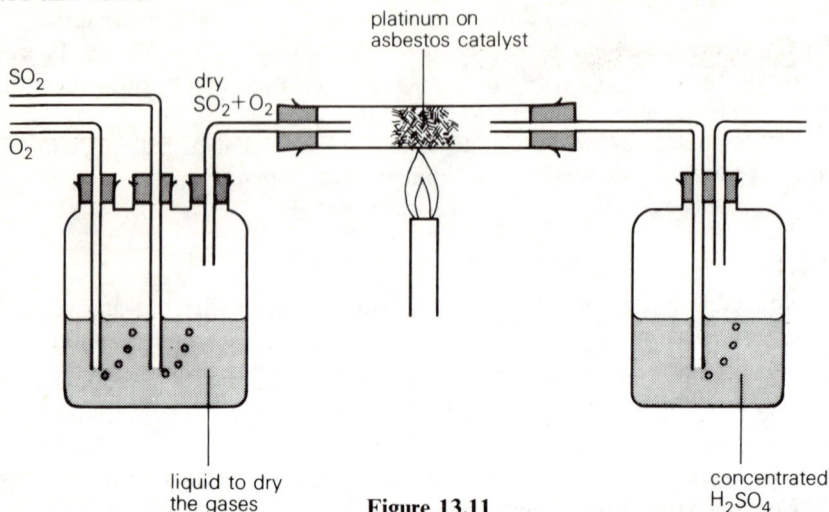

Figure 13.11

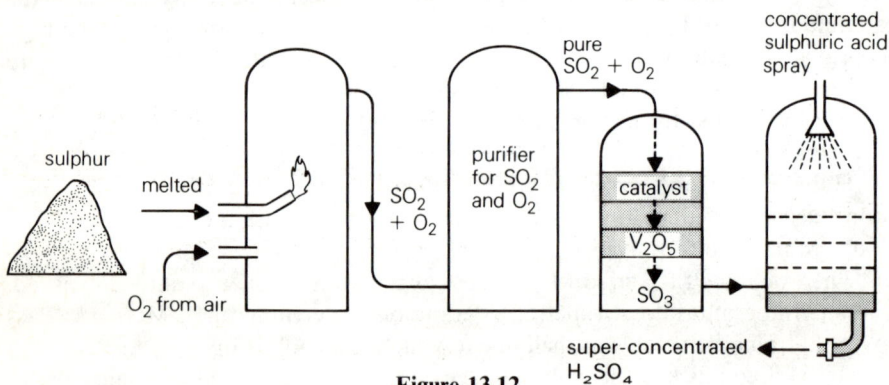

Figure 13.12

New words you have met in this chapter

Reversible reaction   a reaction in which the products can turn back into the reactants again. A reaction of this kind eventually arrives at a balance in which the rate of the forward reaction equals the rate of the backward reaction.

Catalyst   a substance added to a reaction mixture which allows the balance between the forward and backward reactions to be achieved more quickly. It is not itself used up in the reaction.

Strong acid   see the end of Chapter 14.

Weak acid   see the end of Chapter 14.

14

Sulphuric acid

14.1

In the last chapter we found out how sulphuric acid is made, but we have not yet seen why it is so important. Apart from the bottles in your school laboratory, you probably have never seen sulphuric acid and yet it has almost certainly played some part in the manufacture of many things in your home—metals, plastics, paints, fabrics, dyes, and even foodstuffs. The only sulphuric acid in your home will be the acid in the battery of a car or motorbike.

We shall spend this chapter looking at the behaviour of this remarkable and important acid.

14.2

To begin with we shall examine its small scale behaviour in the laboratory.

In its concentrated form sulphuric acid is a dense, oily liquid which must be handled with the greatest of care. **Goggles should be worn** when this liquid is handled.

Its chemical behaviour comes into three main categories:

(a) it is a strong acid;
(b) it has a strong attraction for water;
(c) it is an electron acceptor (a good oxidizing agent).

14.3 Strong acid

It is a common fault to confuse the meaning of the terms 'strong acid' and 'concentrated acid'.

A **strong acid** is one which, in solution, is almost completely ionized. (A concentrated acid is one in which there are many moles of the acid in each litre of solution. For example, concentrated sulphuric acid contains about 18 moles per litre.)

In its very concentrated form, sulphuric acid is only slightly ionized, but in its more dilute forms it is almost entirely ionized into hydrogen ions (protons) and sulphate ions.

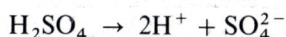

$$H_2SO_4 \rightarrow 2H^+ + SO_4^{2-}$$

The other strong acid which we met earlier was hydrochloric acid. Sulphuric acid has much in common with it.

Dilute sulphuric acid reacts with:

(a) *metals above hydrogen in the Reactivity Series*, releasing hydrogen and giving sulphates.

$$Mg + H_2SO_4 \rightarrow MgSO_4 + H_2$$
$$(Mg + 2HCl \rightarrow MgCl_2 + H_2)$$

(b) *metal oxides* to give sulphates and water.

$$ZnO + H_2SO_4 \rightarrow ZnSO_4 + H_2O$$
$$(ZnO + 2HCl \rightarrow ZnCl_2 + H_2O)$$

(c) *metal hydroxides* to give sulphates and water.

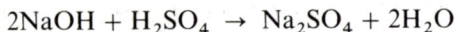

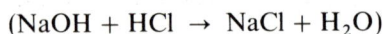

$$2NaOH + H_2SO_4 \rightarrow Na_2SO_4 + 2H_2O$$
$$(NaOH + HCl \rightarrow NaCl + H_2O)$$

(d) *metal carbonates* to give sulphates, water, and carbon dioxide.

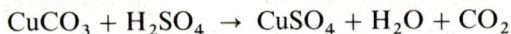

$$CuCO_3 + H_2SO_4 \rightarrow CuSO_4 + H_2O + CO_2$$
$$(CuCO_3 + 2HCl \rightarrow CuCl_2 + H_2O + CO_2)$$

Notice that, in these pairs of equations, two moles of HCl are required to do the job of one mole of H_2SO_4. This is because HCl has only one mole of hydrogen ions (protons) per mole whereas H_2SO_4 has two moles of hydrogen ions per mole.

Acids like HCl with one mole of protons per mole are said to be **monoprotic** (or monobasic).

Acids like H_2SO_4 with two moles of protons per mole are said to be **diprotic** (or dibasic).

Concentrated sulphuric acid has a high boiling point and this gives it some extra properties which are useful in the laboratory and in industry. For example, other acids can be made by adding concentrated sulphuric acid to one of their compounds and warming the mixture. Since most acids have a lower boiling point than sulphuric acid, they distill off and can be collected, leaving any sulphuric acid behind. Here are some examples.

(a) $H_2SO_4 + 2NaCl \rightarrow Na_2SO_4 + 2HCl(g)$
hydrochloric
acid gas

$\underset{\text{(any chloride)}}{H_2SO_4 + 2XCl} \rightarrow X_2SO_4 + 2HCl(g)$

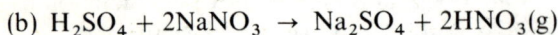

(b) $H_2SO_4 + 2NaNO_3 \rightarrow Na_2SO_4 + 2HNO_3(g)$
nitric acid
vapour

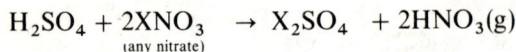

$\underset{\text{(any nitrate)}}{H_2SO_4 + 2XNO_3} \rightarrow X_2SO_4 + 2HNO_3(g)$

(c) $3H_2SO_4 + 2Na_3PO_4 \rightarrow 3Na_2SO_4 + 2H_3PO_4$
phosphoric
acid

$3H_2SO_4 + 2X_3PO_4 \rightarrow 3X_2SO_4 + 2H_3PO_4$
(any phosphate)

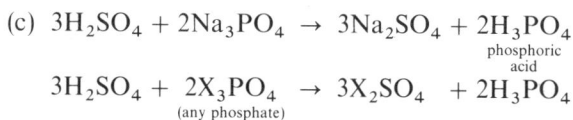

Phosphoric acid for the fertilizer industry is made this way from phosphate rock which is mainly calcium phosphate $Ca_3(PO_4)_2$ (see Section 14.7).

14.4 Strong attraction for water

Concentrated sulphuric acid has the ability to absorb water and as it does so, it gives out heat. This can happen so fiercely as to be dangerous.

(a) **On no account must water be added to concentrated sulphuric acid.** The heat generated turns the water instantly to steam. The steam has a volume at least 1000 times greater than the water it came from. This causes the acid to spurt and splash dangerously.

The acid can be diluted by adding **it** *slowly* to water and stirring it vigorously. The large amount of water heats up, but does not get hot enough to turn into steam.

(b) Sulphuric acid can absorb water which is already present in other substances and so it can be used to dry them. For example, gases can be dried by bubbling them through the concentrated acid.

The blue colour in copper sulphate crystals is caused by the presence of water molecules in the crystals. If a crystal of blue copper sulphate is dropped into concentrated sulphuric acid, the blue colour disappears as the water is withdrawn from the crystals into the acid.

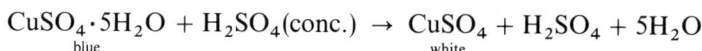

$$CuSO_4 \cdot 5H_2O + H_2SO_4(conc.) \rightarrow CuSO_4 + H_2SO_4 + 5H_2O$$
blue   white

(c) Even if substances do not contain water as such, but contain hydrogen and oxygen, concentrated sulphuric acid can draw out these elements to make water. An example of this can be seen in the experiment shown in Fig. 14.1.

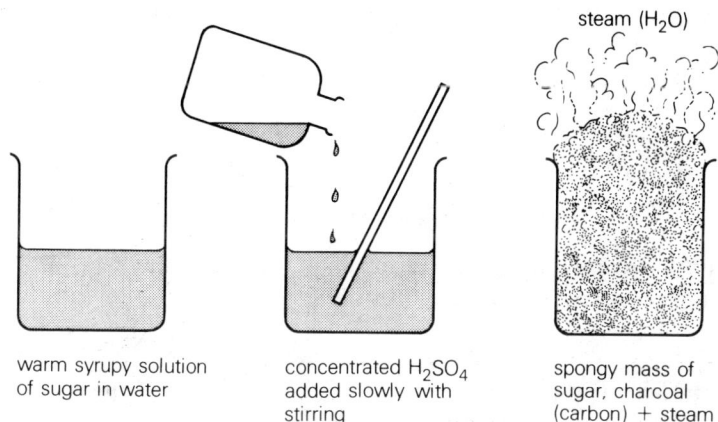

warm syrupy solution of sugar in water

concentrated H_2SO_4 added slowly with stirring

steam (H_2O)

spongy mass of sugar, charcoal (carbon) + steam

Figure 14.1

Sucrose

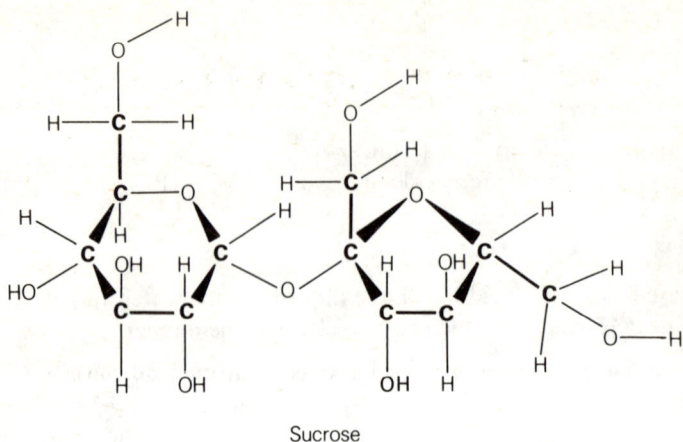

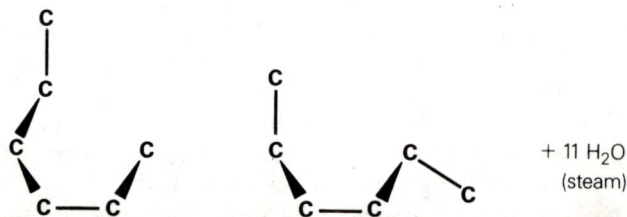

Carbon 'skeleton'

Figure 14.2

What has happened is that the hydrogen and oxygen atoms have been removed, leaving the black mass of carbon.

14.5 Electron acceptor (oxidizing agent)

Dilute sulphuric acid reacts with metals as mentioned in Section 14.3, page 149, but the warm concentrated acid can also react with metals below hydrogen in the Reactivity Series. This time, however, hydrogen is not pushed out by the metal.

The metals, as usual, lose electrons to become ions; for example

$$Cu - 2e \rightarrow Cu^{2+}$$

but the electrons are taken up by the acid as a whole.

$$H_2SO_4(conc.) + 2e \rightarrow SO_3^{2-} + H_2O$$

Sulphites in the presence of warm acid give SO_2 (Section 13.4(b)).
The complete equation can be written as:

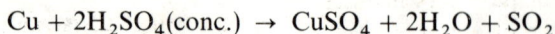

$$Cu + 2H_2SO_4(conc.) \rightarrow CuSO_4 + 2H_2O + SO_2$$

Concentrated sulphuric acid also attacks *non-metals* and gives sulphur dioxide.

$$C + 2H_2SO_4 \rightarrow CO_2 + 2SO_2 + 2H_2O$$

14.6

More than 100 years ago a famous chemist called Justus von Liebig said, 'It is no exaggeration to say we may fairly judge the commercial prosperity of a country from the amount of sulphuric acid it consumes.'

Table 14.1 gives the figures for the consumption of sulphuric acid in Britain in the latter part of this century. As you can see these figures are related to the changes in prosperity of our country. Our industry was booming in the '50s and '60s and, although there has been some growth since, it has recently ceased.

Table 14.1 Consumption of sulphuric acid in Britain

Year	Consumption (tonnes)	Increase on previous figure (tonnes)
1950	1 802 700	
1960	2 701 400	+898 700
1970	3 298 600	+597 200
1974	3 855 000	+556 400
1975	3 500 000	−355 000

14.7 How is sulphuric acid used in industry?

(a) About a third of the sulphuric acid in Britain goes into the fertilizer and agriculture industry. The common fertilizers have been ammonium sulphate, made by adding sulphuric acid to ammonia, and superphosphates, made from sulphuric acid and calcium phosphate rock.

Recently the calcium superphosphates have been overtaken by the ammonium phosphates, for example, $(NH_4)_2HPO_4$, as our main phosphate fertilizer.

The phosphoric acid is released from phosphate rock (Section 14.3) by concentrated sulphuric acid and then allowed to react with ammonia.

Since fertilizers control our food supply, you can see how sulphuric acid plays its part in feeding the nation.

(b) About 15% of the sulphuric acid is used in the production of pigments which give 'body' and covering power to paints. Notably, titanium dioxide is purified by sulphuric acid and this forms the base of 'brilliant white' paints. Paints with this base stay brighter and keep their colour longer than the old lead-based paints.

(c) A sulphuric acid and nitric acid mixture is necessary for nitrating the substance toluene to give trinitrotoluene (TNT). Explosives have both bad and good uses. Quarrying, mining, and road building use large amounts of explosives for peaceful purposes.

(d) Another 10% of our sulphuric acid is used in the production of soaps and detergents (Section 20.7).

(e) Rayon fibres are used in the manufacture of clothing and the cords and fibres in tyres are often made of it. The other form of rayon which you will have seen is the transparent wrappings used for displaying goods in supermarkets.

Rayon is a cellulose (carbohydrate) material which (when dissolved in an alkaline solution) can either be squirted through holes to make a fibre or spread on rollers to make a thin film. The alkali is then neutralized by sulphuric acid and the fibre or film is ready for use.

Each day about 13 000 tonnes of sulphuric acid are used in Britain and more than 95% of it is made from sulphur by the Contact Process.

New words you have met in this chapter

Strong acid	an acid in which *most* of the molecules are broken down into positively charged hydrogen ions and other negatively charged ions. The word *strong* has nothing to do with the word *concentrated*.
Concentrated acid	a solution of an acid in which the proportion of the acid is high.
Weak acid	an acid in which *few* of the molecules are ionized into H^+ and another negatively charged ion. The word *weak* has nothing to do with *dilute*.
Dilute acid	a solution of an acid in which the proportion of the acid is low.
Oxidizing agent	a substance which makes another substance lose electrons (become oxidized). An easy way to remember about oxidation and its opposite (reduction) is the word OILRIG:

                    Oxidation
                    Is
                    Loss of electrons
                    Reduction
                    Is
                    Gain of electrons

Monoprotic acid	an acid which contains one mole of H^+ ions per mole of acid (HCl).
Diprotic acid	an acid which contains two moles of H^+ ions per mole of acid (H_2SO_4).

Chemistry in Action 5 (*continued from p. 147*)

In this short story, you have been asked to 'think scientifically'. There are many ways of finding answers to questions. We could look up books or listen to others. We could even make guesses or just decide what we'd *like* the answer to be.

For many problems there is a special way which helps us find the answer. This is known as the scientific way, and it nearly always means that we have to carry out an experiment or perhaps many experiments.

As Bob, Mary, and Joe found out, deciding which is the *right* experiment is not always easy. Their experiment was not really the right one because the high conductivity that they obtained could be explained in several ways. In the scientific way of solving problems, we *must* choose the right experiment, often called the *critical* experiment, which will give an answer with only one explanation.

In the problem of aluminium chloride the critical experiment might be to check the conductivity of aluminium chloride, either as a gas or as a liquid (which could be obtained by heating under slight pressure). In either case, if there were any ions present, they might be set free under these conditions. In other words, we *suggest* that aluminium chloride *might* be ionic and then carry out an experiment which could only give a conductivity reading *if*, in fact, the aluminium *is* ionic!

Scientists often work in this way and part of the skill of a good scientist is to be able to design the critical experiment.

15

Nitrogen—the unreactive element?

H							He
Li	Be	B	C	$_7\mathbf{N}^{14}$	O	F	Ne
Na	Mg	Al	Si	P	S	Cl	Ar

Figure 15.1

15.1

About four-fifths of the air around us is made up of the gas nitrogen. When we breathe air in and out the amounts of oxygen and carbon dioxide change, but the nitrogen seems to be unchanged.

However, in Chapter 17 we shall see that our bodies are made up largely of nitrogen compounds. Our muscles, blood, hair, and nails are proteins containing nitrogen atoms. Clearly nitrogen is important to us, yet when we breathe it in, it does not get involved in chemical reactions in our bodies. In the next few chapters we shall investigate the processes by which we make nitrogen part of us.

15.2 Nitrogen is fairly unreactive

In most of the chemical processes we associate with air such as breathing, burning, and rusting, nitrogen takes no part. If we look at the Periodic Table we find nitrogen in column 5 which suggests that it can form three or even five bonds. Molecules of nitrogen gas in the air go around in pairs (N_2) and the atoms are held together by three bonds, represented as $N\equiv N$. To break these three bonds requires much effort (energy). If nitrogen is going to combine easily with something else we would expect that the sum of the strengths of the new bonds formed would have to be stronger than the $N\equiv N$. However, in most cases when nitrogen combines with something else there is a loss of energy (Fig. 15.2).

The energy used up in the first step is greater than the energy released in the second. Therefore, unless we have another source of energy which we can supply

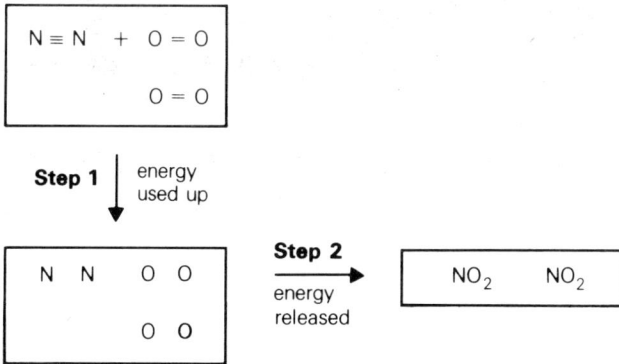

$N \equiv N \quad + \quad O = O$

$O = O$

Step 1 | energy used up

N N   O O

O O

Step 2 energy released → $NO_2 \quad NO_2$

Figure 15.2

continuously, nitrogen tends to stay as nitrogen gas rather than combine with other elements.

This can be shown in an experiment in which we allow electric sparks to pass through air for a few minutes. Soon a brown gas, nitrogen dioxide (NO_2), can be seen (Fig. 15.3).

On a much larger scale this happens in a thunderstorm where the energy is supplied by the lightning. A man-made version of this occurs in every car engine (Fig. 15.4). Here the air in the petrol–air mixture meets high energy sparks from the spark plugs, some of the nitrogen combines with the oxygen, and oxides of nitrogen come out with the exhaust gases.

These oxides of nitrogen (there are several of them) can cause as much harmful pollution as the carbon monoxide which is made at the same time.

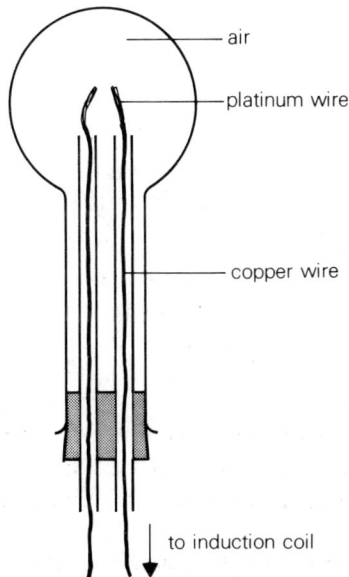

air

platinum wire

copper wire

to induction coil

Figure 15.3

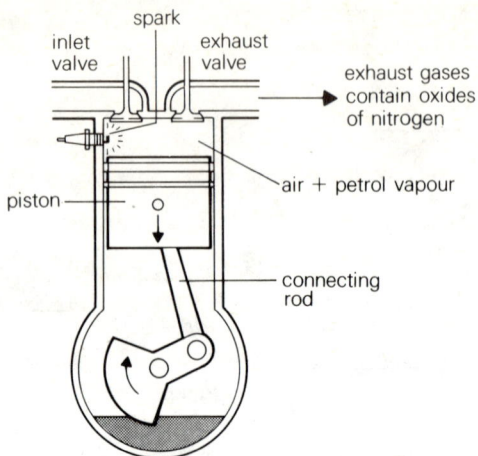

Figure 15.4

Nitrogen dioxide dissolves in water to give nitric acid.

$$NO_2 + H_2O \rightarrow HNO_3$$

This introduces us to a new ion, the nitrate ion, written as NO_3^-. This is a flat triangular ion with nitrogen in the middle and with a single negative charge spread over it.

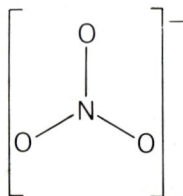

Plants can absorb and use nitrates in their growth.

Here is the first clue to the answer to the problem mentioned in Section 15.1. Nitrogen enters the food chain as the nitrate ion in plants.

15.3 Another route to nitrates

If there is a cheap and plentiful supply of electricity, it should be possible to use man-made lightning in a factory to make nitrogen and oxygen combine. The nitrogen dioxide can be used to give nitric acid, which can be neutralized to give nitrates, which are used as fertilizers. The snag is that most countries do not have such an electricity supply. If we are going to be able to use nitrogen, another pathway must be found.

War sometimes provides the pressure for research and the development of new chemical techniques. This was the case in the First World War when Germany, cut off by a shipping blockade, had to find new sources of nitrates for fertilizers and explosives. The air above Germany contained all the nitrogen required, but the problem was how to make it combine with another element easily and cheaply. The problem had been largely solved by Fritz Haber in 1908, who found a way of making nitrogen and hydrogen combine to make ammonia (NH_3). However, it was not until 1916 that the combined efforts of Haber and Bosch got it into industrial production.

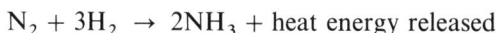

$$N_2 + 3H_2 \rightarrow 2NH_3 + \text{heat energy released}$$

Here was a process in which the energy problem seemed to have been solved. The breaking of the strong $N\equiv N$ bonds and the H—H bonds was more than

balanced by the heat released when the $H\diagdown\underset{H}{\overset{N}{|}}\diagup H$ bonds were made.

But there always seems to be a snag. Energy was required to separate nitrogen from the air and energy was required to get hydrogen from its most common compound, water. When the whole process was summed up, there was a net energy loss (Fig. 15.5) and this would cost money.

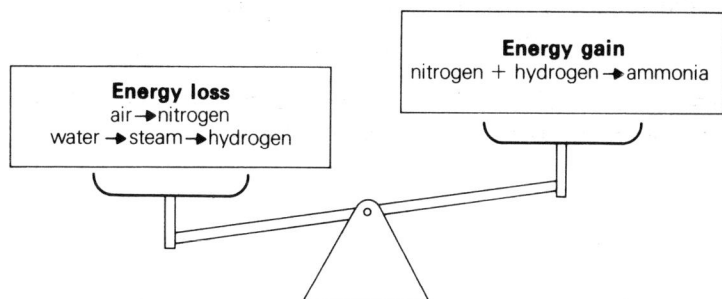

Figure 15.5

However, there was a need for ammonia in the war effort and so the expense had to be met regardless. Haber's method is still used today, except that the way that hydrogen is obtained has changed. It is easier to get it from methane (North Sea gas) and other hydrocarbons than from steam alone.

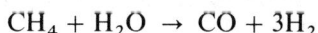

$$CH_4 + H_2O \rightarrow CO + 3H_2$$

15.4 Haber's problem

Let us spend just a little longer on looking at Haber's method.

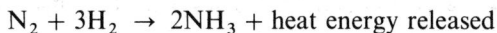

$$N_2 + 3H_2 \rightarrow 2NH_3 + \text{heat energy released}$$

He reasoned that, if the molecules of nitrogen and hydrogen were to meet and bump into each other, this would be helped by squashing them together into a smaller space. In other words, he argued that increasing the pressure should help the reaction. This turned out to be true. Look along any horizontal strip of Table 15.1. As the pressure increases the maximum yield of ammonia increases.

Table 15.1 Maximum percentage of NH_3 available with varying temperature and pressure

Pressure (atm)	25	50	100	200	400
Temperature (°C)					
100	91.7	94.5	96.7	98.4	99.4
200	63.6	73.5	82.0	89.0	94.6
300	27.4	39.6	53.1	66.7	79.7
400	8.7	15.4	25.4	38.8	55.4
500	2.9	5.6	10.5	18.3	31.9

For many chemical reactions you have met, increasing the temperature seems to help. Heating the molecules makes them speed up and bump into each other harder. Look back at Table 15.1 and see what happens as you go down any vertical column, that is, as the temperature increases.

The yield of ammonia drops as the temperature rises. Heat must make the ammonia molecules break up and return to nitrogen and hydrogen.

It would therefore seem sensible to do the reaction at very high pressures, such as 400 times atmospheric pressure, and at a low temperature. However, there is a snag here too. To get the maximum yield of ammonia at low temperatures takes a very long time, too long to be of any use. This reminds us of a similar problem we met in Section 13.7 when we were looking at the manufacture of sulphur trioxide. In that case the trouble was overcome by using a catalyst. The same solution is possible here. This time the catalyst used is made up of fine particles of iron in the presence of an alkali such as potassium hydroxide. This catalyst operates efficiently only between 400 °C and 540 °C. Table 15.1 shows us that at these temperatures the maximum yield of ammonia will not be much better than 30%. To use very high pressures is costly because very thick-walled reaction vessels are required and the pumping is also expensive. Most manufacturers settle for pressures of 80–350 atmospheres, giving a maximum yield of ammonia of about 15%. This is not as bad as it sounds because the ammonia is formed quickly and can be removed easily by condensing it from the unchanged nitrogen and hydrogen. These can then be sent round the process again and again, converting more of them into ammonia each time, while more nitrogen and hydrogen are pumped into the reactor to keep the pressure the same.

A reminder

Notice that the catalyst has *not given us more ammonia*, but has given it *more quickly*.

15.5 Why bother with ammonia?

This is a good point at which to investigate the behaviour of ammonia. We will then be able to understand how it links to nitric acid, nitrates, fertilizers, plants, and us.

In the laboratory small samples of ammonia can be made easily without the problems of high pressure, temperature, and the catalyst. A family of compounds related to ammonia are available and from them the gas can be generated. These ammonium salts have NH_4^+ as their positive ion. This is a tetrahedral ion with a single positive charge spread over it (Fig. 15.6).

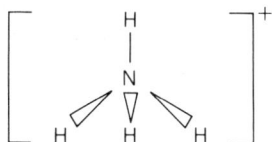

Figure 15.6

When an ammonium salt is heated with a strong alkali (many OH^-) ammonia gas is released as an H^+ is pulled away from the ammonium ion by the OH^- (Fig. 15.7).

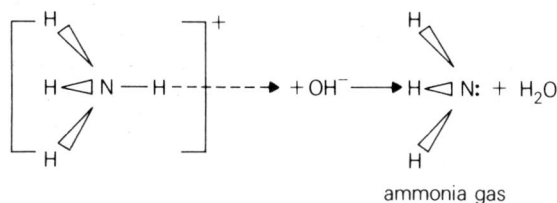

ammonia gas

Figure 15.7

Make some ammonia from ammonium chloride or ammonium sulphate and sodium hydroxide solution.

Carry out the following tests on it.

(a) Very carefully, smell it.
(b) Collect some in a test-tube and cover the mouth of it. Immerse it in water and open the tube (see Fig. 13.4). The water rushes in, showing that the gas is very soluble in water. Keep the solution for the next test.
(c) Test the solution with indicator paper. The pH should be quite high. The spare pair of electrons on the ammonia attracts an H^+ from water. This gives the ammonium ion NH_4^+ and leaves OH^- free in solution. These give the solution a high pH value (Fig. 15.8).

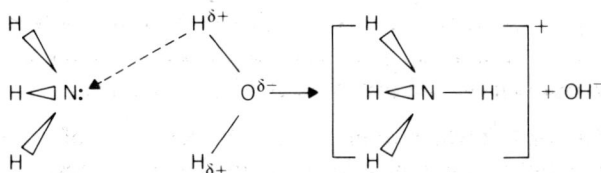

Figure 15.8

(d) *Oxidizing the ammonia.* We still have not managed to link ammonia (NH_3) with the nitrate ion (NO_3^-) which we said earlier was required by plants. Somehow we have to introduce oxygen.

To obtain a steady supply of ammonia we can use the apparatus shown in Fig. 15.9. Soda lime is just a solid form of a strong alkali and calcium oxide is there to dry the ammonia gas.

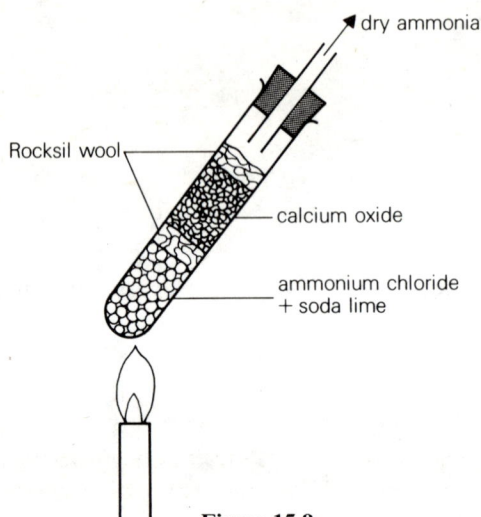

Figure 15.9

We have learned that when things are burnt, they combine with oxygen.

(i) Let us try to burn ammonia (Fig. 15.10) and then test the air above it with pH paper for signs of the acid gas, NO_2.

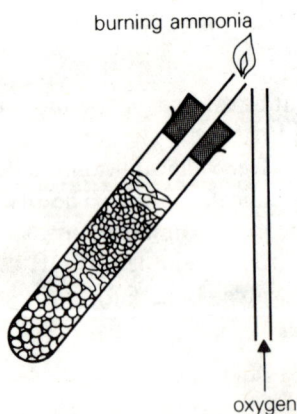

Figure 15.10

Ammonia does burn quite well in an atmosphere of oxygen but you are unlikely to find any NO_2.

$$NH_3 + O_2 \rightarrow N_2 + H_2O$$

(ii) Another source of oxygen is the oxide of an unreactive metal such as copper. Pass a stream of ammonia over hot copper(II) oxide (Fig. 15.11).

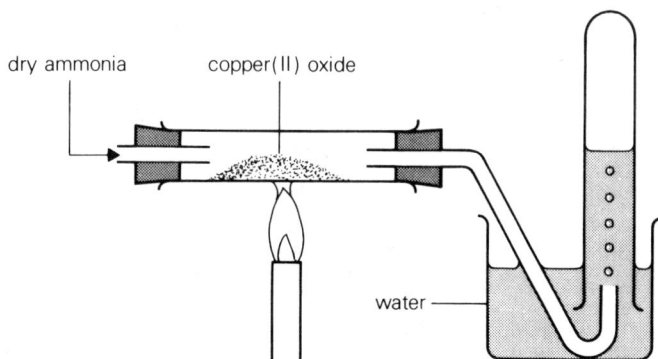

dry ammonia   copper(II) oxide

water

Figure 15.11

Perhaps the ammonia will take the oxygen from the copper(II) oxide. Does the water in the dish become acid? Do brown fumes appear?

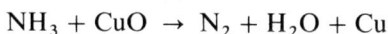

$$NH_3 + CuO \rightarrow N_2 + H_2O + Cu$$

Once again the hydrogen of the ammonia has joined with oxygen, but the nitrogen appears as nitrogen gas uncombined with oxygen.

(iii) Perhaps we have to turn again to a catalyst to help us. A chemist called Ostwald noticed that when a mixture of air and ammonia was passed over hot platinum wire, a brown gas (NO_2) was formed. This reaction gave out so much heat that the platinum continued to glow red-hot without any further heating.

$$NH_3 + O_2 \rightarrow NO_2 + H_2O$$

Here is the link we have been seeking.

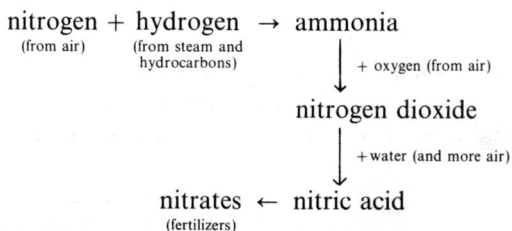

nitrogen + hydrogen → ammonia
(from air)   (from steam and
            hydrocarbons)   + oxygen (from air)

nitrogen dioxide

+ water (and more air)

nitrates ← nitric acid
(fertilizers)

This process, in which nitrogen from the air is combined with other elements and then made into useful compounds, is called **nitrogen fixation**.

Summing up so far

1 Nitrogen gas is fairly unreactive, but it can be made to combine directly with oxygen to give oxides of nitrogen. This requires large amounts of electrical energy.

2 Nitrogen can be combined with hydrogen with the help of a catalyst operating at high pressures and moderate temperatures.

3 Another catalyst, platinum, allows ammonia to combine with oxygen to give oxides of nitrogen.

4 Nitrogen dioxide and water together give nitric acid. This is the basis of fertilizers.

New words you have met in this chapter

Nitrogen fixation   the process by which nitrogen in the air is made to combine with other elements to make useful compounds.

Chemistry in Action 7

Contact with cleaner air

You will remember that sulphur trioxide is made from sulphur dioxide by the Contact Process (see p. 147). A mixture of sulphur dioxide and air is passed through a vanadium oxide catalyst at 425 °C and sulphur trioxide is formed. The trioxide is dissolved in concentrated sulphuric acid, which is then diluted with water. It sounds simple, but it turns out to be rather complicated. Let us look at some of the problems in a real industrial process.

Here is the reaction: $2SO_2 + O_2 \rightarrow 2SO_3$

The graph shows the percentage conversion to the trioxide at various temperatures. You can see that at 425 °C the percentage conversion is around 98%.

We cannot run our process at a lower temperature since it would take too long for the reaction to occur.

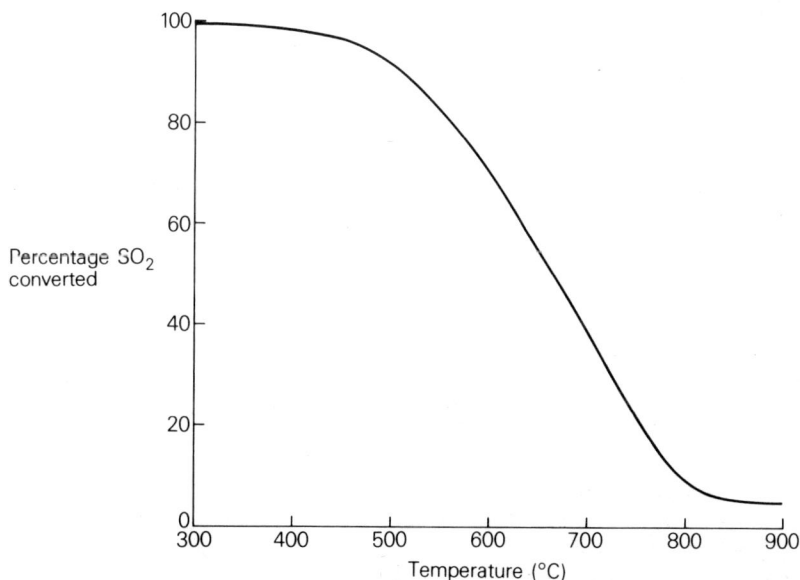

First problem

When the mixture of sulphur dioxide and air is passed through the catalyst at 425 °C the reaction takes place. However, as it does so, it produces heat! The temperature of the catalyst rises to above 600 °C. At this temperature the conversion is reduced to around 65% (see the graph). We cannot start at less than 425 °C because the reaction would be too slow. We cannot achieve better than 65% conversion because of this extra heating. How can we solve this problem?

You will remember that, in the Haber process for making ammonia, we recycled the unchanged gases (Section 15.4, p. 160). In the Contact Process there is little point in putting the mixture back through an overheated catalyst. Cooling the catalyst to around 425 °C is not successful either.

Here is a picture of our process so far.

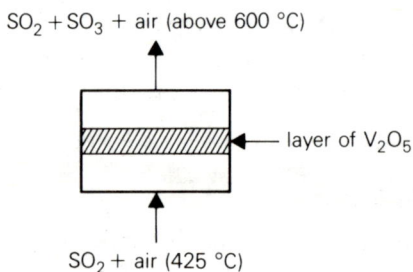

$SO_2 + SO_3$ + air (above 600 °C)

layer of V_2O_5

SO_2 + air (425 °C)

Now *form a group* with two or three members of your class. Discuss how you might attempt to achieve a much better percentage conversion. You may find it helpful to make a rough drawing of your ideas.

When you have decided what you might do, turn to page 174.

16

Nitric acid and fertilizers

At this stage we can do a number of simple reactions with nitric acid to see how it compares with other acids we have met. It comes in a very dangerous, concentrated form which contains about 17 moles of the acid per litre of solution. This attacks most common materials such as wood, skin, clothing, and paper, and **must be handled very carefully**. Your teacher will probably demonstrate these reactions for you and will probably use a much more dilute form of it. Nitric acid is a strong acid, that is, it is almost completely ionized in solution.

16.1 Neutralization

Nitric acid, like other acids, can react with alkalis to give *salts* (see Chapter 19). In this case the salts are *nitrates*.

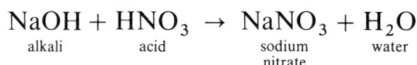

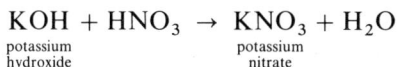

$$\underset{\text{alkali}}{\text{NaOH}} + \underset{\text{acid}}{\text{HNO}_3} \rightarrow \underset{\substack{\text{sodium}\\\text{nitrate}}}{\text{NaNO}_3} + \underset{\text{water}}{\text{H}_2\text{O}}$$

$$\underset{\substack{\text{potassium}\\\text{hydroxide}}}{\text{KOH}} + \text{HNO}_3 \rightarrow \underset{\substack{\text{potassium}\\\text{nitrate}}}{\text{KNO}_3} + \text{H}_2\text{O}$$

If you do these experiments, the solutions can be set aside to crystallize.

16.2 An electron acceptor

Many acids are electron acceptors. This can be seen when we add a reactive metal like magnesium to them.

The magnesium atoms each lose two electrons and give magnesium ions.

$$\text{Mg} - 2e \rightarrow \text{Mg}^{2+}$$

These electrons are picked up by the hydrogen ions of the acid and hydrogen gas is given off.

$$2\text{H}^+ + 2e \rightarrow \text{H}_2$$

(a) If we place some magnesium ribbon in a test-tube half full of water and add a few drops of nitric acid, this *very dilute* acid reacts with the magnesium as expected.

$$\text{Mg} + 2\text{HNO}_3 \rightarrow \text{Mg(NO}_3)_2 + \text{H}_2$$

(b) If we repeat the experiment with *dilute* nitric acid we do not get hydrogen, but a colourless gas comes off which turns brown near the mouth of the test-tube. Once again the magnesium (and most other common metals) lose electrons and become ions. Where do the electrons go this time? It must be the nitrate ion which receives the electrons.

In the first case (Fig. 16.1) the electron of the negative charge plus an electron from the metal go to one of the oxygen atoms to give O^{2-} and leave NO_2.

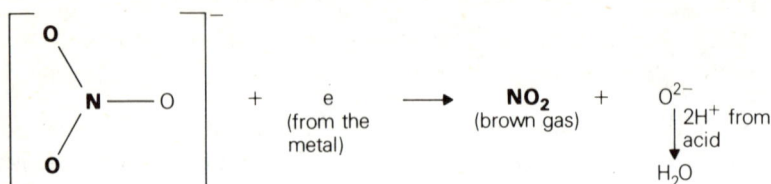

Figure 16.1

In the second case (Fig. 16.2) the electron of the negative charge plus three electrons from the metal go to two of the oxygen atoms to give two O^{2-} ions and leave NO (nitric oxide).

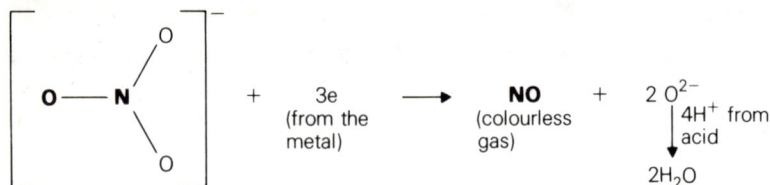

Figure 16.2

When NO reaches the air at the mouth of the tube it picks up oxygen to become brown NO_2.

$$2NO + O_2 \rightarrow 2NO_2$$

(c) If the acid is concentrated the metal displaces mainly brown NO_2. It was mentioned in the last chapter (Section 15.2) that oxides of nitrogen were pollutants in car exhaust gases. Care should be taken not to inhale these gases in the laboratory.

16.3 The behaviour of nitrates

Before we return to the importance of nitric acid and nitrates in industry let us look at the behaviour of nitrates.

(a) First of all, they all dissolve well in water.
(b) When the dry crystals of a variety of nitrates are heated, four different types of reaction occur.

(i) *Nitrates of sodium and potassium*

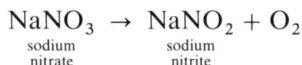

$$NaNO_3 \rightarrow NaNO_2 + O_2$$

sodium   sodium
nitrate   nitrite

These reactive metals hold on to most of the nitrogen and oxygen and release only some oxygen. The NO_2^- ion which is left is the *nitrite* ion.

(ii) *Nitrates of most other metals*

$$Cu(NO_3)_2 \rightarrow CuO + NO_2 + O_2$$

Here most of the nitrate ion is lost as NO_2 and oxygen and the metal is left with only some oxygen.

(iii) *Nitrates of the least reactive metals*

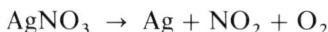

$$AgNO_3 \rightarrow Ag + NO_2 + O_2$$

In these cases the whole of the nitrate ion is lost and the metal is left alone.

(iv) *Ammonium nitrate* This compound has a behaviour all of its own when heated. Nothing is left in the tube and at the end of the heating there is sometimes a mild explosion.

$$NH_4NO_3 \rightarrow N_2O(g) + H_2O(g)$$

nitrous   steam
oxide

Ammonium nitrate in some of its crystalline forms is quite a strong explosive in its own right. It is also used in conjunction with other explosives to give very violent explosions. On the other hand it is an extremely useful fertilizer.

(c) *Test for a nitrate* If a suspected nitrate is dissolved in water and mixed with iron(II) sulphate solution, a greenish solution is left. If some concentrated sulphuric acid is added by slowly running it down the inside of the tube wall, a brown ring appears (Fig. 16.3). This is a test for a nitrate.

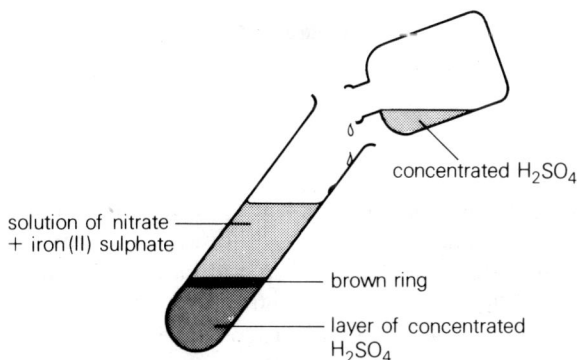

concentrated H_2SO_4

solution of nitrate + iron(II) sulphate

brown ring

layer of concentrated H_2SO_4

Figure 16.3

16.4 Ammonium nitrate fertilizer

In Section 16.1 you may have made a small sample of ammonium nitrate by a method very similar to that used industrially.

Fairly concentrated nitric acid, made by the Ostwald process (Section 15.5) is neutralized by blowing ammonia gas (Haber process) into it. This releases a large amount of heat which causes much of the water to evaporate. If the mass is allowed to crystallize of its own accord, the crystals tend to cake together and the lumps are useless for spreading evenly as a fertilizer. An ingenious method has been devised (Fig. 16.4) to overcome this problem.

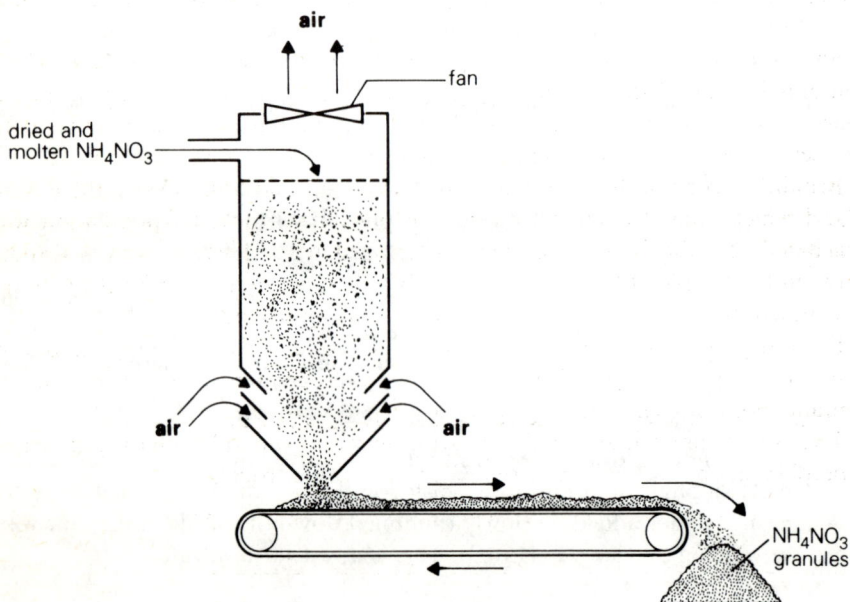

Figure 16.4

The remainder of the water in the mass is evaporated and the ammonium nitrate is then melted and allowed to drop down a tall tower as tiny droplets about 2 mm in diameter. The tower is about as high as an eight-storey building. The droplets are chilled by a stream of air drawn up the tower by a fan. They arrive at the bottom of the tower as little spheres which are safe to handle and which do not cake together in storage. When needed on the farm, they can be distributed evenly and easily by mechanical spreaders.

16.5 Other fertilizers

Ammonium nitrate is very rich in nitrogen. Let us calculate the percentage of nitrogen in it.

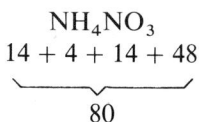

$$\underbrace{NH_4NO_3}_{80} \quad 14 + 4 + 14 + 48$$

The formula weight is 80, of which 28 parts are nitrogen.

$$\% \, N = \frac{28}{80} \times 100 = 35\%$$

Other fertilizers are required for a variety of purposes. A simple example is ammonium sulphate $(NH_4)_2SO_4$. Calculate the percentage of nitrogen in this compound.

In column 5 of the Periodic Table, just below nitrogen, we find another important element for plants, namely phosphorus. The main source of phosphorus is phosphate rock, a fairly complex compound with a formula $Ca_{10}(PO_4)_6F_2$.

So important is this rock that governments compete for territory which contains it. One of the largest deposits of it is in North-West Africa. In recent years the countries in that area have been disputing borders in what appears to be useless desert, but large deposits of phosphate rock are really the prize.

Britain's record in this is not entirely perfect. In the Indian Ocean there is an island which consisted almost entirely of phosphate rock. Its population was evacuated and the island was literally stripped bare. There is now a dispute between the people of the island and the British Government about the amount of compensation to be paid for the ruin of their homeland.

From the rock, phosphoric acid (H_3PO_4) is made. This can be neutralized by ammonia to give $(NH_4)_2HPO_4$, ammonium hydrogen phosphate. This fertilizer contains both nitrogen and phosphorus for plant growth.

Two other phosphate fertilizers are common; superphosphate and triple superphosphate; but neither of them contains any nitrogen.

16.6 Back to nature

Before the days of chemists with their synthetic fertilizers, Nature must have somehow managed to make her own fertilizers. The natural fertilizers were animal manure and rotten plant compost. In addition to this, some plants, members of the pea family (Leguminosae), have a mechanism for fixing nitrogen directly from the air, converting it to ammonia and to nitrates which the plant can then use.

The bacteria perform this wonderful reaction without high pressures or high temperatures. It is known that they use a system of natural catalysts which chemists are now trying to understand. So far, only part of the process is understood, but one of the world's most important discoveries will have been made when chemists can imitate the plants by fixing nitrogen easily and cheaply.

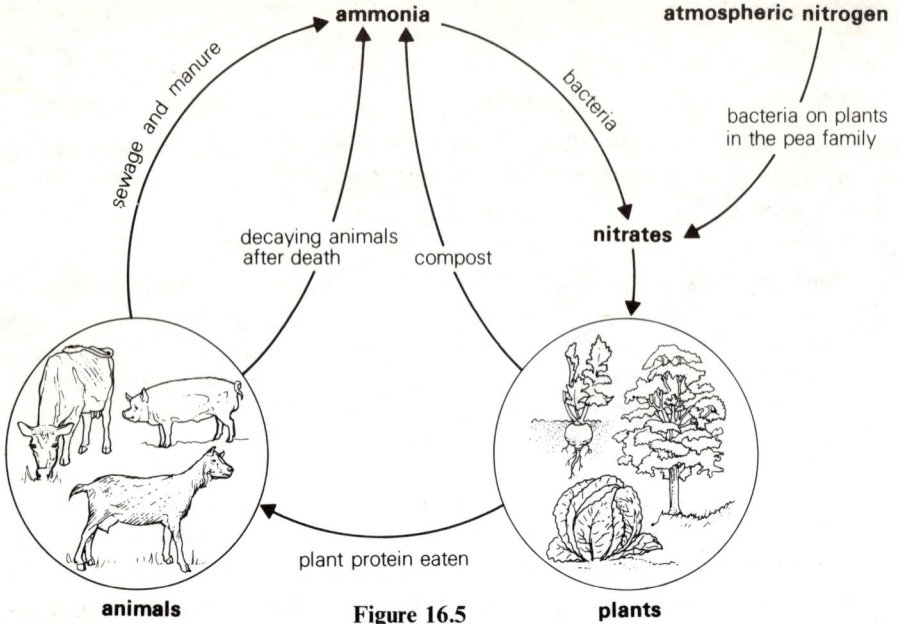

Figure 16.5

The natural situation is shown in Fig. 16.5. Ammonia in sewage and compost is converted by bacteria into nitrates which plants can use. This is supplemented by nitrogen from the air through plants of the pea family. Plants are eaten by animals and the nitrogen and phosphorus compounds of the plants are passed on to make animal flesh and bone and to provide complex compounds to help in their body energy cycles. The unused nitrogen and phosphorus compounds return to the soil as manure and so the cycle is complete.

What has happened to upset this wonderful balance? Why can't we leave Nature to get on with things?

The first major problem is the **growth in world population** and the second the **movement of people into towns and cities**.

(a) As long as each family had its own piece of fertile land on which they grew all their food (plant and animal) and to which they returned all their compost and sewage, things were in balance. To supplement his nitrogen supply the farmer sowed one quarter of his land with clover (a member of the pea family) each year and rotated this round all of his ground in a four-year cycle.

This situation no longer exists. There is not enough fertile land for every family and most families are engaged in occupations other than farming. The bulk of our population lives in towns and cities, far from the areas which are producing the food.

(b) The food-producing areas are far from the food-consuming areas. The bulk of the world's wheat is grown in North America where the crop can be efficiently grown. It is then transported all over the world. But how do the nitrogen and phosphorus compounds get back to the American soil? We would need to transport sewage across the world and put it back into the soil. This is clearly not a practical proposition. Within a small region it is perhaps possible. Much of the sewage which is dumped in our rivers and estuaries could be used locally as a fertilizer, but on a world scale the expense would put this practice out of the question.

These are the reasons why the chemist has been obliged to step in and use the freely available nitrogen of the air to restore the natural balance. It is quite wrong to think of synthetic fertilizers as being nasty and inferior to natural fertilizers. They are in fact very closely related materials. Without them there is no way in which the world could sustain the population it has, let alone the population it may have by the end of this century.

There is no way by which the world can 'go back to Nature'. Some people pay for 'natural foods'—produced by an industry which suggests that 'synthetic' means 'harmful'. The vast majority of us need to live by the ingenuity of the chemist.

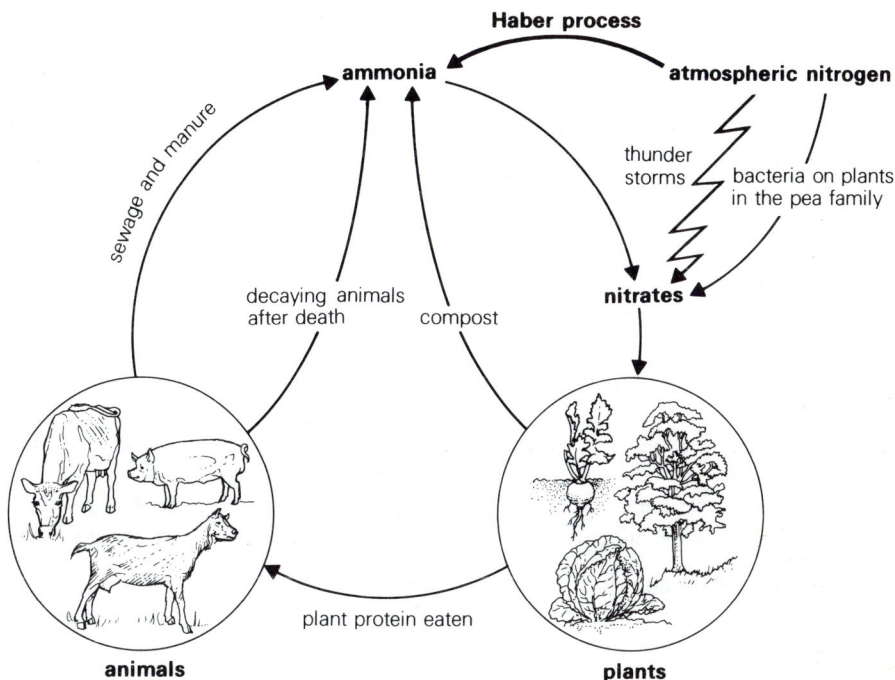

Figure 16.6

The nitrogen cycle in our modern society needs the chemist as much as it needs the green plants and the animals (Fig. 16.6).

In the next chapter we shall see how nitrogen compounds are used in living things.

Chemistry in Action 7 (*continued from p. 166*)

Second problem
One way to increase the conversion rate is to repeat the catalysis step, cooling the gases in between. In fact, many factories use four stages, like this:

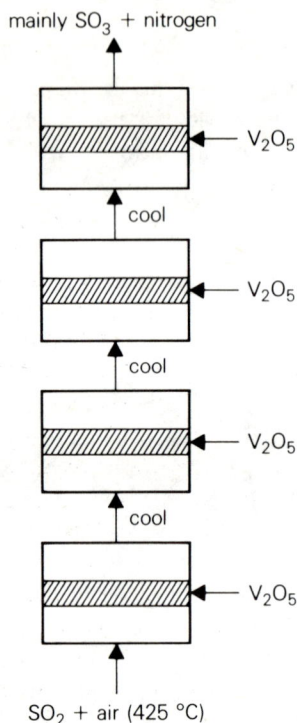

mainly SO_3 + nitrogen

$\leftarrow$ V_2O_5

cool

$\leftarrow$ V_2O_5

cool

$\leftarrow$ V_2O_5

cool

$\leftarrow$ V_2O_5

SO_2 + air (425 °C)

After four stages the percentage conversion is around 98%, which is much better. But is it good enough? Many factories use around 650 tonnes of sulphur dioxide each day! Let us consider what such large quantities mean in practice.

1 Assuming 100% efficiency, how much sulphuric acid does such a factory produce each day?
2 If the process is 98% efficient, how much sulphur dioxide is left unchanged?

Any unchanged sulphur dioxide is passed out of the factory to the atmosphere. The present law insists that factories must be 99.5% efficient in their use of sulphur dioxide. So 98% is not good enough! Can you think of a way to improve the 98% efficiency to give better than 99.5%? Sulphur dioxide is such a harmful gas that large amounts must not be allowed to escape into the atmosphere. The gas causes corrosion of metals, severe damage to plants and trees, and damage to the lungs (Section 13.3, p. 139).

17

Nitrogen in living things

17.1

We have now seen that nitrogen enters into the living world via ammonia and nitrates, but what is its job?

In Section 15.5 we discovered a way of obtaining ammonia from ammonium compounds. By heating them with a strong alkali it is possible to release the ammonia. It can be detected with wet pH paper. Let us see if we can do something similar with parts of living things.

Try to obtain samples of as many of the following substances as you can: wool, hair, meat, egg white, gelatin, finger nail cuttings, peas, beans. Break each sample up into small pieces, put them into a test-tube, and add about twice the bulk of soda lime (a mixture of sodium and calcium hydroxides). Heat each sample with the soda lime and hold a piece of wet pH paper near the mouth of the test-tube. In each case you should get evidence for the presence of an alkaline gas (high pH) like ammonia. The gases are not simply ammonia itself, but are related to it because they all contain **nitrogen**.

If we had heated starch or sugar with soda lime in the same way we would *not* have obtained an alkaline gas. These *nitrogen*-containing materials are called proteins and have to do with the building of our body structure. Some proteins also contain *sulphur*, hence the need for *sulphates* in our fertilizers. Our bodies are supported by bones which are mainly composed of calcium *phosphate* and so we need *phosphates* in fertilizers.

Notice, however, that all of these elements come to us from plants or from other animals which have fed on plants. The plants take up these elements from the soil and so they must constantly be replaced. Once again we have come upon the major importance of fertilizers.

17.2 How proteins are made up

There are very many different kinds of protein, as we have seen in our previous experiment. There is no obvious connection between egg white and wool, between finger nails and gelatin, and yet all of them reacted similarly with a strong alkali.

Proteins consist of large molecules which can be broken down to simpler ones, rather like the carbohydrates we met in Chapter 6. This is done by boiling

175

them with acid. These simpler fragments can be detected by chromatography (Fig. 17.1).

Each spot corresponds to one of the building units of proteins. When you compare the chromatograms from different protein materials you will see similarities between them, but no two patterns will be the same.

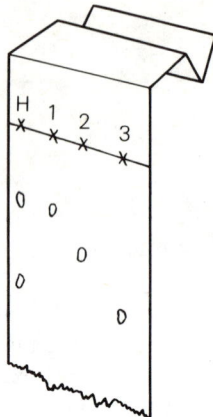

Spot H: protein hydrolysate

Spots 1,2 and 3: known amino acids

Figure 17.1

These simpler units are called **amino acids** (*amino* shows their link with ammonia). In natural materials there are twenty-four kinds of these amino acids. Depending upon how these are strung together in the protein molecules, we can get the huge variety of protein materials there are in the world. This is similar to the many thousands of words which can be obtained from the twenty-six letters of the alphabet or the many ways in which twenty-four different types of bead could be strung into a necklace.

17.3 Breaking down and building up

Now we have almost the whole story of how nitrogen, an apparently inactive element, plays a vital part in the natural world.

Ammonia is converted by bacteria into nitrates which plants absorb, reconvert to ammonia, and use to make a variety of amino acids. All of the amino acids have in common an amino group (NH_2) and an acid group (CO_2H). These two groups are attached to a variety of structures which need not concern us now. We can represent an amino acid, as in Fig. 17.2, with a

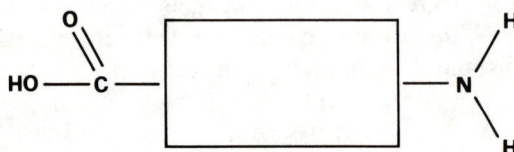

Figure 17.2

different 'box' for each of the twenty-four different amino acids which occur naturally. These acids have almost a press-stud mechanism by which they can link together.

You have already met the idea that acids and alkalis (bases) react together to produce water as well as a salt (Section 16.1).

Amino acids have an acid group (CO_2H) and a basic group (NH_2) attached to the same carbon atom. Under some circumstances an amino acid can combine with itself! When an acid and a base react with each other they are said to **neutralize** each other (Chapter 19).

If we have a pair of amino acid molecules lined up like this they can neutralize each other (Fig. 17.3).

If the amino group (NH_2) gives up a hydrogen atom and the acid group (CO_2H) gives up an **OH** group, these can come together to form water. This leaves the nitrogen with a spare electron and the carbon with a spare electron. These electrons can be shared between the nitrogen atom and the carbon atom to give a new bond (Fig. 17.4).

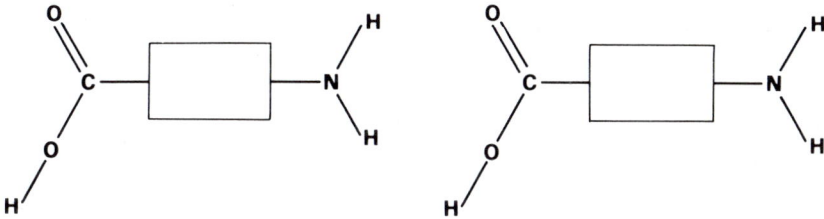

Figure 17.3

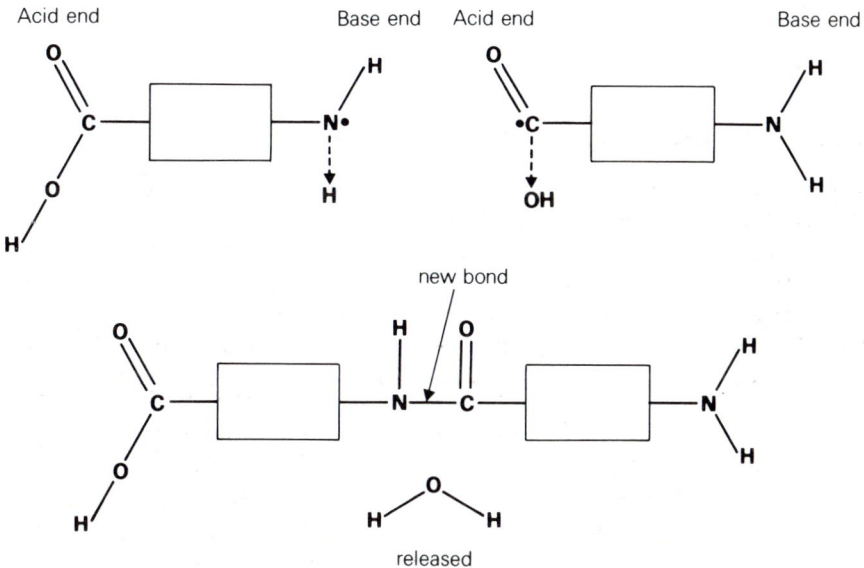

Figure 17.4

This process can be repeated over and over again until large chains of amino acids give us proteins. The number and arrangement of the amino acid units produce the huge variety of proteins.

The assembling of these chains is called **condensation** (that is, a gathering together). The process of breaking up the chains into the separate amino acids is called **hydrolysis** (because water is inserted into each link).

17.4 Putting it all together

Plants make a range of amino acids from which they assemble their own proteins. Animals, including ourselves, eat plant proteins. However, the arrangement of the plants' amino acids does not suit us, so we dismantle (hydrolyse) the plant proteins into separate amino acids and reassemble them as human protein to suit our own needs. We do the same to animal protein by dismantling it to give a selection of amino acid pieces which we then reassemble. We do not dismantle them by the rather fierce process we used in the laboratory—boiling them with acid. Enzymes, natural catalysts within our bodies, enable us to do this at normal body temperatures.

Provided we get a good supply of all the necessary amino acids, we can maintain our body health, but if there is a shortage of all the amino acids we are in trouble. We can also have a problem if we have an adequate supply of amino acids, but one essential one is missing. Both of these unhappy situations lead to diseases which, fortunately, are rare in Britain. In some countries, however, they are very common and cause a great deal of misery. An example is the disease kwashiorkor. This inhibits growth of muscle, hair, and even the brain. Children suffering from this disease typically have a swollen abdomen and thin, wasted limbs. It occurs often when babies are weaned from their mother's milk, which is rich in protein, on to a mainly starchy, carbohydrate diet. The children need not be starving in the sense of being hungry, but their bodies are crying out for amino acids from which to build healthy tissue.

The whole process is like building with 'Lego'. Perhaps we have been given a magnificent bridge, beautifully constructed, but we want to make a windmill. We dismantle the bridge and can make the windmill provided that the bridge contains all the kinds of pieces we need. If, however, we need a window or a door for the mill it is unlikely that we will have the right pieces and our mill must remain incomplete.

As you have seen in these chapters on nitrogen, chemistry is very much part of our lives. It takes place in our bodies in a way over which we have little control, except that we can provide the correct chemical substances in our food. A good and varied diet is essential to provide all the building units. A knowledge of chemistry also enables us to live in our kind of society by restoring and maintaining the balances of Nature in agriculture and food production.

New words you have met in this chapter

Amino acids these are the building units in proteins. In the same molecule there is an acid group (**CO$_2$H**) and a basic group (**NH$_2$**). There are twenty-four amino acids essential for human growth.

Proteins large molecules made by linking amino acids into long chains. The normal human proteins are flesh, hair, nails, blood, and skin.

Condensation the process by which small molecules link to each other by losing a molecule of water between them.

Hydrolysis the process by which large molecules are dismantled by inserting water molecules to release the smaller units.

Neutralization the process by which an acid and a base combine to form a new compound (often a salt) and water.

Revision section for Chapters 13–17

Answers to this section will be found on page 245.

1 By referring to Chapters 4 and 13 find out as many similarities as you can between SO_2 and CO_2. Write equations for any reactions you use.

2 If Britain's sulphur supplies were cut off what things would become scarce in our shops? (Refer to Chapters 13 and 14 if necessary.)

3 How is it possible to have a dilute solution of a strong acid? (Refer to Chapter 14.)

4 Write equations for the action of heat on
    (a) sodium nitrate   (b) lead nitrate   (c) mercury nitrate.

5 A white crystalline material has been found in an unlabelled bottle. It is known to be either sodium carbonate, sodium sulphite, or sodium sulphate. Read the evidence below and fill in the right-hand column for each part. (Chapters 13 and 14 will help you.)

What was done to the substance	The result	Conclusion about the identity of the crystals
(a) Crystals shaken with water	Dissolved easily	
(b) Crystals dissolved in water. $BaCl_2$ solution added	White precipitate forms	
(c) Dilute HCl added to solid in (b)	Solid dissolves and a gas is given off	
(d) Gas from (c) tested with lime water	Lime water does not turn milky	
(e) Dilute HCl added to some crystals and warmed	Choking smell	

6 You are given three jars each containing a different colourless gas. The gases are oxygen, nitric oxide (NO), and nitrogen. From the following description work out which gas is in which jar.

Jar 1 The lid was opened to admit a little air. There was no visible effect.

Jar 2 The lid was opened to admit a little air. There was no visible effect.

Jars 2 *and* 3 These were placed mouth to mouth and the lids opened. There was no visible effect.

7 Gelatin is a protein which is the basis of most jellies. However, if your *only* source of protein is jellies your diet would not be good enough to maintain your health. Why might this be so?

A fertilizer to order

Part I

A small company supplies fertilizer mixtures to farmers. The company buys in the necessary compounds and then sells mixtures as required. For many crops three elements must be present in the mixture: nitrogen, phosphorus, and potassium. The company needs to make up a suitable mixture as cheaply as possible. To do this, they ask for your advice.

The table opposite gives the necessary information. Unfortunately, some of the information is missing. **Work as a group** (sharing out the calculations) and complete the spaces shown with a dotted line in the table.

* * *

You can see that there is only one compound which contains potassium, but you will have to *choose* a compound which contains phosphorus and choose another which contains nitrogen. Look at *all* the information in the table and *discuss* which compounds to choose. Draw up a table like the one below and fill in your choices.

When you have completed this, turn to page 237.

Choice	Compound	% of element in chosen compound
For K For P For N	KCl	52

| Compound | Formula | Formula mass | Percentages | | | Solubility $(g\,l^{-1}, 20\,°C)$ | Melting point | Cost* per kg | Cost† per kg of | | |
			N	P	K				N	P	K
Ammonia	NH_3	17	82	—	—	530	−78	12	14.6	—	—
Potassium chloride	KCl	74.5	—	—	52	347	770	10	—	—	19.2
Ammonium nitrate	NH_4NO_3	30	...	—	—	2700	170	20	...	—	—
Ammonium phosphate	$(NH_4)_2HPO_4$	132	...	...	—	660	155	30	...	...	—
Urea	$(NH_2)_2CO$	60	...	—	—	1000	135	18	...	—	—
Calcium phosphate	...	...	—	...	—	0.02	1670	13	—	...	—
Ammonium sulphate	...	...	...	—	—	750	235	15	...	—	—
Calcium dihydrogen phosphate	$Ca(H_2PO_4)_2$	234	—	...	—	18	109	28	—	...	—

* Expressed in an imaginary currency called the 'groat'.
† How to calculate the last column:
Ammonia costs 12 groats per kg and contains 82% nitrogen by weight.
Using ammonia: 0.82 kg nitrogen would cost 12 groats

1.00 kg nitrogen would cost $\dfrac{12 \times 100}{82}$ groats

$= 14.6$ groats

18

Acids and alkalis in water

18.1

When elements burn in oxygen, compounds called **oxides** are formed. At room temperature some oxides are solids, others are liquids, and some are gases.

Oxides formed from metals are usually solids. Oxides formed from non-metals are often either liquids (water—hydrogen oxide) or gases (sulphur dioxide).

Not all oxides dissolve in water, but those which do dissolve give either acids or alkalis (Fig. 18.1).

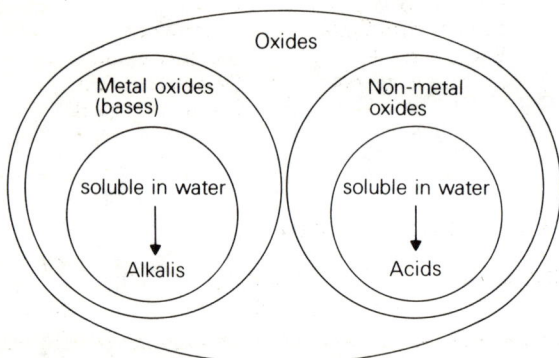

Figure 18.1

An **alkaline** solution is formed when a **metal oxide** dissolves in water. The solution turns litmus or pH paper blue.

An **acidic** solution is formed when a **non-metal oxide** dissolves in water. The solution turns litmus or pH paper red.

18.2 Alkalis—the common factor

Metal oxides (or hydroxides) are called **bases**. Those of them which dissolve in water give solutions called **alkalis** (Fig. 18.1)

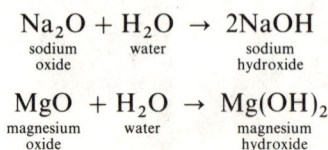

$$Na_2O + H_2O \rightarrow 2NaOH$$

sodium oxide   water   sodium hydroxide

$$MgO + H_2O \rightarrow Mg(OH)_2$$

magnesium oxide   water   magnesium hydroxide

184

These alkalis have in common the hydroxide (OH^-) ion. This is a negative ion just like a chloride ion. When the hydroxide is dissolved in water the OH^- ions are attracted to the positive ends of water molecules. An OH^- attached to water is written as $OH^-(aq)$.

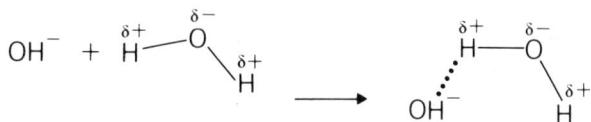

Look at column 1 of Table 18.1. Where, on the Periodic Table, do these metals comes from? Is there a pattern?

Table 18.1

Soluble bases	Insoluble bases
Magnesium oxide	Iron oxide
Calcium oxide	Copper oxide
Potassium oxide	Cobalt oxide
Calcium hydroxide	Zinc Oxide
Barium hydroxide	Silver oxide
Sodium oxide	Mercury oxide
Strontium oxide	Cadmium oxide
	Aluminium oxide

18.3 Acids—the common factor

An acid is a hydrogen-containing compound which yields hydrogen ions when it is dissolved in water. Not all acids are poisonous or corrosive. The common factor is that they can release H^+ ions to other substances with which they come in contact. A hydrogen ion is really just a proton—a very positively charged scrap of material. It has to find something negative to attach itself to. Since we meet most acids dissolved in water, the proton is often attached to the negative end of polar covalent water molecules (Section 7.2, p. 78). When the hydrogen ion is in water we write it $H^+(aq)$. This means that water molecules are clustered round the hydrogen ions.

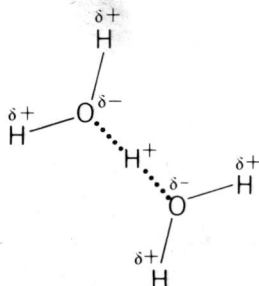

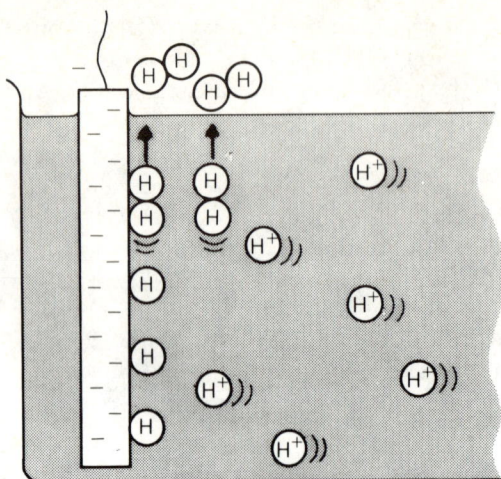

Figure 18.2

When electricity is passed through solutions of acids (Fig. 18.2) hydrogen gas is always given off at the negative electrode or cathode (Section 10.2, p. 109).

At the cathode, hydrogen ions receive electrons and become hydrogen atoms

$$H^+ + e \rightarrow H$$

These single atoms pair up and form hydrogen gas.

$$H + H \rightarrow H_2$$

Hydrogen gas is made up of many millions of these diatomic (two atom) hydrogen molecules.

Acids behave like each other in several ways which make them fairly easy compounds to detect.

(a) Dilute acids react with magnesium and give off hydrogen gas (Fig. 18.3).

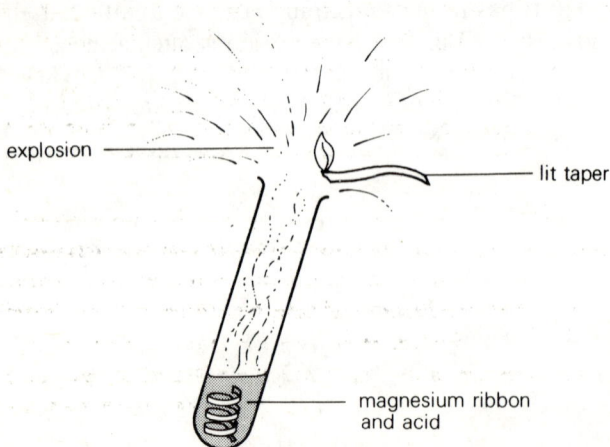

explosion

lit taper

magnesium ribbon and acid

Figure 18.3

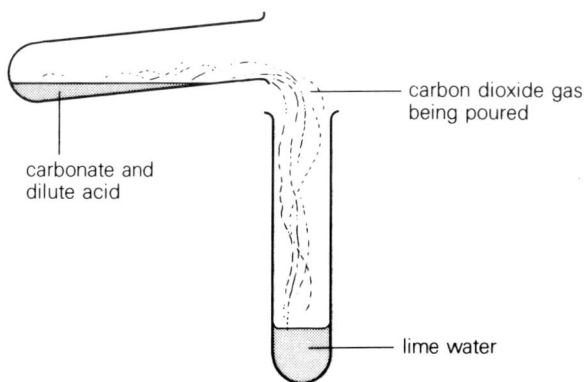

Figure 18.4

(b) Dilute acids react with carbonates and give off carbon dioxide gas (Fig. 18.4). If some of the carbon dioxide gas is collected and shaken with a little clear lime water, the limewater should turn chalky.

$$Ca(OH)_2 + CO_2 \rightarrow CaCO_3$$
$$\text{(chalk)}$$

Summing up so far

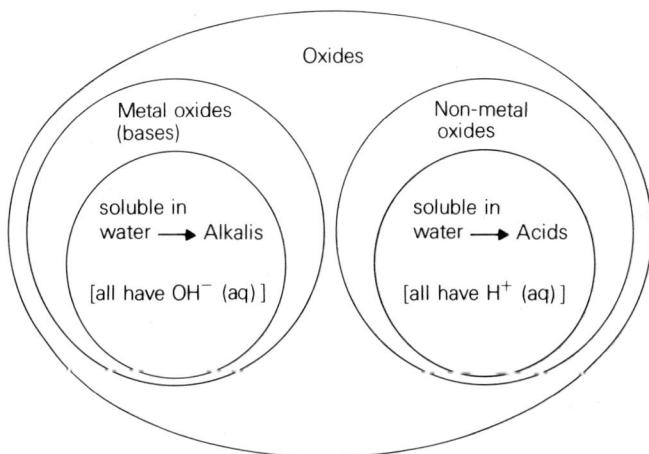

Figure 18.5

18.4 Making solutions

In Chapter 11 you learned about the use of the term 'mole' in chemistry. At that time we were referring to the gram formula weight of substances, but we were not concerned about their state. Since most chemical reactions occur in solution, the idea of the mole has had to be extended to deal with this situation.

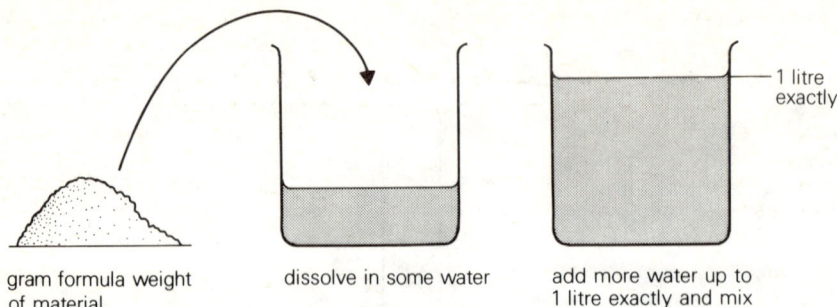

gram formula weight   dissolve in some water   add more water up to
of material   1 litre exactly and mix

1 litre
exactly

Figure 18.6

If we weigh out *1 mole* of a substance (its gram formula weight), dissolve it in some water, and then make the solution up to *exactly one litre* (1000 cm^3) with more water *and mix thoroughly*, we form what is known as a **molar solution** (Fig. 18.6). This is usually shortened to a 1 M or M solution.

1 mole of the substance is contained in the 1 litre of solution. Using a litre of this solution is the same as using a mole of the dissolved substance.

We say that the **concentration** of the solution is 1 mole per litre. It is a molar or M solution.

Let us take an example.

To prepare a molar solution of sodium chloride, NaCl, we have to weigh out the gram formula weight of the compound. In this case it is 58.5 g (23 for Na and 35.5 for Cl) of the compound. This quantity of NaCl has to be dissolved in some water and the solution made up to 1 litre with more water and mixed. This litre of solution contains 1 mole of NaCl. It is called a molar or M solution.

It will not always be necessary to prepare 1 litre of a molar solution. When a smaller volume only is required, the weight of the dissolved substance has to be adjusted before it is dissolved in water and made up to the required volume.

For instance, to make 500 ml (0.5 l) of molar sodium chloride, only half of the gram formula weight (0.5 mole or 0.5 × 58.5 g) need be used.

All the diagrams in Fig. 18.7 apply to a molar solution of sodium chloride.

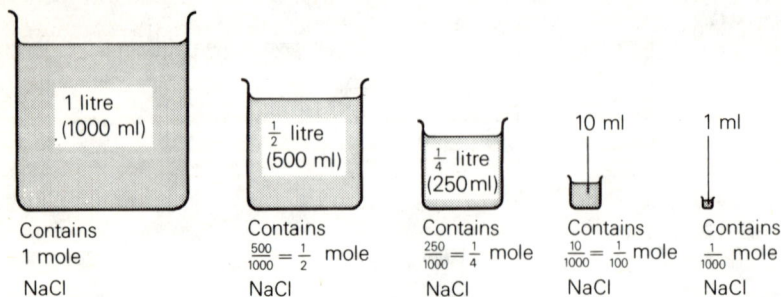

1 litre
(1000 ml)

Contains
1 mole
NaCl

$\frac{1}{2}$ litre
(500 ml)

Contains
$\frac{500}{1000} = \frac{1}{2}$ mole
NaCl

$\frac{1}{4}$ litre
(250 ml)

Contains
$\frac{250}{1000} = \frac{1}{4}$ mole
NaCl

10 ml

Contains
$\frac{10}{1000} = \frac{1}{100}$ mole
NaCl

1 ml

Contains
$\frac{1}{1000}$ mole
NaCl

Figure 18.7

More concentrated than molar

Normally you will not experiment in class with solutions which are much more concentrated than M, but such solutions can be prepared for substances which are sufficiently soluble.

For instance, if 2 moles of a substance are weighed out, dissolved in some water, and then made up to 1 litre with more water, the solution obtained will be 2 molar or 2 M solution.

A litre of 5 M solution of a compound will contain 5 moles (5 × gram formula weight) of the dissolved substance.

It is worth pointing out that *the number of moles of dissolved substance* in any volume of a solution is equal to the *molarity of the solution multiplied by the volume in litres* (Fig. 18.8).

Notice that the solutions shown in Fig. 18.8(b), (c), and (d) all contain 1 mole of sodium chloride.

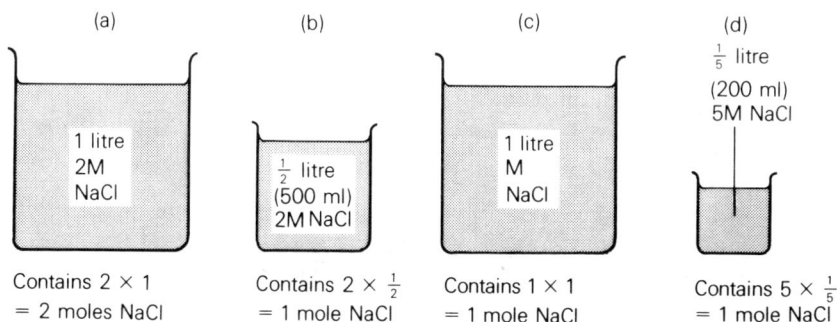

(a)	(b)	(c)	(d)

(a) 1 litre 2M NaCl — Contains 2 × 1 = 2 moles NaCl

(b) $\frac{1}{2}$ litre (500 ml) 2M NaCl — Contains 2 × $\frac{1}{2}$ = 1 mole NaCl

(c) 1 litre M NaCl — Contains 1 × 1 = 1 mole NaCl

(d) $\frac{1}{5}$ litre (200 ml) 5M NaCl — Contains 5 × $\frac{1}{5}$ = 1 mole NaCl

Figure 18.8

Less concentrated than molar

The solutions which you use in your practical work will often be less concentrated than M.

For instance, a 0.1 M solution of a substance is one-tenth as concentrated as a M solution. To prepare such a solution you need to weigh out only 0.1 mole of the substance (one-tenth of its gram formula weight). If this quantity is then dissolved in water, made up to exactly 1 litre with more water, and stirred, the molarity of the solution is 0.1 M; its concentration is 0.1 moles per litre.

Similarly, one litre of a 0.5 M solution of a substance contains only one-half the gram formula weight (0.5 of a mole) of the substance dissolved in water.

Chemists often have to carry out calculations which involve the ideas we are now discussing—the number of moles and the number of grams of a dissolved substance in a solution. These will not confuse you if you get the pattern right.

There are two important things to remember.

(a) $\begin{bmatrix} \text{the number of} \\ \textbf{moles} \\ \text{of substance} \\ \text{dissolved} \end{bmatrix} = \begin{bmatrix} \text{the volume of} \\ \text{solution in} \\ \textbf{litres} \end{bmatrix} \times \begin{bmatrix} \text{the molarity} \\ \text{of the} \\ \text{solution} \end{bmatrix}$

(b) $\begin{bmatrix} \text{the number of} \\ \textbf{grams} \\ \text{of substance} \\ \text{dissolved} \end{bmatrix} = \begin{bmatrix} \text{the number of} \\ \text{moles of} \\ \text{substance} \\ \text{dissolved} \end{bmatrix} \times \begin{bmatrix} \text{the gram formula weight} \\ \text{of the substance} \\ \text{dissolved} \end{bmatrix}$

Let us see how these calculations work out in practice.

Example 1
How many moles of HCl are dissolved in 100 ml of 2 M HCl?
  This is a one-stage piece of arithmetic.

$$\begin{bmatrix} \text{the number of} \\ \text{moles} \\ \text{dissolved} \end{bmatrix} = \begin{bmatrix} \text{volume of} \\ \text{solution} \\ \textbf{in litres} \end{bmatrix} \times \begin{bmatrix} \text{the molarity} \\ \text{of the} \\ \text{solution} \end{bmatrix}$$

$$= \frac{100}{1000} \times 2$$

$$= \frac{1}{5} \text{ or } 0.2 \text{ mole}$$

Example 2
How much NaCl is contained in 250 ml of 2 M solution?
  When the number of grams of a substance has to be calculated, you must first work out the number of *moles* of substance dissolved—as in the example above.

$$\begin{bmatrix} \text{the number of} \\ \text{moles} \\ \text{dissolved} \end{bmatrix} = \begin{bmatrix} \text{volume of} \\ \text{solution} \\ \textbf{in litres} \end{bmatrix} \times \begin{bmatrix} \text{the molarity} \\ \text{of the} \\ \text{solution} \end{bmatrix}$$

$$= \frac{250}{1000} \times 2$$

$$= 0.5 \text{ mole}$$

Then you are able to use the second step:

$$\begin{bmatrix} \text{the number of} \\ \text{grams of} \\ \text{substance} \\ \text{dissolved} \end{bmatrix} = \begin{bmatrix} \text{the number of} \\ \text{moles of} \\ \text{substance} \\ \text{dissolved} \end{bmatrix} \times \begin{bmatrix} \text{the gram formula weight} \\ \text{of the substance} \end{bmatrix}$$

$$= \underset{\text{(as found in Step 1 above)}}{0.5} \times 58.5 \text{ g}$$

$$= 29.25 \text{ g}$$

The weight of NaCl contained in 250 ml of a 2 M solution is, therefore, 29.25 g.

  You will see that when the *number of grams* of a substance has to be calculated, there are *two* steps to the problem.

Step 1 Calculate the number of *moles* of the substance dissolved (volume in litres × molarity).
Step 2 Calculate the number of grams (number of moles dissolved × gram formula weight)

  Now try the following examples:

(a) How many moles of NaCl are dissolved in 500 ml of 4 M NaCl solution?
(b) How many moles of H_2SO_4 are dissolved in 15 ml of 2 M H_2SO_4?
(c) How many moles of $AgNO_3$ are dissolved in 100 ml of M $AgNO_3$?

Acids and alkalis in water **191**

(d) How many grams of NaOH are required to make 1 litre of 0.1 M solution?
(e) What weight of NaCl is required to make 500 ml of 0.5 M solution?
(f) What weight of sodium carbonate is required to make 250 ml of 0.1 M solution?
(g) If one mole of NaOH is dissolved in 500 ml of solution, what is the concentration of the solution?
(h) 0.5 mole of silver nitrate is dissolved in 250 ml of solution. What is the concentration of the solution?

18.5 Conductivity and concentration

In Chapter 7 we found a simple way to detect ions in solution. We noticed that solutions containing ions carried an electric current. It would seem reasonable to suppose that solutions of the same substance, but of different concentrations, would conduct differently. Look at the situation in Fig. 18.9.

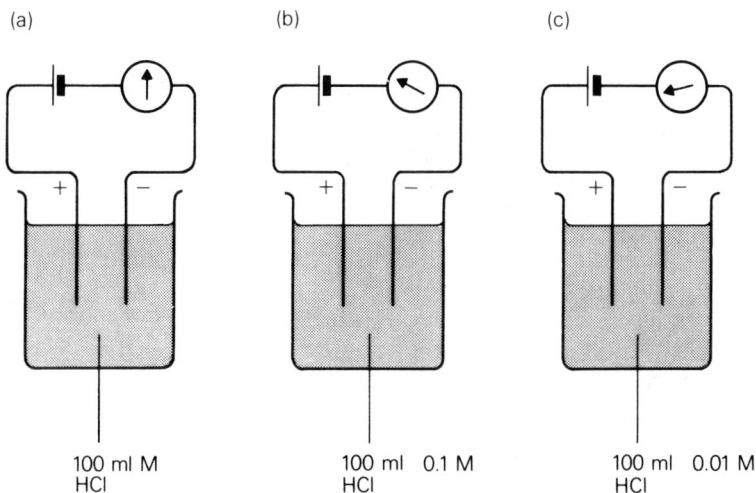

(a)   (b)   (c)

100 ml M HCl   100 ml 0.1 M HCl   100 ml 0.01 M HCl

Figure 18.9

The number of ions in solution (b) will be only one-tenth of the number in solution (a). Since the same kind of ions are present in both solutions, the conductivity depends on the number of ions present.

For the same reason, the conductivity of the solution in beaker (c) will be less than either of the others because it contains fewer ions.

18.6 Race between ions

In solid ionic compounds the ions are not free to move very much. One way of getting the ions to drift apart is to dissolve them in water (Section 7.5) and so your experiments in this section will be carried out on solutions of ionic substances.

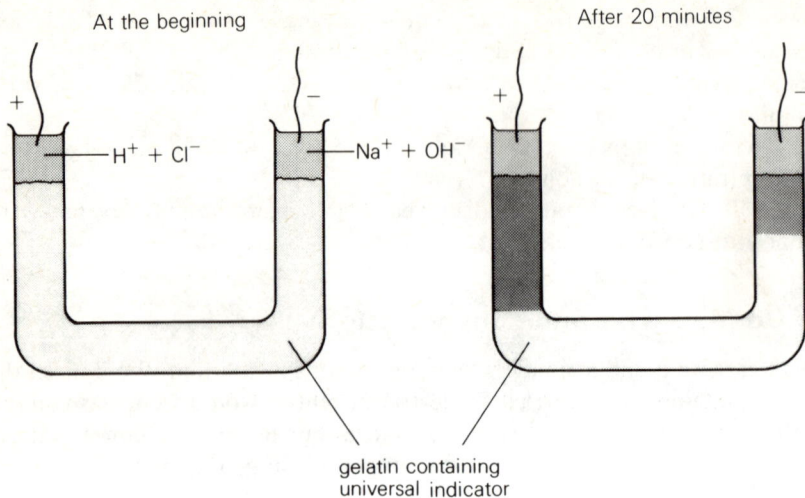

Figure 18.10

The arrangement shown in Fig. 18.10 gives one way of comparing the mobilities (rate of movement) of hydrogen ions and hydroxide ions.

About 20 minutes after switching on the battery the hydrogen ions will have moved approximately twice as far as the hydroxide ions. They are, therefore, about twice as fast, or as we say, twice as mobile.

You can obtain more evidence for the different mobilities of ions by using the conductivity apparatus shown in Fig. 18.9.

If you measure the conductivity of 100 ml M HCl and then, using the same circuit, measure the conductivity of 100 ml M NaCl and of 100 ml M NaOH, you will be able to make a number of comparisons. These results are compared in Fig. 18.11.

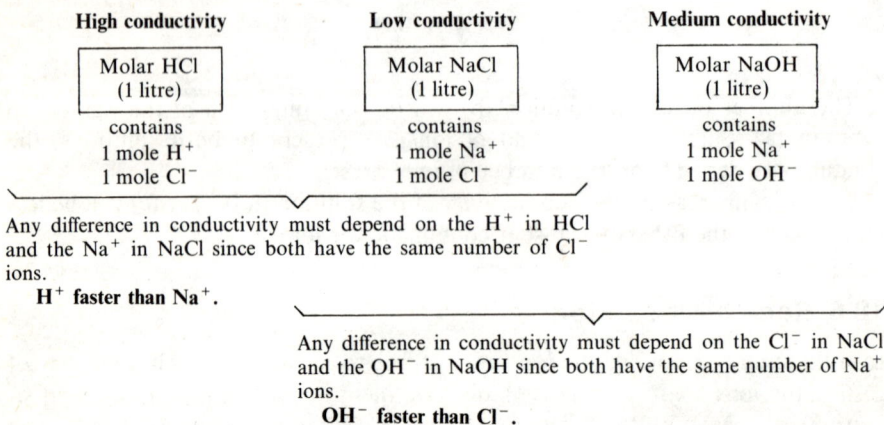

High conductivity	**Low conductivity**	**Medium conductivity**
Molar HCl (1 litre)	Molar NaCl (1 litre)	Molar NaOH (1 litre)
contains 1 mole H^+ 1 mole Cl^-	contains 1 mole Na^+ 1 mole Cl^-	contains 1 mole Na^+ 1 mole OH^-

Any difference in conductivity must depend on the H^+ in HCl and the Na^+ in NaCl since both have the same number of Cl^- ions.

H^+ faster than Na^+.

Any difference in conductivity must depend on the Cl^- in NaCl and the OH^- in NaOH since both have the same number of Na^+ ions.

OH^- faster than Cl^-.

Figure 18.11

We noticed in Fig. 18.10 that H^+ ions travel faster than the OH^- ions. Now we know that OH^- ions travel faster than Cl^- ions.

Therefore H^+ ions are faster than OH^- ions which are faster than Cl^- ions.

Summary

(a) If the mobility of the hydrogen ion is taken as 10, then the mobility of the hydroxide ion is about 5 and that of other ions (e.g. sodium ion and chloride ion) is about 2. Look back to Fig. 8.3 to remind yourself of the 'ion race'.

(b) There are two main factors which control the conductivity of a solution.
  (i) the number of ions present in the solution and
  (ii) the speed or mobility of these ions.

  We shall need these two ideas in the next chapter when we investigate what happens when acids and alkalis are mixed.

18.7 Two important ions and the pH scale

The indicators which you have used to tell whether a substance is acidic or alkaline—such as litmus, pH paper, or universal indicator—can also tell us something about the concentration of the hydrogen and hydroxide ions in the solutions tested.

Pour a few drops of universal indicator, or dip a piece of pH paper, into each of seven test-tubes which contain the solutions of hydrochloric acid shown in Table 18.2. Quickly compare the colour from each test-tube with the colours on the packet. In this way you will be able to give a number to each solution. Can you see any connection between the molarity of the solutions and the pH number? (See p. 198.)

Table 18.2

Molarity of HCl solution (M)	pH number
1/10	
1/100	
1/1000	
1/10 000	
1/100 000	
1/1 000 000	
1/10 000 000	

The numbers known as pH numbers are used when we are describing acids in which the concentration of hydrogen ions is very low (usually 0.1 M or less). The pH number for distilled water is 7, which tells us that there are very few hydrogen ions present.

In pure water, only one molecule in 500 million is broken up into an H^+ ion and an OH^- ion (Section 7.6, p. 85). The scientific word usually used instead of 'broken up' is **dissociated**.

One in 500 million is a very small number. One way to visualize it is to look at Fig. 18.12.

Three hundred water molecules are shown there, with one of them dissociated. On average, 7000 books the size of this one, with all of their pages covered with water molecules, would have to be 'read' before another dissociated water molecule turned up!

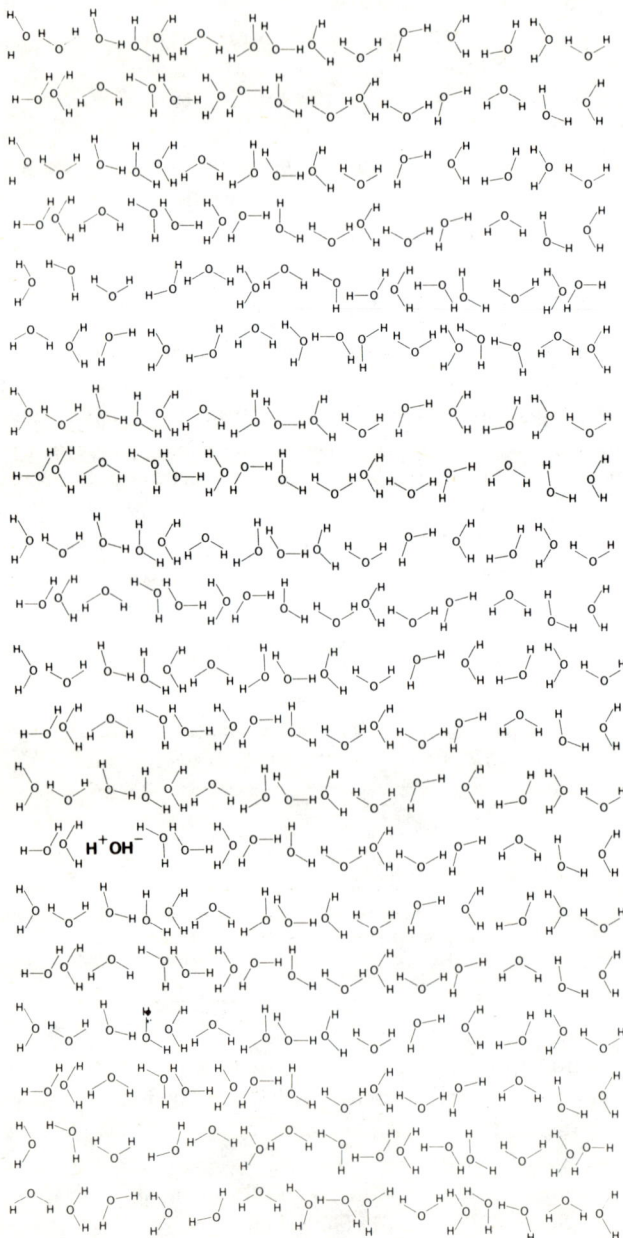

Figure 18.12

The pH values shown on the packet of pH paper go beyond 7. This cannot be because of further dilution with water because adding more water (of pH 7) would not increase the pH. And yet the pH scale on most papers goes up to 13.

If you tested diluted solutions of M NaOH with indicator, in the same way as the M HCl was tested previously, you will find that each dilution will bring you down the pH scale until you reach pH 7 once more and no more dilution will take you beyond pH 7.

When a water molecule breaks up it must give one hydrogen ion for every hydroxide ion. Similarly, for water to be made, one hydrogen ion must team up with one OH$^-$:

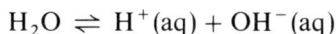

$$H_2O \rightleftharpoons H^+(aq) + OH^-(aq)$$

Therefore at pH 7 the number of hydrogen ions and hydroxide ions must be the same.

The pH scale is very important biologically. Many body fluids will operate properly only if the pH is of a certain value. Enzymes (the natural catalysts) function only where certain values of pH exist. Certain plants will grow well only in soil of a definite pH value. For example, rhododendrons and azaleas grow in acid soil (pH 5) while other plants require calcium hydroxide (lime) which gives the soil a pH greater than 7. In gardening shops you can buy indicator paper with which you can test the pH of your garden soil.

The pH values of some common substances are shown in Fig. 18.13.

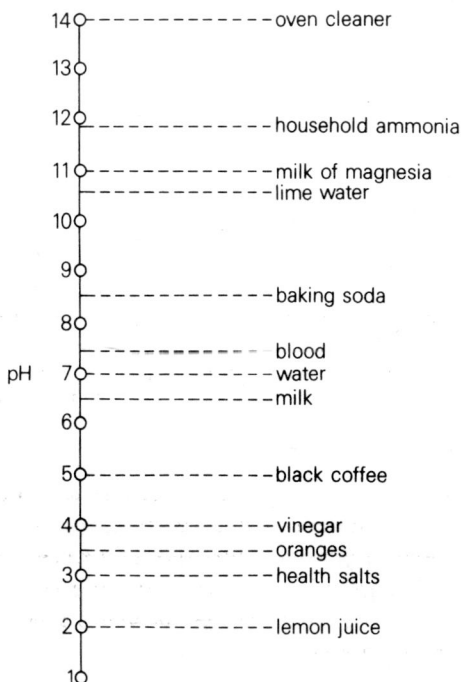

pH	
14	oven cleaner
13	
12	household ammonia
11	milk of magnesia
	lime water
10	
9	
	baking soda
8	
	blood
7	water
	milk
6	
5	black coffee
4	vinegar
	oranges
3	health salts
2	lemon juice
1	

Figure 18.13

Summary

The hydrogen ion makes a compound an acid. It affects certain dyes, which we call indicators, and makes them change colour. The colour change depends upon the concentration of the hydrogen ion.

The hydroxide ion is common to all alkalis and, together with the hydrogen ion, it forms water.

$$H^+(aq) + OH^-(aq) \rightarrow H_2O$$

The concentration of these ions is placed on the pH scale, from 1–14.

When the concentration of hydrogen ions and hydroxide ions is equal, the pH is 7 because water has been formed.

New words you have met in this chapter

Acids   these substances give hydrogen ions to other substances. Oxides of non-metals which dissolve in water give acids, e.g.
$$H_2O + SO_3 \rightarrow H_2SO_4 \rightarrow 2H^+(aq) + SO_4^{2-}(aq)$$

Bases   these are the oxides (or hydroxides) of metals

Alkalis   these oxides (or hydroxides) of metals dissolve in water. They release $OH^-(aq)$ into solution.

Electrolyte   an ionic substance which carries an electric current when it is molten or in solution.

Conductivity the ability of a substance to carry electricity.

Mobility   the speed at which an ion moves.

Dissociate   a molecule dissociates when it breaks up into smaller parts such as ions.

ANSWERS TO QUESTIONS IN CHAPTER 18

On page 190

(a) number of moles = volume of solution in litres × molarity

$$= \frac{500}{1000} \times 4$$

$$= 2 \text{ moles}$$

(b) volume of solution $= \frac{15}{1000}$ litre

molarity of solution $= 2$ M

number of moles $= \frac{15}{1000} \times 2$

$$= 0.03 \text{ mole}$$

(c) number of moles $= \frac{100}{1000} \times 1$

$$= 0.1 \text{ mole}$$

(d) When the number of grams of a substance has to be calculated, the two-step process is necessary. First, find the number of moles of the substance, as in the other examples.

$$\text{number of moles} = 1 \times 0.1$$
$$= 0.1 \text{ mole}$$

This number then has to be multiplied by the gram formula weight of NaOH, which is 40.

number of grams of NaOH
$$= \text{number of moles} \times \text{gram formula weight NaOH}$$
$$= 0.1 \times 40 \text{ g}$$
$$= 4 \text{ g}$$

(e) number of moles NaCl $= \dfrac{500}{1000} \times 0.5$
$$= 0.25 \text{ mole}$$

number of grams NaCl $= 0.25 \text{ mole} \times 58.5 \text{ g}$
$$= 14.6 \text{ g}$$

(f) number of moles $Na_2CO_3 = \dfrac{250}{1000} \times 0.1 = 0.025 \text{ mole}$

number of grams $Na_2CO_3 = 0.025 \times 106 \text{ g}$
$$= 2.65 \text{ g}$$

(g) In this calculation there is a slight variation in what is known.

number of moles of substance dissolved = volume in litres × molarity

$$1 = \dfrac{500}{1000} \times \text{molarity}$$

So
$$\text{molarity of the solution} = \dfrac{1}{0.5} = 2 \text{ M}$$

This means there is a concentration of 2 moles of dissolved substance per litre. Therefore the concentration of this solution is $2 \times 40 = 80 \text{ g l}^{-1}$.

(h) We know the number of moles used and the volume of the solution in litres.

number of moles of substance used = volume in litres × molarity

$$0.5 = \dfrac{250}{1000} \times \text{molarity}$$

$$\text{molarity} = \dfrac{0.5}{0.25}$$
$$= 2 \text{ M}$$

1 mole $AgNO_3$ weighs 170 g.
Therefore, the concentration of the solution $= 2 \times 170 \text{ g l}^{-1}$
$$= 340 \text{ g l}^{-1}$$

On page 193

The pH number corresponds to the number of zeros in the molarity.

$$pH = 1 \quad \text{for} \quad \frac{M}{10}$$

$$pH = 2 \quad \text{for} \quad \frac{M}{100}$$

$$pH = 6 \quad \text{for} \quad \frac{M}{1\,000\,000}$$

19

Acids and alkalis together

When alkalis and acids are put together their ions react with each other to give new materials called **salts**.

sodium hydroxide + hydrochloric acid → sodium chloride + water

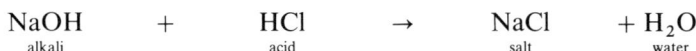

$$\underset{\text{alkali}}{\text{NaOH}} \quad + \quad \underset{\text{acid}}{\text{HCl}} \quad \rightarrow \quad \underset{\text{salt}}{\text{NaCl}} \quad \underset{\text{water}}{+ \text{H}_2\text{O}}$$

The salt has been made by replacing the hydrogen ion in the acid by the sodium ion from the alkali.

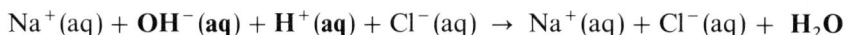

$$\text{Na}^+(\text{aq}) + \textbf{OH}^-(\textbf{aq}) + \textbf{H}^+(\textbf{aq}) + \text{Cl}^-(\text{aq}) \rightarrow \text{Na}^+(\text{aq}) + \text{Cl}^-(\text{aq}) + \textbf{H}_2\textbf{O}$$

19.1 Naming salts

All *sulphates* are formed from sulphuric acid (hydrogen *sulphate* solution).
All *chlorides* are formed from hydrochloric acid (hydrogen *chloride* solution).
All *nitrates* are formed from nitric acid (hydrogen *nitrate* solution).

The parent acid gives its negative ion (anion) to the salt; this is rather like a family in which all the children have their father's surname.

This pattern can be extended to include phosphates, carbonates, sulphites, nitrites, ethanoates, and so on. But a salt also contains a positive ion (cation)—either a metal ion or the ammonium ion.

The alkali *sodium* hydroxide will give *sodium* salts.
The alkali *potassium* hydroxide will give *potassium* salts.
The alkali *ammonium* hydroxide will give *ammonium* salts.

However, alkalis are not the only source of a positive ion (or cation). There are four possible sources of this part:

(a) a *metal* itself,
(b) a *metal* oxide,
(c) a *metal* carbonate,
(d) a *metal* hydroxide.

All these methods of forming salts have one thing in common. In each case the hydrogen ions released by the acid in solution have been taken away. When the salt crystallizes, the negative ions from the acid settle out with the positive ions from the metal to form crystals of the salt.

It is not difficult to get evidence for this. To do so, we take equal volumes of molar sodium hydroxide and molar hydrochloric acid and put them in the apparatus shown in Fig. 19.1.

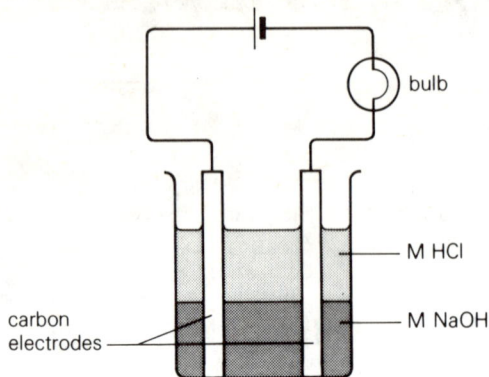

Figure 19.1

It is possible to float one solution on top of the other with almost no mixing. When the carbon electrodes are lowered to the bottom of the beaker the bulb glows brightly because the many ions in both solutions are carrying current very well. If the layers are now stirred so that the acid and the alkali mix thoroughly, the bulb becomes much dimmer. This can only be explained when we realize that, whenever an $H^+(aq)$ meets an $OH^-(aq)$, water is made. We learned in Section 7.6, page 85, that water is a very poor conductor of electricity. If all the $H^+(aq)$ and $OH^-(aq)$ team up to form water, only the $Na^+(aq)$ and $Cl^-(aq)$ will be left to carry the current, and so the bulb will become dim. Evaporating the solution to dryness gives a white solid which tastes of salt (sodium chloride).

A bulb does not tell us about the current very precisely. We can say that the bulb has become dimmer, but is it half as dim or one third as dim? We cannot really say.

Another way of tackling this comes from our work in the previous chapter (Section 18.6, p. 191). You will recall that, of all the ions in solution, $H^+(aq)$ moves fastest in an electric field. All other positive ions are slow by comparison. By using the conductivity apparatus we would be able to 'see' the effect of replacing the fast $H^+(aq)$ with the slow $Na^+(aq)$. If the sodium ions were added slowly we would expect a slow fall in conductivity. Let us investigate this possibility.

(a) *Metal and acid*
Let us replace the $H^+(aq)$ of sulphuric acid by Mg^{2+} from Mg metal.

Half fill the conductivity beaker with water and add five drops of dilute sulphuric acid. Switch on the current and, when the meter reading is steady, stir in some magnesium powder. Bubbles of hydrogen gas will escape and the conductivity of the solution will change. The changes in conductivity can be shown on a graph like the one in Fig. 19.2.

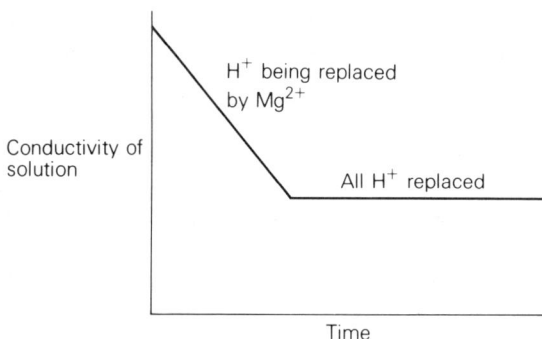

Figure 19.2

Two things have happened.

(i) Magnesium metal has reacted with the acid. It forms magnesium ions and releases electrons.

$$Mg \rightarrow Mg^{2+} + 2e$$

(ii) Hydrogen ions from the acid accept these electrons to form hydrogen atoms—a change which we discussed when dealing with the behaviour of nitric acid in Chapter 16.2.

$$H^+ + e \rightarrow H$$

These hydrogen atoms pair and bubble out of the solution as hydrogen gas.

$$H + H \rightarrow H_2$$

The drop in conductivity shows that the mobile hydrogen ions are being replaced by the slower moving magnesium ions. When all the hydrogen ions have been replaced, the conductivity stops falling.

$$Mg + H_2SO_4 \rightarrow MgSO_4 + H_2$$

(b) *Metal oxide and acid*

(c) *Metal carbonate and acid*

Similar results are found if the experiment is repeated with a metal oxide—for instance with copper(II) oxide and sulphuric acid, or with calcium carbonate and hydrochloric acid (Fig. 19.3).

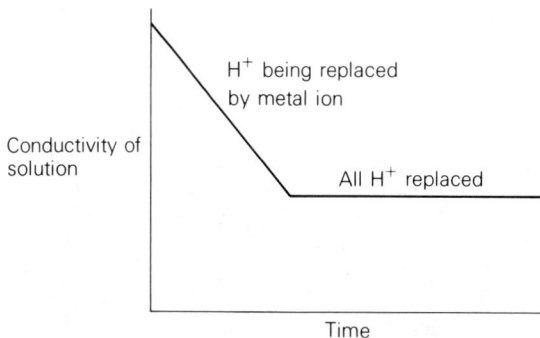

Figure 19.3

The mobile hydrogen ions from the acid are replaced by the slower moving copper(II) ions. This leads to a drop in conductivity. When all the hydrogen ions have been replaced, the conductivity stops falling. In this case no hydrogen is released, but water is formed. It has a very low conductivity.

$$CuO + H_2SO_4 \rightarrow CuSO_4 + H_2O$$

In the other case, the mobile hydrogen ions are replaced by the slower moving calcium ions and the same reasoning can be applied to explain the fall in the conductivity. However, in this case carbon dioxide gas is formed, but its effect on the conductivity is too small to be noticed.

$$CaCO_3 + 2HCl \rightarrow CaCl_2 + H_2O + CO_2$$

(d) *Soluble metal hydroxide and acid*

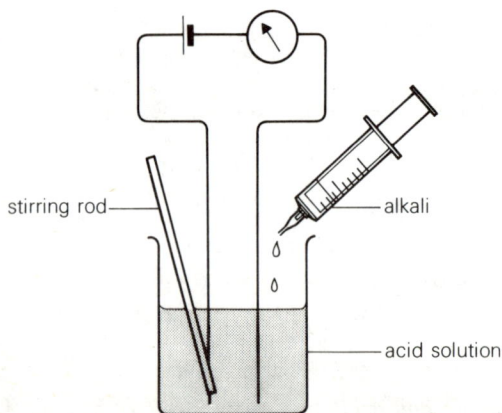

Figure 19.4

As the alkali is added to the acid solution drop by drop (Fig. 19.4), the mobile hydrogen ions are replaced by the slow-moving sodium ions. Conductivity results are shown in Fig. 19.6. A solution of sodium chloride is formed, along with water.

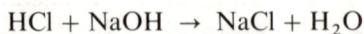

$$HCl + NaOH \rightarrow NaCl + H_2O$$

When all the hydrogen ions have been replaced by sodium ions (i.e. when conductivity reaches a minimum), the alkali is said to have **neutralized** the acid (Fig. 19.5). The volume of acid required to do this can be read from the scale on the syringe (or burette).

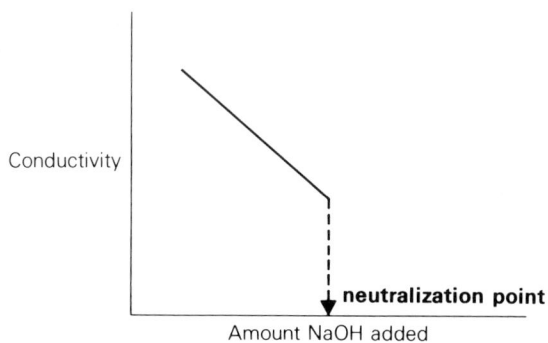

Figure 19.5

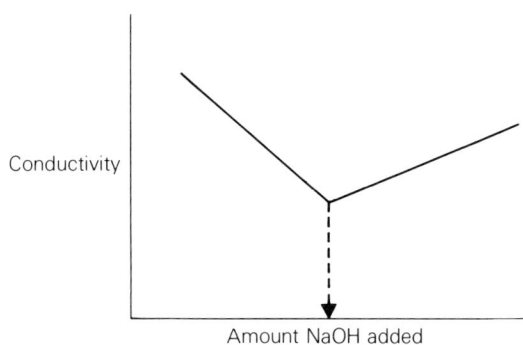

Figure 19.6

If we go on adding drops of alkali after neutralization has taken place, the conductivity rises again (Fig. 19.6) because there are no $H^+(aq)$ left to trap the $OH^-(aq)$ being added along with the $Na^+(aq)$. These extra ions help the solution to carry current.

A similar experiment can be carried out using only the apparatus shown in Fig. 19.7.

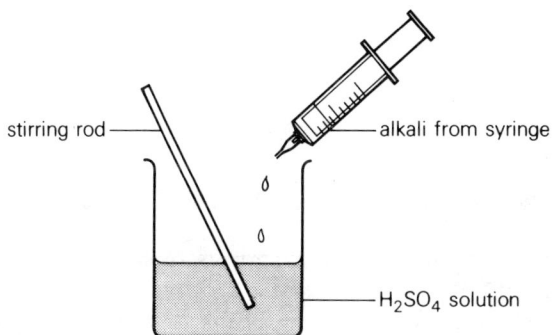

Figure 19.7

If a few drops of methyl orange indicator are added to the acid solution, a change of colour from red to yellow occurs when neutralization has taken place.

When the conductivity experiment is repeated with a few drops of indicator in the acid solution, the conductivity graph and the colour change match (Fig. 19.8).

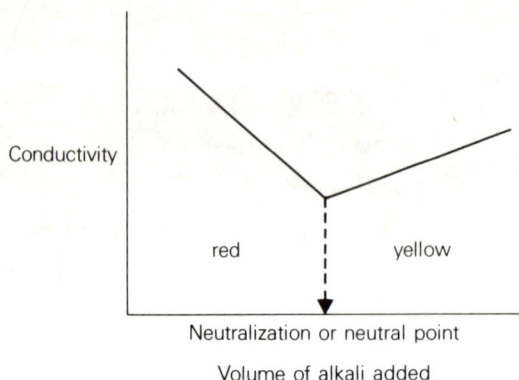

Figure 19.8

Neutralizations without indicators

When you are neutralizing an acid with an alkali, one solution is added to the other until an indicator in them just changes colour. In all of the other examples of neutralization we have a *solution* (the acid) and a *solid* (the metal, the oxide, or the carbonate). How can we tell when the neutralization is complete? Indicators are no use in this case.

The method normally used has the following steps.

(a) Warm the acid.
(b) Add the solid a little at a time and allow it to dissolve.
(c) Keep on adding the solid until no more will dissolve.
(d) Filter off this extra (excess) solid.
(e) The solution of the salt is now left to cool and crystallize.

Summary

In neutralization, the hydrogen ions released by an acid solution either collect an electron each and go off into the air as hydrogen gas, or they go to form water.

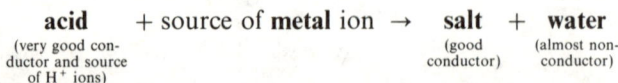

$$\underset{\substack{\text{(very good con-}\\\text{ductor and source}\\\text{of } H^+ \text{ ions)}}}{\textbf{acid}} + \text{source of } \textbf{metal} \text{ ion} \rightarrow \underset{\substack{\text{(good}\\\text{conductor)}}}{\textbf{salt}} + \underset{\substack{\text{(almost non-}\\\text{conductor)}}}{\textbf{water}}$$

The main point about neutralization is that as water is formed during the process, each H^+ ion becomes locked up with one OH^- ion.

Neutralization is complete when all the $H^+(aq)$ of an acid have joined with *exactly the same number* of $OH^-(aq)$ of an alkali to form water.

19.2 Counting ions

Imagine a beaker of acid sitting on the bench in front of you. How would you find out how many hydrogen ions it contained? Since ions are so tiny and since there are so many of them it might be easier to count them not as separate ions but in large groups. A very useful grouping is the **mole**. At least it is possible to weigh out and look at a mole of materials. Let us re-frame our question. Looking at the beaker of acid, *how would you find out the number of moles of* $H^+(aq)$ *ions in it?*

Back in Chapter 18, page 190, we noticed that, if you know the molarity of an acid it is possible to find the number of moles of acid in it.

> number of moles of acid in a solution
> $$= \text{volume of the solution } \textit{in litres} \times \text{molarity}$$

We are nearer to answering our question, but we are not quite there. The question is about the *number of moles of* $H^+(aq)$ in the beaker of acid, not just the number of moles of acid.

Acids like HCl, HNO_3, and HBr give **one** mole of $H^+(aq)$ for every mole of themselves because each has one H^+ per formula.

Acids like H_2SO_4, H_2CO_3, and H_2SO_3 give **two** moles of $H^+(aq)$ for every mole of themselves because each has two H^+ per formula.

Similarly, H_3PO_4 would give **three** moles of H^+ for every mole of substance. We now have the answer to our question.

> number of moles of $H^+(aq)$ in our beaker
> $$= \text{volume of acid in litres } \times \text{ molarity}$$
> $$\times \text{ the number of } H^+ \text{ in the formula of the acid}$$

Let us try some examples.

1 How many moles of $H^+(aq)$ are there in 200 ml 2 M HCl?

$$\text{number of moles } H^+ = \underbrace{\frac{200}{1000}}_{\substack{\text{volume in} \\ \text{litres}}} \times \underbrace{2}_{\text{molarity}} \times \underbrace{1}_{\substack{\text{number of } H^+ \\ \text{in the} \\ \text{formula HCl}}}$$

$$= 0.4 \text{ moles } H^+$$

2 How many moles of $H^+(aq)$ are there in 300 ml M H_2SO_4?

$$\text{number of moles } H^+ = \underbrace{\frac{300}{1000}}_{\substack{\text{volume in} \\ \text{litres}}} \times \underbrace{1}_{\text{molarity}} \times \underbrace{2}_{\substack{\text{number of } H^+ \\ \text{in the formula} \\ H_2SO_4}}$$

$$= 0.6 \text{ mole } H^+$$

In a similar way the number of moles of OH^- in any alkaline solution will depend on three things:

(a) the volume of the solution;
(b) the molarity of the solution;
(c) the number of OH^- ions in each formula of the alkali.

Here are two examples.

1 How many moles of OH^- ions are there in 250 ml M NaOH?

$$\text{number of moles } OH^- = \underbrace{\frac{250}{1000}}_{\substack{\text{volume in} \\ \text{litres}}} \times \underbrace{1}_{\text{molarity}} \times \underbrace{1}_{\substack{\text{number of } OH^- \\ \text{ions in the} \\ \text{formula NaOH}}}$$

$$= 0.25 \text{ mole } OH^-$$

2 How many moles of OH^- are there in 20 ml 0.1 M $Ba(OH)_2$?

$$\text{number of moles } OH^- = \underbrace{\frac{20}{1000}}_{\substack{\text{volume in} \\ \text{litres}}} \times \underbrace{0.1}_{\text{molarity}} \times \underbrace{2}_{\substack{\text{number of } OH^- \\ \text{ions in the} \\ \text{formula } Ba(OH)_2}}$$

$$= 0.004 \text{ mole } OH^-$$

Here are some examples for you to try yourselves. The answers are on page 219.

1 How many moles of H^+ are in 50 ml 2 M HCl?

2 How many moles of H^+ are in 100 ml M H_2SO_4?

3 How many moles of OH^- are in 25 ml 2 M NaOH?

4 How many moles of OH^- are in 1 litre 0.1 M NaOH?

5 How many moles of H^+ are in 500 ml 0.2 M HCl?

6 How many moles of H^+ are in 250 ml 0.25 M H_2SO_4?

Now that we have learned how to calculate the number of moles of H^+ in an acid and the number of moles of OH^- in an alkali we can return to the idea of neutralization.

The important thing to remember about any neutralization is that when neutralization is complete,

number of H^+ ions from the acid solution

$$= \text{number of } OH^- \text{ ions from the alkali solution}$$

number of moles of H^+ from the acid

$$= \text{number of moles of } OH^- \text{ from the alkali}$$

19.3 Finding the unknown quantity

Suppose we have a beaker of acid containing 0.5 moles H^+ and another beaker of alkali containing 0.5 moles OH^- (Fig. 19.9).

If we add a few drops of methyl orange indicator to the acid, it will turn red. Now imagine that we pour the alkali slowly into the acid and stir it. The OH^- of the alkali will seek out and combine with the H^+ in the acid to form water. When the last drop of the alkali is added the number of OH^- will be exactly

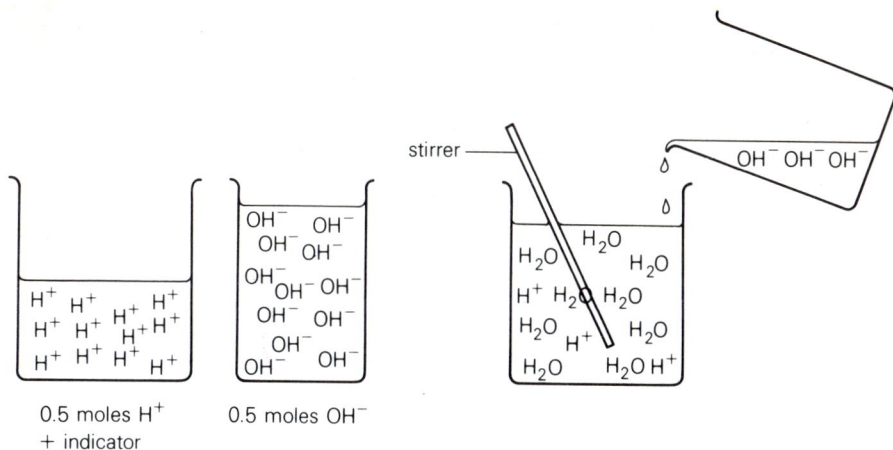

Figure 19.9

equal to the number of H^+ and the indicator will be ready to change. If we could add one extra drop of alkali the number of OH^- would *just* be greater than the number of H^+ and the solution would turn yellow.

This gives us a very useful tool for analysing solutions of acids and alkalis.

If we have an acid and we know its *volume*, its *molarity*, and the *formula* of the acid, we can easily calculate the number of moles of H^+ in it.

If we have an alkali and we know its *formula* and its *molarity* we can find out what *volume* of it would exactly neutralize the acid mentioned above.

Let us use some figures to show you this more clearly.

Suppose we have 25 ml 2 M H_2SO_4 and we want to know what volume of 3 M NaOH would be required to neutralize it. Look at the acid first. How many moles of H^+ are there in it?

number of moles H^+

$$= \text{volume in litres} \times \text{molarity} \times \text{number of } H^+ \text{ in formula } H_2SO_4$$

$$= \frac{25}{1000} \quad \times \quad 2 \quad \times \quad 2$$

$$= 0.1 \text{ mole}$$

Now consider the alkali. Let the volume of NaOH required to neutralize the acid be x. How many moles of OH^- are there in it?

number of moles OH^-

$$= \text{volume in litres} \times \text{molarity} \times \text{number of } OH^- \text{ in formula NaOH}$$

$$= \quad x \quad \times \quad 3 \quad \times \quad 1$$

$$= 3x \text{ moles}$$

For neutralization the number of moles H^+ = number of moles OH^-

$$3x = 0.1$$

$$x = \frac{0.1}{3} \text{ litres}$$

$$= \frac{100}{3} \text{ ml}$$

$$= 33.3 \text{ ml}$$

The volume of alkali required to neutralize the acid is 33.3 ml.

Let us work through a second example.

25 ml M sodium hydroxide requires 15 ml of a solution of sulphuric acid to neutralize it. What is the molarity of the acid solution?

number of moles H^+ in the acid
$$= \text{volume in litres} \times \quad \text{molarity} \quad \times \text{ number of } H^+ \text{ in formula } H_2SO_4$$

$$= \frac{15}{1000} \qquad \times \text{ acid molarity} \times \qquad 2$$

$$= \frac{30 \times \text{acid molarity}}{1000}$$

number of moles of OH^- in the alkali
$$= \text{volume in litres} \times \text{molarity} \times \text{number of } OH^- \text{ in formula NaOH}$$

$$= \frac{25}{1000} \qquad \times \quad 1 \quad \times \qquad 1$$

$$= \frac{25}{1000}$$

For neutralization the number of moles of H^+ = number of moles of OH^-

$$\frac{30 \times \text{acid molarity}}{1000} = \frac{25}{1000}$$

$$\text{acid molarity} = \frac{25}{30} \text{ M}$$

$$= 0.83 \text{ M}$$

Here are some other examples for you to try. The pattern is the same in all of them. You will find the answers on page 219.

1 25 ml of 1.25 M H_2SO_4 were found to neutralize 30 ml of a solution of NaOH. What is the molarity of the NaOH solution?

2 How many ml of 1.5 M NaOH will be required to neutralize 17 ml of 0.5 M H_2SO_4?

3 20 ml of M NaOH required
(a) 15 ml of HCl to neutralize it in one experiment;
(b) 20 ml of H_2SO_4 to neutralize it in another; and
(c) 30 ml of HNO_3 to neutralize it in a third experiment.
Calculate the molarity of each of these acids.

4 How many ml of 2 M H_2SO_4 will be required to neutralize 40 ml of 0.5 M NaOH?

5 What is the molarity of $Ca(OH)_2$ when 100 ml of it can be exactly neutralized by 12.5 ml of 0.5 M HCl?

19.4 Making salts which do not dissolve very well in water

The salts which we were discussing in Section 19.1 were all dissolved in water. To recover them as solids you just had to allow a solution of the salt to evaporate until crystals were deposited.

We usually think of substances as being either soluble or insoluble in water but, strictly speaking, *everything* is soluble to some extent—even glass!

In practice, some salts are so very slightly soluble in water that we regard them as being insoluble. Because of this they are not made by adding acids to alkalis: a new technique is required.

Barium sulphate is an insoluble salt. To make it we have to find some way of getting barium ions and sulphate ions to meet. As soon as they meet, they join together as a solid which settles out at the bottom of the reaction dish. The new salt can then be filtered off.

For these ions to meet we must find a soluble compound containing barium ions (for example, barium chloride) and a soluble compound containing sulphate ions (for example, sodium sulphate). Each is dissolved separately in water to allow the ions to move about freely in solution. When the solutions are mixed, barium ions can meet with sulphate ions and make the required salt.

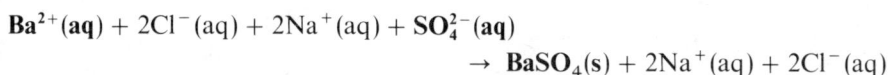

$$Ba^{2+}(aq) + 2Cl^-(aq) + 2Na^+(aq) + SO_4^{2-}(aq)$$
$$\rightarrow BaSO_4(s) + 2Na^+(aq) + 2Cl^-(aq)$$

The barium sulphate settles out as a solid precipitate (Fig. 19.10), while the sodium and chloride ions stay in the solution. These can now be separated from the barium sulphate by filtration. The solid precipitate is left in the paper.

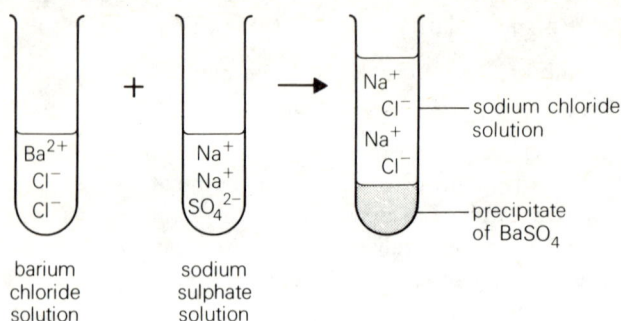

Figure 19.10

Sodium ions and chloride ions are free before and after mixing. The only ions which have reacted are barium ions and sulphate ions.

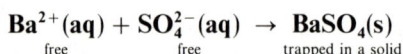

$$Ba^{2+}(aq) + SO_4^{2-}(aq) \rightarrow BaSO_4(s)$$

free   free   trapped in a solid

The sodium ions and chloride ions which do not react are sometimes called 'spectator ions'.

General method

These '*precipitation reactions*', as they are called, always begin with two soluble compounds in solution so that all the ions are free. On mixing these, we are left with a solid containing two kinds of ions locked together and a solution containing two kinds of ions which are free.

$$A^+ + B^- + X^+ + Y^- \rightarrow AY(s) + X^+ + B^-$$

or more simply, leaving out the 'spectator ions' from both sides,

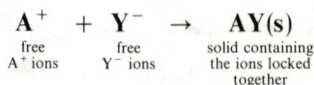

$$A^+ + Y^- \rightarrow AY(s)$$

free   free   solid containing
A^+ ions Y^- ions the ions locked together

This method is fine if you know what is soluble and what is not. In the next section we shall see how to decide this.

19.5 Soluble or insoluble?

Before you decide which method you are going to use to prepare a salt, you must first find out whether it is soluble or insoluble. A soluble salt will be prepared by one of the methods stated in Section 19.1, whereas an insoluble salt will be prepared by precipitation (Section 19.4).

Here is a way of finding out whether the salt which you have been asked to make is soluble or not.

Use the chart in Fig. 19.11, answering the questions and following the arrows.

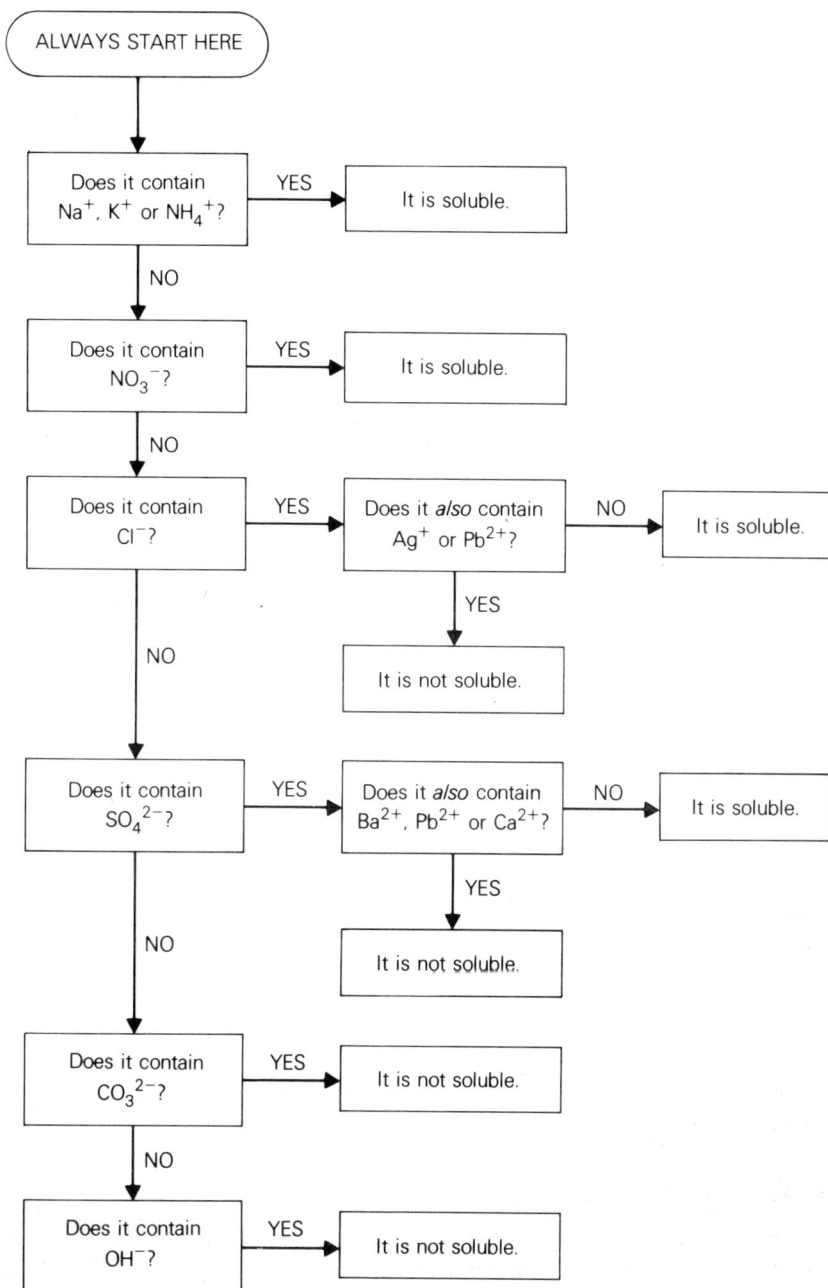

Figure 19.11

As an example for using this flow chart let us find out if **copper chloride** is soluble or not.

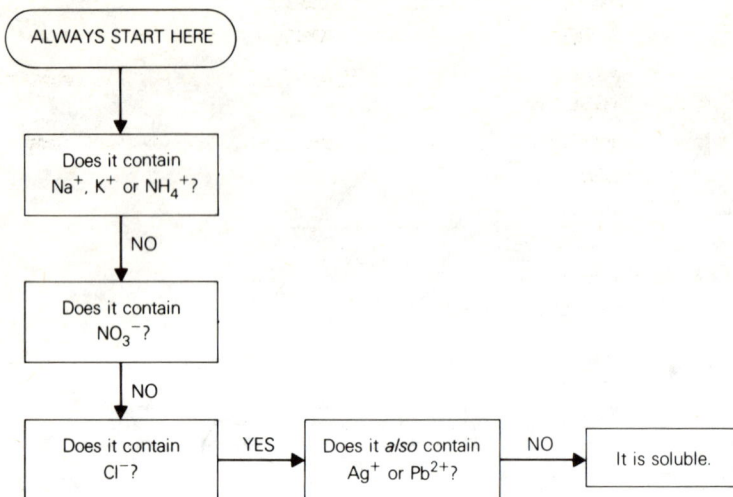

ALWAYS START HERE

Does it contain
Na^+, K^+ or NH_4^+?

NO

Does it contain
NO_3^-?

NO

Does it contain
Cl^-? — YES → Does it *also* contain
Ag^+ or Pb^{2+}? — NO → It is soluble.

Is **zinc carbonate** soluble? Follow the chart in the same way.

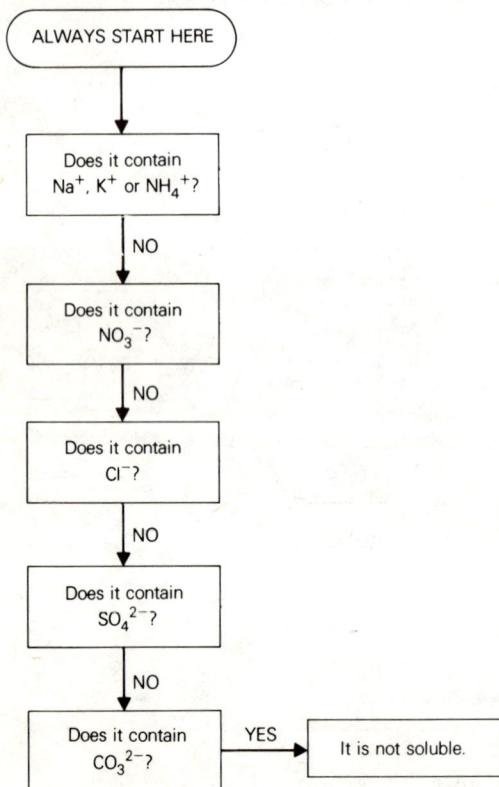

ALWAYS START HERE

Does it contain
Na^+, K^+ or NH_4^+?

NO

Does it contain
NO_3^-?

NO

Does it contain
Cl^-?

NO

Does it contain
SO_4^{2-}?

NO

Does it contain
CO_3^{2-}? — YES → It is not soluble.

When we have decided whether a compound is soluble or not, we have to choose the method for making it.

If it is *soluble* then a *neutralization* method is needed.

If it is *insoluble* then a *precipitation* method is needed.

We can also devise a chart (Fig. 19.12) to help us select the correct method by which to make the salt.

We shall use this flow diagram to select a method to prepare **copper chloride** and **zinc carbonate**.

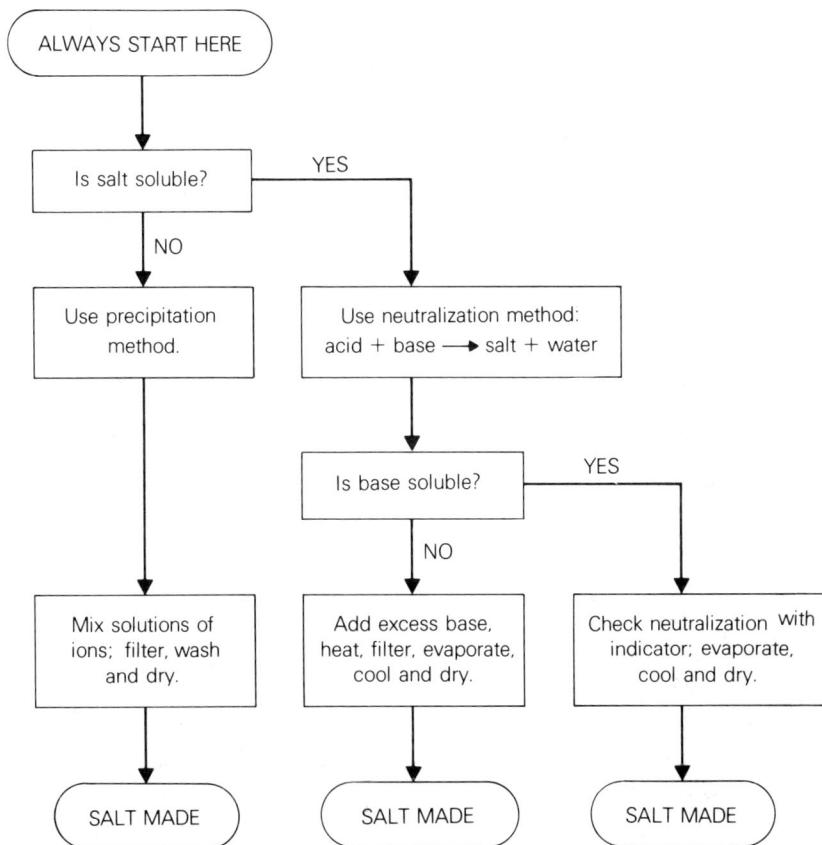

Figure 19.12

Copper chloride
A suitable base is copper oxide (Section 19.1). It has to be added to warm dilute hydrochloric acid (to give a chloride) until no more will dissolve. The mixture is filtered and the solution is allowed to evaporate. On cooling, crystals of copper chloride will be obtained and can be dried on a piece of blotting paper.

We have made **copper chloride**.

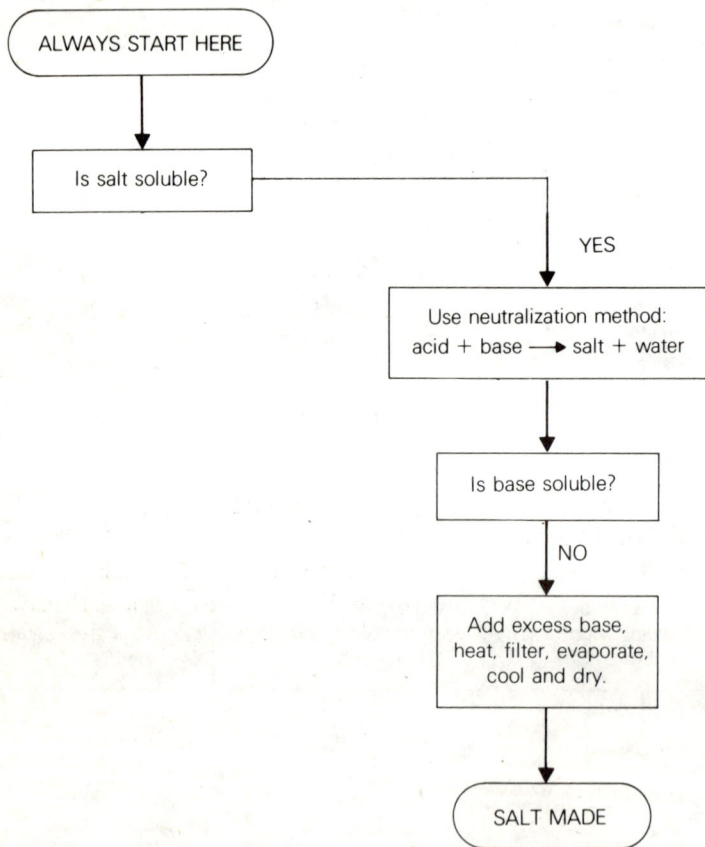

```
        ┌─────────────────────────┐
        │    ALWAYS START HERE     │
        └─────────────────────────┘
                    │
                    ▼
        ┌─────────────────────┐
        │   Is salt soluble?   │──────────────┐
        └─────────────────────┘              │
                                             │ YES
                                             ▼
                          ┌──────────────────────────────────┐
                          │  Use neutralization method:       │
                          │  acid + base ──► salt + water     │
                          └──────────────────────────────────┘
                                             │
                                             ▼
                          ┌──────────────────────────────────┐
                          │        Is base soluble?           │
                          └──────────────────────────────────┘
                                             │ NO
                                             ▼
                          ┌──────────────────────────────────┐
                          │   Add excess base,                │
                          │   heat, filter, evaporate,        │
                          │   cool and dry.                   │
                          └──────────────────────────────────┘
                                             │
                                             ▼
                          ┌──────────────────────┐
                          │      SALT MADE        │
                          └──────────────────────┘
```

Zinc carbonate
We must mix two solutions, one containing zinc ions and the other containing carbonate ions (Section 19.4). Zinc sulphate (see Fig. 19.11) is a soluble salt of zinc. This will do for the first solution.

```
        ╭─────────────────────╮
        │  ALWAYS START HERE  │
        ╰─────────────────────╯
                  │
                  ▼
        ┌─────────────────────┐
        │   Is salt soluble?  │
        └─────────────────────┘
                  │ NO
                  ▼
        ┌─────────────────────┐
        │  Use precipitation  │
        │      method.        │
        └─────────────────────┘
                  │
                  ▼
        ┌─────────────────────┐
        │   Mix solutions of  │
        │  ions; filter, wash │
        │      and dry.       │
        └─────────────────────┘
                  │
                  ▼
        ╭─────────────────────╮
        │     SALT MADE       │
        ╰─────────────────────╯
```

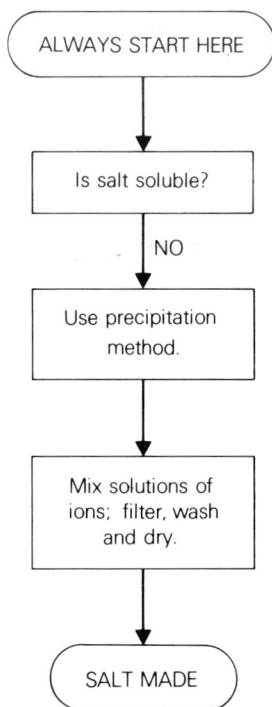

Sodium carbonate is a soluble carbonate (see Fig. 19.11) and so a solution of this compound will be suitable.

These two solutions should be mixed and the precipitate which is made should be filtered, washed with water, and dried. We have made **zinc carbonate**.

Using the same techniques, you should now decide on a method to prepare

(a) calcium carbonate,
(b) magnesium sulphate,
(c) potassium nitrate.

Answers are given on page 220.

19.6 Water—the solvent for everything?

In your work you have received a number of surprises when experimenting with water. One was when you discovered that water could easily free the ions from the rigid arrangement in many ionic solids (Section 7.5, p. 83). The only other way to do this was to melt the solid. In most cases this took a tremendous amount of heat energy. How can water at room temperature so easily break up the ionic arrangement in many compounds? To get the answer we must go back to the structure of the water molecule.

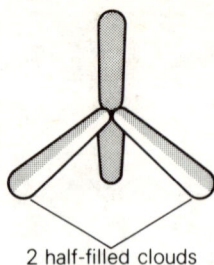

2 half-filled clouds

Figure 19.13

An atom of oxygen has two half-filled clouds (Fig. 19.13) and so requires the electrons from two hydrogen atoms to fill them.

The shape of this water molecule can be pictured in a number of ways (Fig. 19.14). In each O—H bond the pairs of electrons shared by the oxygen and hydrogen atoms are attracted more to the oxygen nucleus than to the hydrogen. This means that these bonds are polar covalent. There is a slightly positive charge at the hydrogen end of each and a slightly negative charge at the oxygen end.

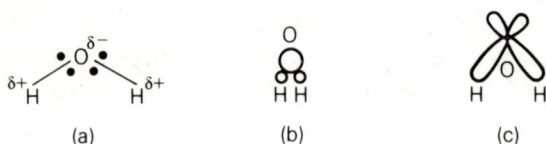

Figure 19.14

How does this structure help the chemist to explain the source of energy which overcomes the attraction between the ions when sodium chloride dissolves in water?

If a sample of sodium chloride, NaCl, is placed in water, the polar water molecules (Section 7.2, p. 78) cluster round the sodium and chloride ions on the surface of the solid (Fig. 19.15).

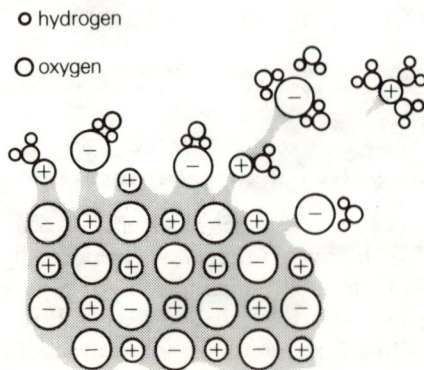

o hydrogen

O oxygen

Figure 19.15

○ hydrogen

○ oxygen

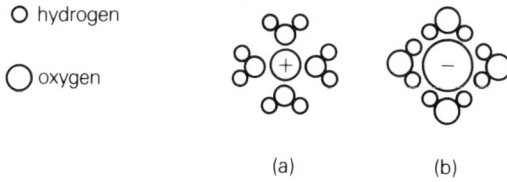

(a)   (b)

Figure 19.16

Moving water molecules swarm round the positively charged sodium ions on the surface of the crystal with their negatively charged oxygen atoms turned toward the cations. They then try to pull the sodium ions off the crystal. In this case they are successful and the sodium ions go into solution as $Na^+(aq)$ (Fig. 19.16(a)).

We have shown four water molecules round the sodium ion, but chemists are not certain how many water molecules hydrate (attach to) each sodium ion.

Similarly, negatively charged chloride ions in the crystal are drawn into solution as hydrated chloride ions by the pull of the positively charged hydrogen atoms in other water molecules (Fig. 19.16(b)).

It is not certain how many water molecules cluster round one chloride ion so we simply write the hydrated chloride ion as $Cl^-(aq)$.

As sodium ions and chloride ions are being hauled off the ionic arrangement into solution, a few of them are attracted back to the crystal lattice and become detached from the swarm of water molecules round them. These ions are redeposited on the crystal surface.

When the solid first dissolves, more ions are being pulled off the crystal than are returning to it. If the number of ions leaving the crystal becomes the same as the number being redeposited, the solution is said to be **saturated**. Because of the constant coming and going of ions, the solid lying at the bottom of a saturated solution is always changing its shape, but not its mass.

Polar water molecules do the same to all ionic solids. If they are able to detach only a very few ions from a solid, the compound is said to be **insoluble**.

19.7 When polar meets polar

Something similar sometimes happens when water molecules meet polar covalent substances.

When hydrogen chloride gas dissolves in water, polar water molecules gather round the polar hydrogen chloride molecules, as shown in Fig. 19.17.

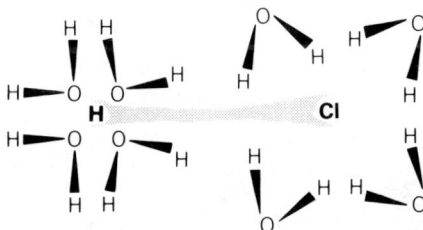

Figure 19.17

A tug-of-war develops which snaps the H—Cl bond and forms hydrated hydrogen ions and chloride ions.

Hydrogen chloride will not give ions in a non-polar solvent because the non-polar molecules are unable to snap the H—Cl bond.

Pure acids contain few ions but, when they dissolve in water, large quantities of hydrogen ions are liberated along with the corresponding negative ions (anions).

Summary

Salts are formed when an acid (a source of H^+ ions) neutralizes an alkali (a source of OH^- ions). During this reaction H^+ ions are usually replaced by slower moving metal cations.

When neutralization is complete:

number of H^+ ions given by the acid = number of OH^- ions given by the alkali

Salts are usually divided into two groups: soluble or insoluble.

Soluble salts   are made by a *neutralization* method.
Insoluble salts are made by a *precipitation* method.

Water is an extremely good solvent because of the way in which its polar covalent molecule can break up the arrangement of ions in a crystal lattice.

New words you have met in this chapter

Conductivity	the conductivity of a solution gives an indication of both the number and the speed of the ions present. The apparatus used to measure this is called a *conductivity apparatus*.
Neutralization	the process by which H^+ ions from an acid are replaced by metal ions. The H^+ ions can escape as hydrogen gas or combine with oxide or hydroxide ions to give water.
Titration	the slow addition of an acid to an alkali (or vice versa) to find the neutralization point. Usually an indicator is used to tell when the neutralization point has been reached.
A molar solution	a molar (M) solution is one which contains the gram formula weight (one mole) of the substance dissolved in 1 litre of solution. A one-tenth molar (0.1 M) solution contains $\frac{1}{10}$ the gram formula weight of the substance dissolved in 1 litre of solution.
Concentration	the concentration of a solution indicates the mass of a substance present in a certain volume of solution.
Precipitation	this occurs when two ions which make up an insoluble compound come together in solution and settle out as a solid.
A saturated solution	a solution which can dissolve no more solute at that particular temperature.

ANSWERS TO QUESTIONS IN CHAPTER 19

On page 206

1 Number of moles of H^+
= volume of acid in litres × molarity × number of H^+ in formula of HCl

$$\text{Number of moles of } H^+ = \frac{50}{1000} \times 2 \times 1$$

$$= 0.1$$

2 Number of moles of $H^+ = \frac{100}{1000} \times 1 \times \underset{\substack{\text{(number of } H^+ \text{ in formula} \\ \text{of } H_2SO_4)}}{2}$

$$= 0.2$$

3 Number of moles of $OH^- = 0.05$

4 Number of moles of $OH^- = 0.1$

5 Number of moles of $H^+ = 0.1$

6 Number of moles of $H^+ = 0.125$

On page 209

1 At neutralization:
number of moles of H^+ present = number of moles of OH^- present

$$\underset{\text{(in litres)}}{\frac{25}{1000}} \times 1.25 \times \underset{(H^+ \text{ in } H_2SO_4)}{2} = \underset{\text{(in litres)}}{\frac{30}{1000}} \times \underset{\substack{\text{(to be} \\ \text{calculated)}}}{\text{unknown molarity}} \times \underset{\substack{\text{(number of } OH^- \text{ in} \\ \text{formula of NaOH)}}}{1}$$

$$\frac{25}{1000} \times 1.25 \times 2 = \frac{30}{1000} \times \text{unknown molarity}$$

So $30 \times \text{unknown molarity} = 25 \times 1.25 \times 2$

$$\text{unknown molarity} = \frac{25 \times 1.25 \times 2}{30}$$

$$= 2.08 \text{ M}$$

2 The equation to arrive at here is:
number of moles H^+ = number of moles OH^-

$$\frac{17}{1000} \times 0.5 \times 2 = x \times 1.5 \times 1$$

Can you see where the figures come from?
In this example we have to find the volume of the NaOH solution required.
Let x litres be this volume.

$$\frac{17}{1000} \times 0.5 \times 2 = 1.5x$$

$$\frac{17}{1000} = 1.5x$$

$$x = \frac{17}{1.5 \times 1000} \text{ litre}$$

$$= 11.3 \text{ ml}$$

3 (a) Molarity of HCl = 1.3 M
  (b) Molarity of H_2SO_4 = 0.5 M
  (c) Molarity of HNO_3 = 0.67 M

4 Volume of 2 M H_2SO_4 required = 5 ml

5 You must first decide the number of OH^- in the formula of $Ca(OH)_2$.
Then the number of moles of H^+ = number of moles of OH^-
The only quantity not known is the molarity of the $Ca(OH)_2$ solution.
This turns out to be 0.03 M.

On page 215

(a) *Making calcium carbonate*

From Fig. 19.11 you will find that calcium carbonate is insoluble and so it must be made by a precipitation method.
   For this we need a soluble *calcium* salt and a soluble *carbonate*.
   Calcium chloride and sodium carbonate will do (check in Fig. 19.11). Make solutions of these two salts and mix them. Insoluble calcium carbonate will settle to the bottom. Filter it off, wash it with water, and leave it to dry.

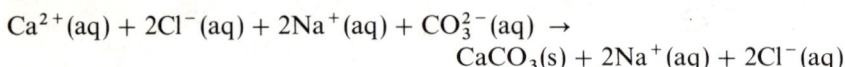

$$Ca^{2+}(aq) + 2Cl^-(aq) + 2Na^+(aq) + CO_3^{2-}(aq) \rightarrow$$
$$CaCO_3(s) + 2Na^+(aq) + 2Cl^-(aq)$$

(b) *Making magnesium sulphate*

From Fig. 19.11 you will find that magnesium sulphate is soluble and so it is made by a neutralization method. The acid which will give us the sulphate ion is sulphuric. The magnesium ions can come from magnesium metal, or magnesium oxide, or magnesium carbonate. These are all solids.
   Warm some sulphuric acid. Add the solid you have chosen a little at a time till no more will dissolve. Filter off the extra and leave the solution to crystallize.

$$MgO + H_2SO_4 \rightarrow MgSO_4 + H_2O$$

(c) *Making potassium nitrate*

From Fig. 19.11 you will find that potassium nitrate is soluble and so it is made by a neutralization method.
   Potassium hydroxide is an alkali and so a solution of it will provide the potassium ions. The nitrate ions will come from nitric acid. We have a situation in which an indicator can be used.
   Place some potassium hydroxide solution in a flask, add an indicator, and then add the nitric acid slowly, mixing the solution all the time. Continue until the indicator just changes colour.
   Allow the solution to evaporate to give potassium nitrate crystals.

Chemistry in Action 9

Solubility and successful separations

Look at the Table of Solubilities on the next page and then answer the questions underneath it.

* * *

Different compounds tend to dissolve in water to different extents. Chemists find this very useful in separating mixtures of compounds into fairly pure compounds. For example, sea water contains large amounts of dissolved magnesium compounds. It would be useful to be able to obtain these magnesium compounds from the sea. But the sea contains so many other dissolved compounds, including compounds of sodium, potassium, and calcium. What we want to do is to be able to obtain the magnesium *without* it being mixed up with compounds of other metals. Look at the Table of Solubilities. Can you see any magnesium compounds which are much less soluble than the compounds of sodium, potassium, and calcium?

Yes, magnesium fluoride, carbonate, sulphite, oxalate, and hydroxide are all fairly insoluble. All compounds of sodium and potassium are soluble, but only magnesium hydroxide is less soluble than the calcium compound. If you add a source of hydroxide ions to sea water, the first compound which will form an insoluble precipitate will be magnesium hydroxide. The precipitate of magnesium hydroxide can be filtered off and converted to magnesium chloride, which is electrolysed. This is, in fact, one major way used in Britain to obtain magnesium from sea water.

Part I

Work as a group of three or four and see if you can find a way of separating the following two mixtures. After you have decided on some possible ways to achieve the separations, your teacher may let you try them in the laboratory.

(a) A solution contains lead nitrate and sodium nitrate dissolved in water. How could you obtain a solution containing only sodium nitrate?

(b) A solution of magnesium nitrate has been contaminated with silver nitrate and barium nitrate. How could you remove both the silver and barium ions from the solution, leaving reasonably pure magnesium nitrate solution?

Write down the answers your group has obtained and check with your teacher that these are correct.

Table of solubilities of some salts. Figures are expressed in grams per 100 g solution

	OH^-	F^-	Cl^-	Br^-	CO_3^{2-}	NO_3^-	SO_4^{2-}	SO_3^{2-}	$*C_2O_4^{2-}$
Na^+	109	4	36	91	21	87	19	17	3.7
K^+	112	95	35	67	112	32	11	82	33
Mg^{2+}	0.0009	0.008	54	102	0.011	70	33	0.6	0.06
Ca^{2+}	0.16	0.0016	75	142	0.002	129	0.21	0.004	0.0007
Ba^{2+}	4	0.12	36	104	0.002	9	0.0002	0.02	0.009
Pb^{2+}	0.016	0.064	0.99	0.84	0.001	55	0.004	d	0.0002
Ag^+	d	195	0.0001	0.000 008	0.003	217	0.8	d	0.003

d = decomposes on formation.
* = oxalate ion.

1 What can you say about most lead compounds?
2 What can you say about all the nitrates?
3 What can you say about most of the chlorides?

Now go back to page 221.

Part II

In real life this common problem of separating mixtures of compounds is often solved by using differences in solubility. Here are some examples for you to try, *still working as a group.*

(a) In an industrial process making materials for dyes and drugs, a factory uses large amounts of sulphuric acid. The solution left contains both sulphate and sulphite ions. Before this can be pumped into the nearby river, most of the sulphate and sulphite ions must be removed. How might you achieve this?

(b) Oxalate ions ($C_2O_4{}^{2-}$) are very poisonous when dissolved in water, but more or less harmless when in the form of an insoluble oxalate. In a school experiment, a pupil accidentally swallowed a little of a solution containing oxalate ions. His teacher looked up a solubility table to find out what to give the pupil to prevent his being poisoned. What would *you* have given the pupil, and why?

(c) The sea contains large amounts of dissolved sodium, potassium, magnesium, calcium, and chlorine compounds. Would you expect to find large amounts of compounds of any of the following elements dissolved in the sea?
    (i) bromine   (ii) fluorine   (iii) silver

(d) Bauxite ore contains Al_2O_3 mixed with large amounts of Fe_2O_3. Before aluminium can be obtained from the ore, the iron oxide must be completely removed. Look at the following information and discuss how you might do it.

Both oxides are insoluble in water, both dissolve in acid (reacting with the acid), but only Al_2O_3 dissolves in alkali (reacting with the alkali). The reactions can be illustrated for hydrochloric acid and sodium hydroxide:

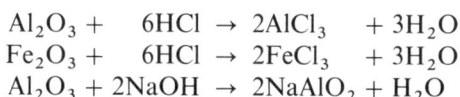

$$Al_2O_3 +\quad 6HCl \rightarrow 2AlCl_3 \quad + 3H_2O$$
$$Fe_2O_3 +\quad 6HCl \rightarrow 2FeCl_3 \quad + 3H_2O$$
$$Al_2O_3 + 2NaOH \rightarrow 2NaAlO_2 + H_2O$$

How would you get the aluminium oxide back again?

20

Big molecules

20.1

In Chapter 5 you learned how large molecules could be formed by linking together many small units. As many as 2000 identical units can be joined by the process called addition. This idea was reflected in the name *poly-mer* (many parts) and several man-made addition polymers were discussed in that chapter. Only this century has much practical use been made of man-made addition polymers.

In Nature, addition polymers exist and have been used for a long time. The commonest of these is rubber. It can consist of up to 20 000 C_5H_8 units, joined together in a chain. This molecule has a formula weight of nearly three-quarters of a million—a big molecule indeed!

20.2 Another way of building big molecules

In Section 6.9 and in Section 17.3 we met the process called **condensation**. This is another way of joining molecules together to form larger ones. It is done by taking out a small molecule, such as water, from between two substances.

If two neighbouring molecules give up a molecule of water between them, the two 'parent' molecules can then use their 'spare electrons' to join together.

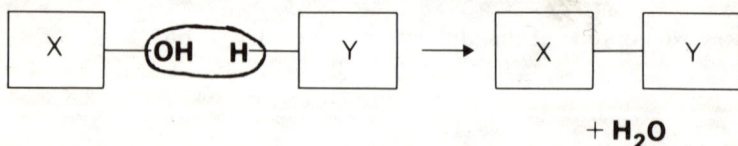

$$+ \, \mathbf{H_2O}$$

In a similar way other small molecules, such as hydrogen chloride (HCl), can be pushed out between two molecules, to form a larger one.

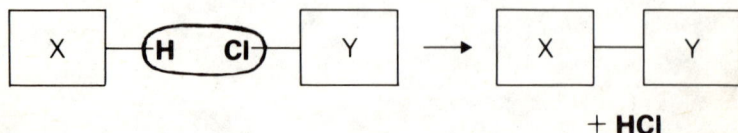

$$+ \, \mathbf{HCl}$$

The reverse of this is known as **hydrolysis**, a reaction which we met in Section 6.3 page 62, and in Section 17.3, page 176. Condensation and hydrolysis are both common types of chemical reactions.

Condensation polymers

Big molecules, which have been formed as a result of a series of condensation reactions, are called **condensation polymers**. For instance the carbohydrate known as cellulose is a naturally occurring condensation polymer and is found in cotton and wood.

The best known man-made condensation polymer is probably Nylon. There are a number of different varieties of Nylon, but the same idea is involved in the manufacture of all of them.

The starting materials, or monomers, used to make Nylon are of two types. One has a string of carbon atoms (X) with an acid group at either end.

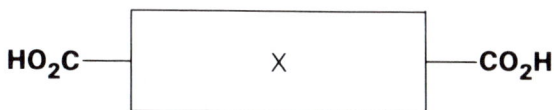

$$HO_2C \boxed{\qquad X \qquad} CO_2H$$

The other has a string of carbon atoms (Y) with an amino group at either end. This is a basic group which can neutralize an acid to give water.

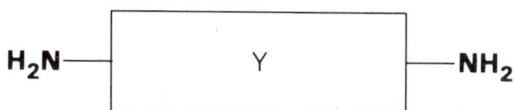

$$H_2N \boxed{\qquad Y \qquad} NH_2$$

These two monomers react together by condensation with the loss of water.

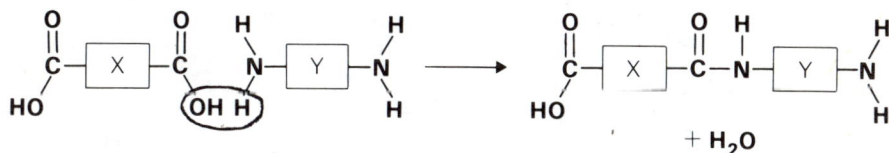

$$+ H_2O$$

In practice it is easier to use the acid chloride instead of the acid itself and so the condensation in this case involves the loss of HCl.

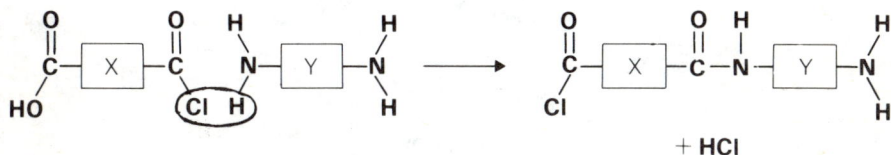

$$+ HCl$$

The $-\overset{\overset{\displaystyle O}{\|}}{C}-\overset{\overset{\displaystyle H}{|}}{N}-$ link in Nylon is similar to that found in all protein fibres, such as hair and silk, and so it is not surprising that Nylon is used in place of them, for example, in Nylon wigs or Nylon tights.

Depending upon the length of the carbon chains in X and Y, we obtain various kinds of Nylon. We can get 6.6 Nylon, 6.10 Nylon, and so on, where the number refers to the number of carbon atoms in the two monomer units.

After it has been made, the Nylon is dried, melted, and squirted through small holes to give fine threads. These threads are then stretched in order to pull all the molecules into line to give a strong, light, flexible fibre.

Terylene is another common condensation polymer, which is similar to Nylon.

Figure 20.1 shows some other well known condensation polymers in use.

Figure 20.1

20.3 Plastics and heat

Both Nylon and Terylene can be melted and then cooled back to their original form. Polythene, Perspex, polystyrene, and polypropylene (polypropene) also behave in the same way. Plastics which soften on heating and harden on cooling are called **thermoplastics**.

There is another group of plastics which harden when they are heated. They do not melt and will not soften again on further heating. They are said to be **thermosetting** plastics. Members of this group are the bakelites which are used for ash trays, electrical plugs, and switches.

The range of plastics now available is almost endless. It contains substances which have been deliberately made because they were needed. Each has its own special properties, in the same way as each metal or each type of wood has its own properties. They are easy to mould and shape in other ways. They can be easily coloured to give them a bright attractive finish or to copy the appearance of natural materials such as wood. They do not rot, are good electrical insulators, are waterproof, and can withstand harsh treatment.

But these advantages can become disadvantages when you want to get rid of them. They cannot be dissolved or left to rot away. It is difficult to smash them up and difficult to re-use them if different types are mixed. Attempts are being made to burn plastic rubbish and to use the heat efficiently.

20.4 The silicones—rocks and plastics?

One of the main drawbacks with many plastics is that they melt and even break down too easily when they are heated. It would be very useful to find substances which behaved like plastics, but which could withstand heat better.

Attention has turned to the element silicon. This is in the same column of the Periodic Table as carbon. It is the element present in most rocks and sand and these substances can withstand high temperatures, but are certainly not soft like plastics.

Perhaps some compound containing both carbon and silicon would meet our requirements.

What has been designed are molecules with the structure shown below.

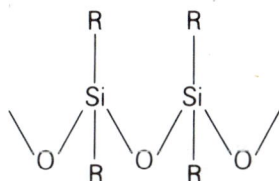

R represents an organic group such as those we met in hydrocarbons, $—CH_3$ or $—C_2H_5$, and so on. The $—Si—O—Si—$ chain is present in rocks and is very strong and heat resistant.

These 'in-between' compounds are called **silicones** and they show the behaviour of their 'oily' hydrocarbon part as well as the heat resistance of the silicon part. They can remain usable in the temperature range from $-80\,^{\circ}$C to $+300\,^{\circ}$C. They are in the form of oils, greases, and rubbers. They are especially good for repelling water, for electrical insulation, and for coating non-stick articles such as pans and mixers.

20.5 Large molecules with ionic behaviour

Soaps and detergents which we use every day have big molecules, but they are not nearly as large as the polymer molecules.

They have only about twenty carbon atoms in their chains. At the end of the chain is an ionic part. The simplest of these is the soap called sodium stearate, $C_{17}H_{35}COO^-Na^+$. It has a long hydrocarbon tail with an ionic head (Fig. 20.2).

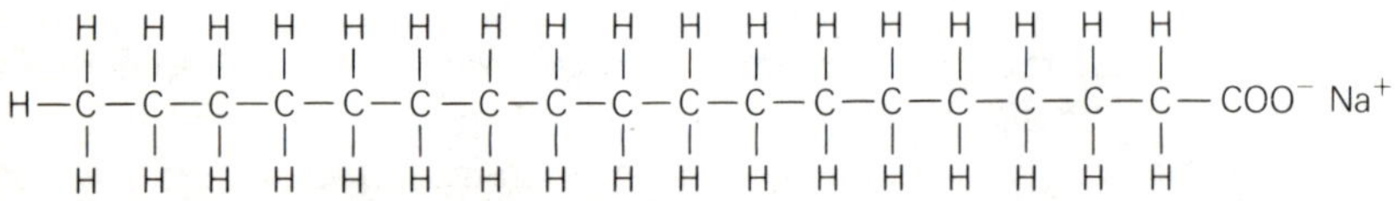

Figure 20.2

How does this 'tadpole-like' structure help water to clean things? The tail of the 'tadpole' is the long non-polar (covalent) hydrocarbon chain, $C_{17}H_{35}$, and its head is the polar (ionic) group **COO$^-$Na$^+$**.

We shall use the symbol ——o to represent such a soap molecule. The polar head, like most ionic compounds, is soluble in water, whereas the non-polar tail is insoluble. Because of its hydrocarbon structure, the tail is attracted to fats, oils, and all solvents for fats.

It is a well-known fact that oil and water do not mix. When oil is shaken with water the particles of oil soon gather together and lie on top of the water.

When soap molecules are added to this they will take up the positions shown in Fig. 20.3, with each tail attracted to the oil and each head attracted to the water.

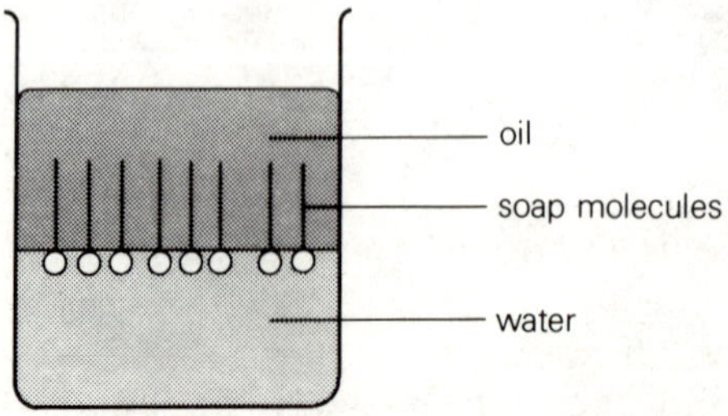

oil

soap molecules

water

Figure 20.3

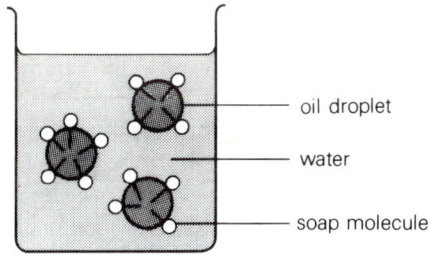

Figure 20.4

When this mixture is shaken, the soap molecules gather round each drop of oil as shown in Fig. 20.4. The sodium ions in each head go into solution, leaving a series of negative charges round each drop (Fig. 20.5).

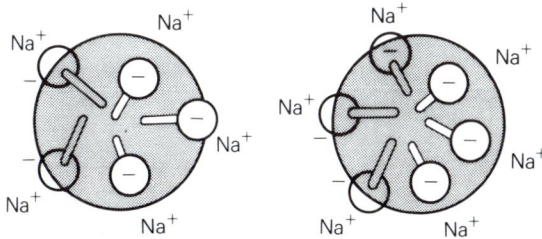

Figure 20.5

This prevents the drops of oil from coming together and so they remain suspended in the water.

Figure 20.6 shows, in stages, what we think happens when soap and water are used to remove grease from a solid surface.

Foaming helps to support the suspended particles of grease, while agitation such as stirring or swirling helps to loosen the grease from the surface to be cleaned.

Finally, the solution and the lather (or suds) which contain the oil and grease, together with the suspended dirt, are rinsed away.

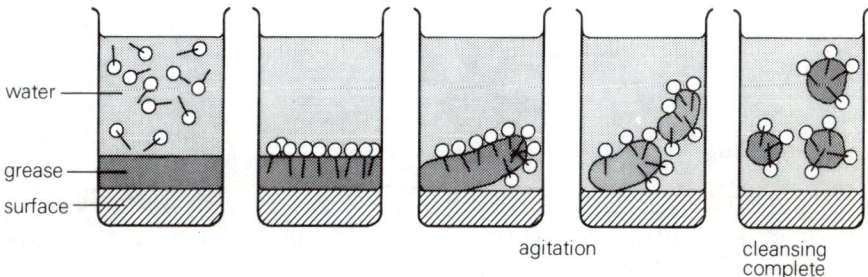

Figure 20.6

20.6 Soaps, scum, and detergents

In many parts of Britain the use of soap is limited because it does not form a lather with the tap water. Instead a grey scum appears which clings to clothes and basins, spoiling their appearance. This kind of water is said to be **hard**.

Hard water occurs in parts of the country in which the tap water passes through chalk or limestone. These rocks are almost insoluble in pure water, but if the water contains carbon dioxide (carbonic acid) it can dissolve the chalk.

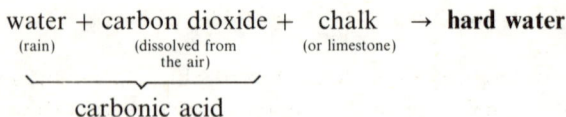

$$\underset{\text{(rain)}}{\text{water}} + \underset{\substack{\text{(dissolved from}\\ \text{the air)}}}{\text{carbon dioxide}} + \underset{\text{(or limestone)}}{\text{chalk}} \rightarrow \textbf{hard water}$$

$$\underbrace{\hspace{7cm}}_{\text{carbonic acid}}$$

The mineral gypsum is slightly soluble in water and this also gives rise to hardness in water.

Chalk and limestone are forms of *calcium* carbonate, while gypsum is *calcium* sulphate. It is the calcium ion which causes the hardness. The magnesium ion in the mineral magnesite (magnesium carbonate) can also produce water hardness—and you will notice that calcium and magnesium are in the same vertical column in the Periodic Table. Why do these ions cause a scum with soap?

Let us take soap to be sodium stearate, a water-soluble substance which contains sodium ions and stearate ions. To simplify matters we shall represent the stearate anion as St^-. When these stearate ions mix with calcium ions in hard water calcium stearate is formed as an insoluble grey scum.

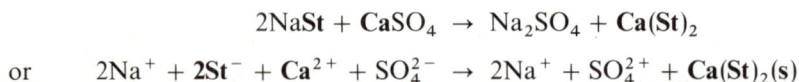

$$2NaSt + CaSO_4 \rightarrow Na_2SO_4 + Ca(St)_2$$

or $\quad 2Na^+ + 2St^- + Ca^{2+} + SO_4^{2-} \rightarrow 2Na^+ + SO_4^{2+} + Ca(St)_2(s)$

It is a typical precipitation reaction in which four types of ion meet freely. Two types combine to form an insoluble solid while the other two remain free (see Section 19.4, p. 209). Magnesium stearate is also insoluble and, by the same process, a scum occurs. The formation of this scum poses a problem for the chemist. There are two ways round it.

(a) The calcium and magnesium ions could be removed from the water.
(b) Another kind of soap could be designed which does not react with either calcium or magnesium ions.

Both lines of investigation have been followed and both have proved successful.

(a) *Removing the offending ions*

(i) One of the simplest ways of removing ions is by a precipitation process.

What is required to solve the problem is a cheap substance, containing a negative ion (anion), which will remove the calcium and magnesium ions as insoluble substances. An ideal compound is sodium carbonate (washing soda) because the carbonate ions precipitate out with the calcium ions as insoluble calcium carbonate.

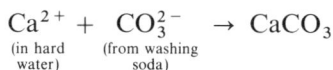

$$Ca^{2+} + CO_3^{2-} \rightarrow CaCO_3$$

(in hard water)   (from washing soda)

The ions which are now left in the solution do not interfere with the washing process. This treatment improves the lathering qualities of the water, but there is still the solid calcium carbonate to contend with.

(ii) An even more ingenious idea avoids the problem of solid precipitates altogether.

Chemists have designed tiny plastic beads which have sodium ions loosely attached to them. These are called **ion exchange resins** and are related to the plastic, polystyrene.

When hard water is allowed to flow through a tube packed with these beads, the calcium ions in the water are exchanged for sodium ions. These do not react with the soap and so a lather forms easily.

Eventually the beads will be completely covered with calcium ions and they will become useless unless the calcium ions can be removed and sodium ions put back. This is done quite readily. A concentrated solution of sodium chloride passed through the tube reverses the process. Calcium ions are flushed out leaving the column ready to perform its task again. You can now see the reason for the name 'ion exchange'.

These beads are almost indestructible and can be used over and over again. They are used on a very large scale industrially to soften water for boilers. The 'distilled water' used in your school may have been made by an ion exchange process instead of by distillation.

(b) *Redesigning the soap—detergents*

This is the second approach to tackling the problem of hard water.

From their knowledge of soap, chemists realized that they would have to prepare a molecule which had a long hydrocarbon chain and was therefore attractive to grease. At the same time they had to design a 'head group' which was attractive to water and yet did not react with calcium or magnesium ions to give a scum.

The outcome of their research was the production of 'soapless' detergents. There was a good supply of long chain hydrocarbons from the petroleum industry and it was found that these could take on a suitable 'head group'. The hydrocarbons chosen have a long carbon chain ending with a ring of six carbon atoms (Fig. 20.7). Treatment with very concentrated sulphuric acid adds an ionic 'head' to the ring.

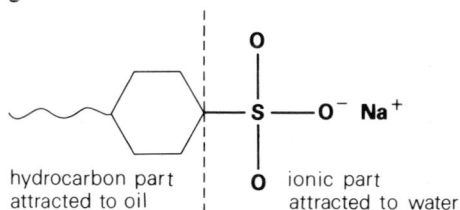

hydrocarbon part attracted to oil   ionic part attracted to water

Figure 20.7

This new sulphonated hydrocarbon ion does not form a precipitate with calcium or magnesium ions, and so forms a lather even with the hardest water.

A blessing or a curse?

The ability of detergents to give a good lather in hard water is very useful for washing clothes and dishes, but when detergents were first used they created a problem for the sewage engineer. When the froth was poured down the drain, the bubbles remained. By the time the water arrived at the sewage plant it often had a 'head' of froth several feet thick!

Chemists have now designed detergents which can be digested by the bacteria in the sewage plants. This means that less frothing occurs, simplifying the task of the sewage engineer.

Another way to overcome the problem of frothing is to add a de-foaming substance to the water. The de-foaming substances used are often the silicones which were mentioned earlier in this chapter.

New words you have met in this chapter

Condensation polymerization a process which joins monomers together by the removal of a small molecule such as H_2O or HCl.

Starch and cellulose are naturally occurring condensation polymers. Nylon and Terylene are man-made condensation polymers.

Addition polymerization in this only one type of monomer, based on ethene,

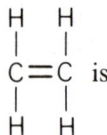

$$
\begin{array}{c}
H \quad H \\
| \quad | \\
C = C \\
| \quad | \\
H \quad H
\end{array}
$$

is used. Identical units join together by breaking one of the carbon-to-carbon bonds (see Section 5.4, p. 45). Rubber is a naturally occurring addition polymer. Polythene and PVC are man-made addition polymers.

Thermoplastic a plastic which can be melted and cooled back to its original form.

Thermosetting plastic a plastic which hardens on heating and does not melt when it is heated later.

Silicones compounds which contain chains of silicon and oxygen atoms, with hydrocarbon groups branching off these chains.

Hard water water which does not form a lather with soap. It normally contains Ca^{2+} or Mg^{2+} ions.

Detergents these substances act like soap but do not form a scum with water which contains Ca^{2+} or Mg^{2+} ions. They give a lather with hard water.

Revision section for Chapters 18–20

Answers to this section will be found on page 246.

1 A solution of barium hydroxide was added to sulphuric acid until it was just neutralized.
  (a) What ions would be free in solution? (**Hint.** Use Fig. 19.11 to check whether $BaSO_4$ is soluble.)
  (b) If a conductivity apparatus were used to measure the conductivity of sulphuric acid as barium hydroxide solution was being added, what would be the shape of the graph of conductivity against amount of barium hydroxide added?
  (c) If some tap water had barium ions in it would you expect it to be hard or not?

2 One of the acid monomers used to make Nylon has a formula weight of 146. 25 ml of a 0.1 M solution of it required 5 ml of M NaOH to neutralize it.
  (a) How many H^+ does this monomer have in its formula?
  (b) Try to work out the formula for this acid which consists of a $-CH_2-CH_2------$ type of chain with one or more $-CO_2H$ groups on it.

3 Make a list of detergents you have at home. Here is a hint to get you started: washing-up liquid, . . .

4 Decide whether a thermosetting or a thermoplastic plastic is better for each of the following products. In some cases both will be suitable; in some cases neither will be.
  (a) Shampoo bottles.
  (b) Dustbins able to take hot ashes.
  (c) Model cars.
  (d) Transparent film for covering food.
  (e) Electrical wall plugs.
  (f) Steering wheels for cars.

Choose a fibre

Fibres today

If you look at the clothes in a shop, you will notice that they are made of many different kinds of fibres. For example, some garments may have a label saying 'Pure Wool'. Others may be labelled 'Polyester' or 'Nylon'. Of course, many clothes are made of mixtures, such as '55% polyester, 45% cotton'.

Before these clothes were made, someone somewhere had to decide which fibre or fibres to use. They had to study the behaviour of the various fibres which were available. Each fibre has its own particular good and bad points, which make it useful for a particular purpose. For example, cotton is useful for many clothes because it lasts well and is pleasant on the skin. Terylene (a polyester) is strong and fairly comfortable to wear, but also has the great advantage that it can be permanently creased to give pleated garments. Combined with wool it is used to make permanently pressed trousers.

The acrylics can be made to 'feel' like wool, and they have the advantage over wool of lasting longer. They do not shrink on washing and, added to this, they can be drip-dried because they do not absorb much moisture. High moisture absorbance fibres do not make good drip-dry garments. However, if a fibre does not absorb moisture well, it cannot absorb perspiration and this makes it feel uncomfortable on the skin.

There are other factors which must also be considered. Some fibres are more expensive than others. Some can be dyed easily, giving colours which will not wash out. Some wash safely with water while others require dry cleaning.

In the table opposite, eight un-named fibres are considered and some information is given about how they behave.

You should *work as a group* of three or four and together choose the best fibres for various purposes. Can you find *two* good fibres for *each* of the following uses?

(a) Running vests for athletes.
(b) Pairs of tights.
(c) Fishing nets.

Start by deciding how the fibre should behave for each use. Then look at the table and try to decide which fibres you would choose.

Fibre	Density (g cm^{-3})	Dry strength (g dec^{-1})*	Wet strength (g dec^{-1})*	% stretch before breaking	Force needed to stretch (g dec^{-1})*	% elastic recovery†	Moisture absorbance	Handle and wear
A	1.31	1.1	0.9	30–45	29	100	16	Warm 'feel', can shrink a lot, moderate wear, can irritate skin
B	1.55	3.2	3.4	5–10	53	70	9	Firm, comfortable, tough, can shrink a little, may crease
C	1.34	3.6	2.6	20–25	63	90	11	Crisp attractive 'feel', very poor resistance to wear
D	1.52	2.4	1.3	17–25	64	60	13	Soft, very good resistance to wear, crease resistant
E	1.30	1.2	0.8	25–28	36	85	3	Crisp sharp 'feel', gives permanent creases
F	1.14	4.5	3.8	23–42	20	100	5	Soft, lasts well, crease-resistant, very tough
G	1.38	4.1	4.1	25–35	60	80	0.5	Lasts well, gives permanent creases, very tough
H	1.16	2.4	2.0	25–45	40	90	2	Soft, warm 'feel', non-shrink, tough, resistant to creasing

* g dec^{-1} = grams per decitex, a measure of force per unit cross section. The decitex replaces the older unit, the denier.
† The extent to which the fibre returns to its original shape after stretching.

Chemistry in Action 11

Dis-solving a problem

A substance known as PETN is made in large amounts in industry. It is used as an explosive in mining and quarrying. The process of manufacture uses nitric acid. Although the crystals of PETN are washed thoroughly in water (in which PETN is almost insoluble), some of this nitric acid remains trapped in the crystals. If the acid were not removed, it would make the PETN decompose slowly. Can you find a way to purify the PETN crystals so that they are dry and contain no nitric acid?

Part 1

Form a group with two or three other members of your class.

You need to find a liquid which dissolves PETN well when hot, but much less well when cold. The impure PETN can then be dissolved in the hot solvent. When the solution cools, crystals of pure PETN will form, leaving the unwanted nitric acid and water in solution. This pure PETN can be filtered off. The solvent must also be able to dissolve water. Here is a picture of what you are trying to do.

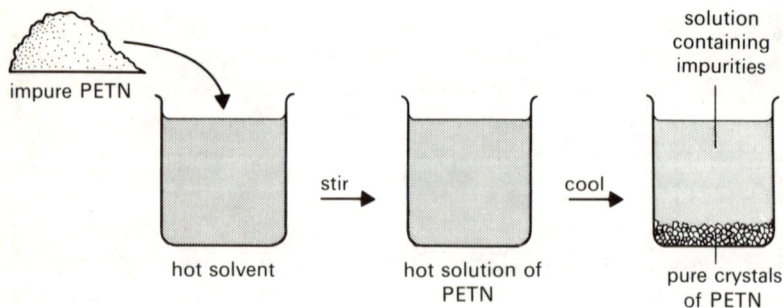

Look at the following information. Six solvents are listed with their boiling points. As a group try to select one solvent which could be used to purify PETN.

A Propanone (b.p. 56 °C) D Toluene (b.p. 113 °C)
B Ethylethanoate (b.p. 77 °C) E Benzene (b.p. 80 °C)
C Pyridine (b.p. 115 °C) F Ethanol (b.p. 78 °C)

Pyridine, propanone, and ethanol dissolve in water and water dissolves in them. PETN is more or less totally insoluble in water at any temperature.

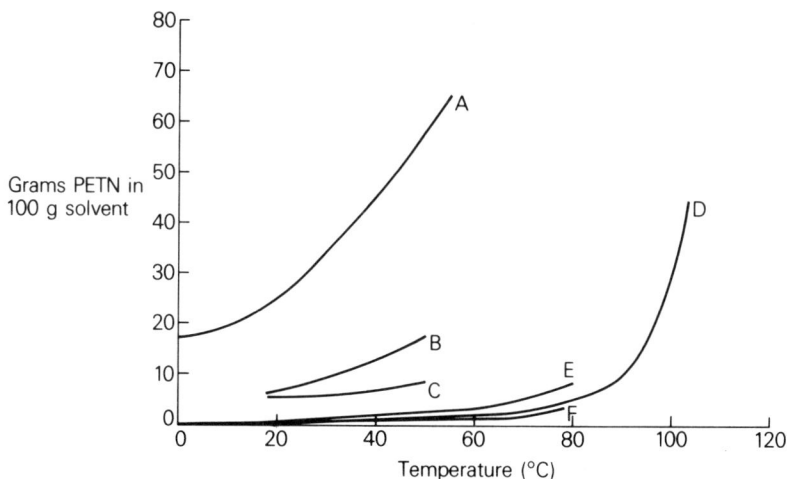

Now turn to page 243.

Chemistry in Action 8 (*continued from p. 182*)

Part II

Check your choices.

(a) For phosphorus, you should have rejected calcium phosphate ($Ca_3(PO_4)_2$) because it is insoluble in water so that plants cannot absorb it. This leaves you with

$(NH_4)_2HPO_4$ at 130.4 groats per kg of phosphorus
$Ca(H_2PO_4)_2$ at 107.7 groats per kg of phosphorus

Although the calcium compound is cheaper, the ammonium compound contains a 'bonus' of nitrogen as well. Either are reasonable choices for you to make.

(b) For nitrogen, you should have rejected ammonia (NH_3) because, being a gas, it cannot be mixed with solids. The cheapest source of nitrogen is urea at 38.3 groats per kg. Unfortunately, the nitrogen in urea is linked by polar covalent bonds (not ionic bonds) and is absorbed only slowly by plants. Before much urea is absorbed it will have been washed out of the soil by rain. This leaves only

NH_4NO_3 at 57.1 groats per kg of nitrogen
$(NH_4)_2SO_4$ at 71.4 groats per kg of nitrogen

On grounds of cost, the nitrate seems to be the best choice, although the sulphate can have some advantages in being easier to handle.

The mixture which is required for potato growing needs to contain the following:

nitrogen	17%
phosphorus	7%
potassium	10%

One tonne of the mixture is needed.

Let us consider three possibilities. Your teacher will ask you to work out one of them, while other groups in your class work out the other two. At the end you can compare answers to see which group made the cheapest mixture.

Mixture I   KCl plus $Ca(H_2PO_4)_2$ plus NH_4NO_3
Mixture II   KCl plus $(NH_4)_2HPO_4$ plus $(NH_4)_2SO_4$
Mixture III   KCl plus $(NH_4)_2HPO_4$ plus NH_4NO_3

Here is how to do the calculation. You need to make one tonne of fertilizer, which will contain:

0.17 tonne nitrogen	(17%)
0.07 tonne phosphorus	(7%)
0.10 tonne potassium	(10%)

1 tonne of KCl contains 0.52 tonne potassium (from your table).
But we only need 0.10 tonne of potassium.

So, we shall need $\dfrac{0.10}{0.52}$ tonne KCl which is 0.19 tonne KCl

Working as a group, carry out the calculations for the other compounds in the mixture your teacher has allocated to you. When you have done this, you can easily work out the cost of making a tonne of the mixture.

Answers to Revision Sections

Answers to revision section for Chapters 1–3

1 **Elements:** iron, tin, lead, sulphur, silver.
   Compounds: starch, Nylon, petrol, Terylene, salt, water, alcohol, methane.
   Remember that elements are the substances listed in the Periodic Table and
   are the basic building units out of which everything else is made.

2 If you have chosen B, C, and E *only* you have the correct idea.
   If you have included A, D, or F in your choice, you still do not have a clear
   idea of the different types of molecules.

Go back to Section 1.2, p. 1.

3 (a) The answer is J.
      All isotopes of an element have the *same atomic number* which appears at
      the bottom left-hand side of the symbol. Both A and J have atomic
      number 92 (i.e. 92 protons).
      If you have chosen C or I you are confusing *atomic number* with *mass
      number* (Chapter 1, p. 6).
   (b) The answers are B, H, K.
      The number of neutrons is the *mass number* minus the *atomic number*.
   (c) A, C, and J.
      The atomic numbers are more than 90.
      atomic number = number of protons = number of electrons
   (d) D, G, K, and L.
      atomic number = number of protons = number of electrons
      mass number − atomic number = number of neutrons (Chapter 1, p. 6.)

4 2)8)2, 2)8)8)1.   (Chapter 2, p. 10.)

5 (a) CS_2 (b) GeO_2 (c) Na_2Se (d) LiI
   (e) $SrBr_2$ (f) Mg_3N_2 (g) Cs_2O (h) SiH_4

$$S = C = S$$

$$\overset{\displaystyle H}{\underset{\displaystyle H}{\overset{|}{\underset{H \diagup \quad \diagdown H}{Si}}}}$$

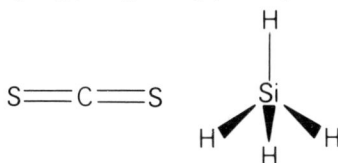

If you have these shapes or formulae wrong go back to Chapter 3, page 21, and
read it again.

Answers to revision section for Chapters 4–6

1 (a) 1, 4, 8, 11. Notice that all compounds containing carbon and hydrogen *only* are hydrocarbons. This includes both saturated (4 and 11) as well as unsaturated compounds (1 and 8).

(b) 4 and 11. Alkanes are saturated hydrocarbons with the general formula C_nH_{2n+2}.

(c) 3 and 7. These contain C, H, and O. The ratio of H to O is 2:1.

(d) 2, 6, 10. These have the general formula $C_nH_{2n+1}OH$ and carry the —COH group.

If you have included 5 or 9 because they have an —OH group notice that the carbon carrying the —OH also is carrying =O. This makes 5 and 9 alkanoic acids, not alcohols.

(e) 5 and 9. These have the $-\overset{\overset{\displaystyle O}{\|}}{C}-OH$ group. This is sometimes written as —CO$_2$H or —COOH.

(f) 12. Here an alcohol $H-\overset{\overset{\displaystyle H}{|}}{\underset{\underset{\displaystyle H}{|}}{C}}-OH$ has linked with an acid

$HO-\overset{\overset{\displaystyle O}{\|}}{C}-\overset{\overset{\displaystyle H}{|}}{\underset{\underset{\displaystyle H}{|}}{C}}-H$ to give the ester called methyl ethanoate.

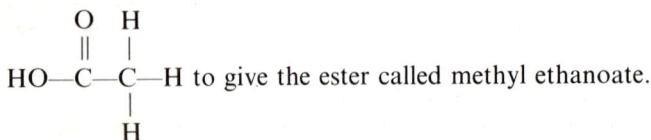

2 The fuel would be some form of coal, that is, carbon. When carbon burns in plenty of air, carbon dioxide is formed. However, if the air supply to the stove was reduced, there may not have been enough oxygen to change all the carbon into CO_2. In this case some carbon monoxide formed. Some of this poisonous carbon monoxide escaped into the bedroom through the cracks in the chimney.

3 Carbon dioxide consists of carbon combined with oxygen. Water vapour (hydrogen oxide) is formed when hydrogen combines with oxygen. The likelihood is that the oxygen required to form these substances came from the air, whereas the carbon and hydrogen could have come only from the oil, suggesting that the oil is a hydrocarbon.

4 C_6H_{14} C_8H_{18}
   hexane   *octane*

5 *Pen*tane is the fifth member of the alkane homologous series. Its formula is C_5H_{12}.

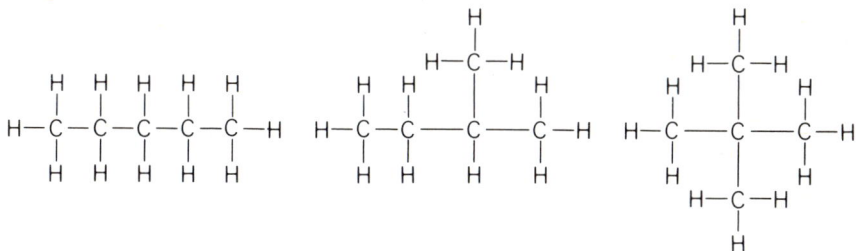

Isomer 1	Isomer 2	Isomer 3

6 It would have to be shaken with bromine water, which is light brown in colour. If the mixture remained coloured, then the liquid under test must have been saturated (Section 4.6, p. 39).

7 (a) Molecules of the monomer ethene (ethylene) can be made to undergo an addition reaction in which they string together (polymerize) to form very large long chain molecules.

(b) The enzyme, ptyalin, in saliva has broken down (hydrolysed) all the starch into simpler sugars.

(c) Many monosaccharide units strung together in the same way as other polymers are made from simpler monomer units.

8 The sort of things you will have in the list are materials made from plastics: bags, certain fabrics, beakers, calculators, car seats, floor covering, rulers, pens, clothing, and so on.

9 The fat molecules have been broken down by the heat (cracked) and new substances (gases) have formed. Bonds have been broken and new bonds formed, some of which are double bonds. This makes the new substances unsaturated.

10 If the alcohol general formula is $C_nH_{2n+1}OH$ then, when $n = 0$, the formula is HOH. It is this hydroxide group which is responsible for the similarity between the chemical behaviour of water and the alcohols. Both are neutral to litmus and both are good solvents.

11 In the first chromatogram the hydrolysis (breaking down) of the starch has produced glucose and maltose (no sucrose). There is also an indication of a more complicated polysaccharide which has not been identified.

  In the second, hydrolysis has been carried out using a different substance and the starch has been hydrolysed *completely* to maltose.

12 *propanol + ethanoic acid → propylethanoate + water

Answers to revision section for Chapters 7–10

1 The general rule is that elements far apart in the Periodic Table tend to form ionic bonding. Elements quite near each other give polar covalent bonds. Bonds between identical non-metal atoms are covalent.

(a) ionic (b) polar covalent (c) ionic (d) ionic

(e) ionic (f) covalent   (g) polar covalent

2 (a) KF or K^+F^-.

(b) SiO_2 (Silicon will form 4 bonds and oxygen 2 bonds.)

(c) $CaBr_2$ or $Ca^{2+}(Br^-)_2$

(d) MgS or $Mg^{2+}S^{2-}$

(e) $BaCl_2$ or $Ba^{2+}(Cl^-)_2$

(f) B_2O_3 (Boron forms 3 bonds and oxygen 2 bonds.)

3 Positive ions come mainly from metals which are on the left of the Periodic Table.

Positive ions are likely to come from zinc, copper, caesium, aluminium, and strontium. The others will probably give negative ions.

4 (a) Iron is more reactive than copper and so it will displace copper from its compounds.

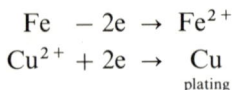

$$Fe - 2e \rightarrow Fe^{2+}$$
$$Cu^{2+} + 2e \rightarrow \underset{\text{plating}}{Cu}$$

(b) Two metals, one reactive and one much less reactive, are in contact. The more reactive one, aluminium, will corrode rapidly giving a pile of white aluminium oxide (Al_2O_3). Rusting is usually accompanied by heat loss, but we do not normally notice it since rusting is such a slow process.

(c) Potassium, to keep it from rusting or corroding, must be kept out of contact with air and moisture. That is why it is kept under oil.

(d) Zinc is more reactive than iron and so it protects the iron by corroding itself. Zinc rust keeps out air and water and so even the corroding of the zinc underneath is slowed down.

(e) This pile of discs is just a battery of cells. Two different metals in contact with a corrosive material, such as water or acid, form a little electric cell. By stacking the cells together the voltage of all the cells adds up enough to cause sparks.

Zinc is more reactive than copper and so will push off more ions into the acid than will the copper. This leaves the zinc with an excess of electrons compared with the copper. In this way the zinc becomes more negative than the copper and electrons flow through the wire from zinc to copper.

5 (a) The metals which react with steam to give hydrogen and the metal oxide are magnesium, aluminium, zinc, iron, tin and, to a very small extent, lead.

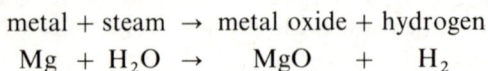

$$\text{metal} + \text{steam} \rightarrow \text{metal oxide} + \text{hydrogen}$$
$$Mg + H_2O \rightarrow MgO + H_2$$

(b) If the reaction is reversed we have

$$\text{hydrogen} + \text{metal oxide} \rightarrow \text{metal} + \text{steam}$$

For this to happen readily, the hydrogen will have to be more reactive than the metal to displace it from its oxide.

A metal which is less reactive than hydrogen is *copper*.

$$H_2 + CuO \rightarrow Cu + H_2O$$

Since tin and lead can hardly displace hydrogen from steam it might be possible to reverse the process:

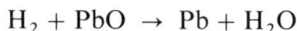

$$H_2 + PbO \rightarrow Pb + H_2O$$
$$H_2 + SnO \rightarrow Sn + H_2O$$

In fact, both of these reactions do occur.

6 (a) When he electrolyses lithium chloride solution, he will get chlorine at the anode and *hydrogen* at the cathode. Since hydrogen is less reactive than lithium it will be released in preference to lithium.

(b) The only way to get lithium metal is to do the electrolysis in the absence of water, i.e. with *molten* lithium chloride.

7 Aluminium is more reactive than silver and so it can displace silver from its compounds.

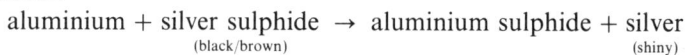

$$\text{aluminium} + \underset{\text{(black/brown)}}{\text{silver sulphide}} \rightarrow \text{aluminium sulphide} + \underset{\text{(shiny)}}{\text{silver}}$$

8 **Substance A** is ionic.

Ionic substances conduct current only when molten or dissolved in water.

Substance B is covalent.

Covalent substances do not conduct current at all.

Substance C is a metal.

Metals conduct well either as solids or when molten.

Chemistry in Action 11 (*continued from p. 237*)

Part 2

The best solvent is propanone. Let us see why this is so. We need a solvent which will also dissolve water (to remove the unwanted nitric acid). Ethylethanoate, toluene, and benzene are therefore unsuitable. This leaves ethanol, pyridine, and propanone. PETN is not very soluble in ethanol at any temperature and PETN does not increase in solubility in pyridine very much as the temperature is raised. This leaves propanone.

However, propanone has problems. Look again at the graph on page 237. At 55 °C, 65 g PETN will dissolve in 100 g propanone. At 20 °C, 25 g PETN dissolves. Suppose we have a solution of 100 g propanone at 55 °C, containing 65 g dissolved PETN. Cooling this solution to 20 °C (roughly room temperature) will give 40 g of crystals of PETN to be filtered off, leaving 25 g of PETN still dissolved.

On an industrial scale, we could dissolve 6.5 tonnes of PETN in the minimum amount of hot propanone (55 °C). How much would remain still dissolved at 20 °C?

To obtain more PETN from this solution at 20 °C, we could either evaporate off some of the propanone, or cool the solution further. However, both of these would be costly. Can you think of another way to obtain more PETN?

Turn now to page 248.

Answers to revision section for Chapters 11 and 12

1 (a) 151, (b) 142, (c) 184, (d) 74, (e) 46.

2 (a) MgS = 56; (b) $BiCl_3$ = 315.5; (c) $SrBr_2$ = 248; (d) Na_3N = 83;
  (e) C_4H_{10} = 58.

3 The gram mole is, of course, the same as the formula weight in grams. The
answers are:
  1(a) 151 g **1**(d) 74 g **2**(b) 315.5 g **2**(e) 58 g

4 (a) Balanced. On each side there is one Pb atom, one O atom, and two H
  atoms.

  (b) Unbalanced. One atom of oxygen is short on the left. To give us this extra
  oxygen atom we need two molecules of FeO.

$$2FeO + C \rightarrow Fe + CO_2$$

  This is still not balanced because we now have one Fe atom short on
  the right. The balanced equation is

$$2FeO + C \rightarrow 2Fe + CO_2$$

  (c) Unbalanced. The left is short of two Cl atoms. This can be remedied by
  taking three HCl molecules.

$$Al + 3HCl \rightarrow AlCl_3 + H_2$$

  The Al and Cl atoms now balance but the right is now short of an H
  atom. But hydrogen atoms need to be in pairs in the gas. We can solve the
  problem as follows.

$$2Al + 6HCl \rightarrow 2AlCl_3 + 3H_2$$

2Al atoms	2Al atoms
6H atoms	6Cl atoms
6Cl atoms	6H atoms

  (d) Balanced.

5

$$PbO + H_2 \rightarrow Pb + H_2O$$
$$\underbrace{207 + 16}_{223} \qquad 207$$

$$223 \text{ g PbO} \rightarrow 207 \text{ g Pb}$$

$$4.46 \text{ g PbO} \rightarrow \frac{207 \times 4.46}{223} \text{ g Pb}$$
$$= 4.14 \text{ g}$$

6

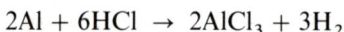
$$2HgO \rightarrow 2Hg + O_2$$
$$\underbrace{2(201 + 16)}_{434 \text{ g}} \rightarrow \qquad \underbrace{2 \times 16}_{32 \text{ g}}$$

$$10.85 \text{ g} \rightarrow \frac{32 \times 10.85}{434} \text{ g} = 0.80 \text{ g}$$

7 From the graph choose a value on the zinc axis which is easily related to the atomic weight of zinc which is 65.

Choose 6.5 g (a tenth of the atomic weight) for zinc. Then the reading for sulphur is 3.2 g.

6.5 g   Zn combine with 3.2 g S
65 g   Zn combine with 32 g S
65 amu   Zn combine with 32 amu S
1 atom Zn combines with 1 atom S

Simplest formula is ZnS.

Answers to revision section for Chapters 13–17

1 (a) Both more dense than air.
(b) Both dissolve in water to give a weak acid:

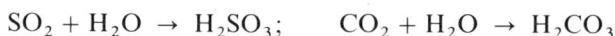

$$SO_2 + H_2O \rightarrow H_2SO_3; \qquad CO_2 + H_2O \rightarrow H_2CO_3$$

(c) Both are reduced by magnesium:

$$SO_2 + 2Mg \rightarrow S + 2MgO; \qquad CO_2 + 2Mg \rightarrow C + 2MgO$$

2 Vegetables (lack of fertilizers) and meat; paints; cellulose sheet in packages.
3 Concentration tells how many molecules are in a given volume.
Strength tells how much the molecules are ionized.
Therefore a strong acid like nitric acid is almost fully ionized, but a very dilute solution containing only a small amount of acid is possible.
4     $NaNO_3 \rightarrow NaNO_2 + O_2$
$Pb(NO_3)_2 \rightarrow PbO + NO_2 + O_2$
$Hg(NO_3)_2 \rightarrow Hg + NO_2 + O_2$

5 (a) All sodium salts dissolve in water therefore no clue from this test.
(b) All three would give a white solid. Most carbonates (including $BaCO_3$) are also insoluble. No clue from this test.
(c) This eliminates Na_2SO_4, but Na_2SO_3 and Na_2CO_3 are possible

$$Na_2SO_3 + HCl \rightarrow SO_2$$

$$Na_2CO_3 + HCl \rightarrow CO_2$$

6 *Jar 1* does not contain nitric oxide (NO).
Jar 2 does not contain NO.
Therefore
Jar 3 contains **NO**.
Jar 2 must contain **N**$_2$ because the contents do not react with NO.
Therefore
Jar 1 contains **O**$_2$.
(d) This eliminates Na_2CO_3 because CO_2 affects lime water. Therefore the unknown substance is probably sodium sulphite.
(e) Choking smell of SO_2 was given off. This confirms sodium sulphite.
7 Gelatin, although it is a protein, does not contain some of the amino acids essential to health. If this was your only protein source you would therefore be unable to build all your own body proteins.

Answers to revision section for Chapters 18–20

1 (a) Almost no free ions would be in solution.
Any Ba^{2+} would precipitate out with SO_4^{2-}.
Any H^+ would combine with OH^- to form water.

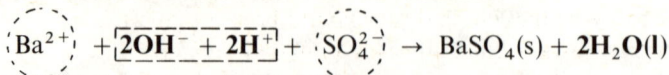

$$Ba^{2+} + 2OH^- + 2H^+ + SO_4^{2-} \rightarrow BaSO_4(s) + 2H_2O(l)$$

(b) When the acid was exactly neutralized there would be no ions to conduct current and so the reading would fall to zero. Any extra $Ba(OH)_2$ added would dissolve, provide ions, and make the reading rise again.

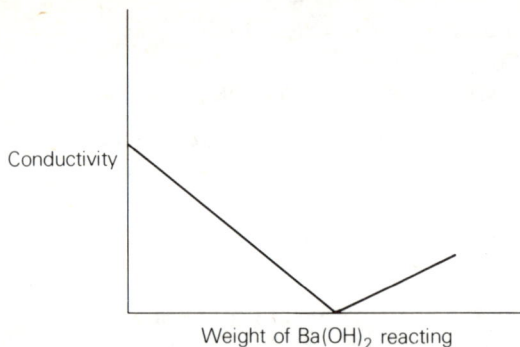

Weight of Ba(OH)$_2$ reacting

(c) Barium is in the same column of the Periodic Table as magnesium and calcium and so its behaviour will be similar to theirs. Water with Ba^{2+} would be hard.

2 (a) Number of moles of H^+ from acid $= 25 \times 0.1 \times$ number of H^+ in 1 molecule of the acid
$= 2.5 \times$ number of H^+
Number of moles of OH^- from alkali $= 5 \times 1 \times 1$
$= 5$
At neutralization $\qquad H^+ = OH^-$
Therefore $\qquad 2.5 \times$ number of $H^+ = 5$
Number of $H^+ = 2$

(b) There must be two $-CO_2H$ groups in the acid.
The formula weight of these two groups $= 2(12 + 32 + 1)$
$= 90$
The weight of the rest of the molecule $= 146 - 90$
$= 56$
Since the rest of the molecule is made up of a string of CH_2 groups each weighing 14, then the number of CH_2 groups $= \dfrac{56}{14} = 4$.

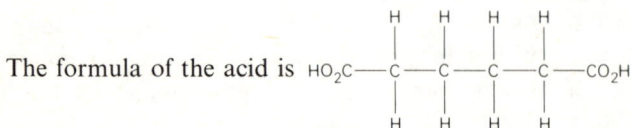

The formula of the acid is

$$HO_2C-\overset{\displaystyle H}{\underset{\displaystyle H}{C}}-\overset{\displaystyle H}{\underset{\displaystyle H}{C}}-\overset{\displaystyle H}{\underset{\displaystyle H}{C}}-\overset{\displaystyle H}{\underset{\displaystyle H}{C}}-CO_2H$$

3 Some of the detergents which you are likely to have at home are: washing-up liquids, shampoos, car wash, hand cleaner, washing powder, dish washer powder, floor and paintwork cleaner, car windscreen washer.

4 (a) Thermoplastic—needs to be soft and squeezy.
    (b) Probably neither—metal bins would be used for this.
    (c) Thermoplastic—must be easily moulded, not brittle.
    (d) Thermoplastic—is not required to withstand high temperatures.
    (e) Thermosetting plastic—must be hard and a good insulator.
    (f) Thermosetting plastic—must be hard and not soften in warm weather.

Chemistry in Action 11 (*continued from p. 243*)

Part 3

Did you think of a good answer? There is a very simple answer—just add water!

PETN does not dissolve in water, but propanone does and so does nitric acid, of course. So adding water will make much more of the dissolved PETN appear as crystals, to be filtered off, leaving the unwanted nitric acid behind dissolved in the mixture of propanone and water. But how much water should be added? Look at the graph below.

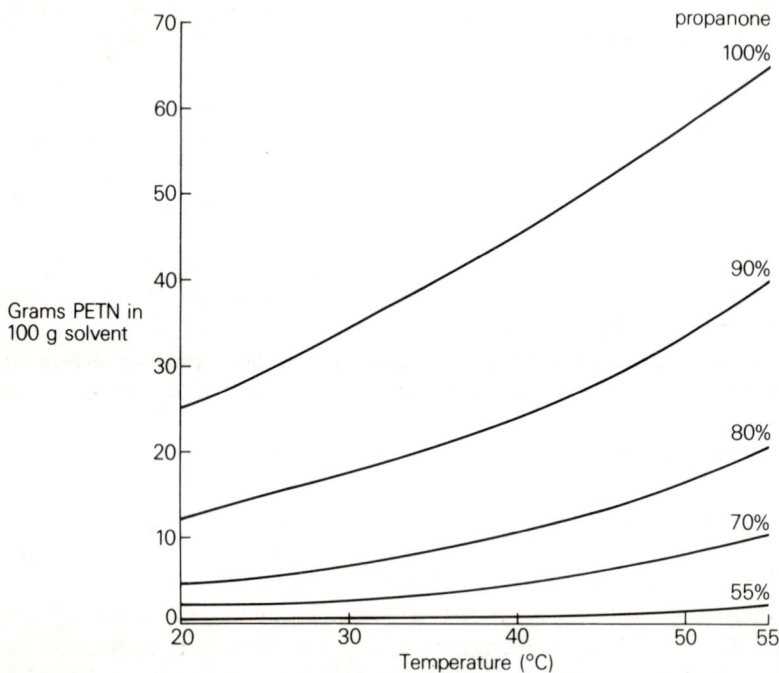

In order to obtain most of the PETN as crystals, the solution at 20 °C must contain less than 55% propanone. About 0.5 g PETN remains dissolved in 100 g propanone/water mixture containing 55% propanone. This may not seem very much, but it means that, in 10 tonnes of such a mixture, 0.05 tonne of PETN will still remain dissolved. This is 50 kg!

Here is what the industry can do. Impure PETN is dissolved in propanone. The temperature is around 45–50 °C. Some sodium carbonate is added—this reacts with the impurity, nitric acid, to form sodium nitrate. Then water is added until a solution containing about 40% propanone is obtained. The temperature drops to around 20 °C. Under these conditions nearly all the PETN appears as crystals, which are filtered off. The unwanted impurities (now sodium nitrate) remain dissolved in the water/propanone mixture. This mixture is warmed up and the propanone boils off at 56 °C, leaving the unwanted water and impurities to be thrown away. The propanone recovered can be used over and over again.

Suggested Answers to Chemistry in Action Sections

Answers to Chemistry in Action 1

1 From your Periodic Table, 59.

2 Top right-hand corner and last column (except for hydrogen).
The elements in the last column were all discovered between 1894 and 1900 and the others between 1766 and 1774.

3 Carbon (C), Calcium (Ca), Chlorine (Cl), Chromium (Cr), Copper (Cu), Cadmium (Cd), Caesium (Cs), Cobalt (Co).
You might have chosen Ce, Cn, Ci, Cm. In fact, Ce has already been used for Cerium (number 58) which is not shown on your Table. Cm is used for Curium (number 98).

4 Tin (stannum), iron (ferrum), strontium (named after the Argyllshire village of Strontian), tungsten (wolfram), silver (argentium). The old names are in brackets.

5 Many compounds of iron, lead, aluminium, and phosphorus are not soluble in water.

6 Iron, copper, silver, gold, platinum, zinc (in alloys like brass), tin, lead, and possibly, mercury.
These are all unreactive or fairly unreactive metals.

7 There are two main reasons why the metal titanium is not used in large quantities today. Firstly, there are few deposits of its compounds on the surface of the Earth which are cheap to mine. Secondly, it is very difficult (and costly) to obtain the metal from its compounds. Although the metal itself is not often used, its oxide—titanium dioxide—is used a lot.

Answers to Chemistry in Action 2

1 Reaction 1 is not favoured because of the high cost of producing ethyne from methane (temperature of 1450 °C).
Reaction 2 is less attractive than Reaction 3 because it uses chlorine instead of hydrogen chloride.
In Reaction 3 the hydrogen chloride produced in the last stage can be used again, thus cutting costs further. The temperature of 270 °C in the middle stage of Reaction 3 is not unfavourable because the mixture has to be heated to 400 °C for the last stage in any case.

2 You should choose a location near a port where oil is coming in and is being refined, because ethene is made by cracked fractions from an oil refinery.

Hydrogen chloride is also required. This is made from rock salt. The major deposit of salt in Britain is in Cheshire. It is easier to move rock salt to the source of ethene than to move ethene gas to the salt.

3 *Advantages*	*Disadvantages*
(a) Cheap; does not depend upon a supply of hides; can be made in large sheets.	Less attractive appearance; not so pleasant to touch; does not allow air to move through it ('breathe').
(b) Does not rot or corrode; cheap; flexible; easily moulded; light for its size.	Can become brittle; does not rot away naturally and so causes a litter problem; less rigid.

4 The main 'bumps' in the production graph occur in the mid and late 70s. The oil crisis of 1973–4 caused oil prices to rise steeply, pushing up the price of PVC, bringing about a fall in demand. There has been some recovery since then. It is worth considering the problems faced by industrial planners when raw material prices suddenly go up. You can also see why some industries suddenly have to reduce their work force, or even close altogether.

Unless an alternative raw material to oil is found, the production of PVC will go down as oil reserves run out.

Answers to Chemistry in Action 4

Metal	Identity
A	Al
B	Ca
C	Cu
D	Au
E	Fe
F	Pb
G	Mg
H	K
I	Sn
J	Ti
K	W

(a) A (aluminium) or J (titanium).
   Aluminium is used because titanium, although stronger, is too expensive.
(b) A (aluminium) or C (copper).
   Copper is a better conductor, but aluminium is cheaper.
(c) C (copper), E (iron), or J (titanium).
   In practice, iron is used despite its corrosion problems. Copper and titanium are too expensive and copper is too dense.
(d) F (lead) or I (tin).
   Often an alloy (mixture) of both is used.
(e) K (tungsten) is very much the favourite, with its high melting and boiling points and great strength.

Notes
(a) One factor which can make a metal expensive is a low percentage in the Earth's crust.
(b) Strictly speaking, pure metals are rarely used. Mixtures (alloys) tend to be more useful.

Answers to Chemistry in Action 5

Aluminium chloride will melt if heated to 193 °C under pressure (just over twice atmospheric pressure). It sublimes at 178 °C under normal pressure. In both liquid and gas forms it turns out to be polar. At higher temperatures the type of bonding present is less certain. When dissolved in water, aluminium and chloride ions exist, but it is possible to argue that a reaction has taken place between the aluminium chloride and the water.

Answers to Chemistry in Action 6

The main thing which Gay-Lussac and his friends did not know was that gases like hydrogen, oxygen, and chlorine possess *two* atoms per particle (molecule). They could not write balanced equations for many of the gas reactions. For example, they wrote, for the ammonia reaction

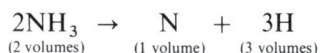

$$2NH_3 \quad \rightarrow \quad N \quad + \quad 3H$$
$$\text{(2 volumes)} \qquad \text{(1 volume)} \quad \text{(3 volumes)}$$

They could not balance this equation.

A few years later an Italian, named Avogadro, suggested ideas which led to the understanding that nitrogen gas contained nitrogen molecules and these molecules were made up of two nitrogen atoms—N_2. Similarly, oxygen and chlorine are O_2 and Cl_2. This allowed the equations to be balanced:

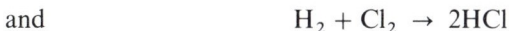

$$2NH_3 \rightarrow N_2 + 3H_2$$

and $$H_2 + Cl_2 \rightarrow 2HCl$$

Having two atoms in a gas molecule is not the only possibility. Three, four, or more atoms per molecule are known. For example, ozone contains *three* oxygen atoms per molecule. It is written as O_3.

Answers to Chemistry in Action 7

A modern factory making sulphuric acid starts by burning sulphur in a flow of air, giving a mixture of sulphur dioxide, oxygen, and nitrogen (1:1:8), which is passed through three consecutive layers of catalyst to achieve a 95–96% conversion to sulphur trioxide. Cooling of the gases takes place between the catalyst layers.

The sulphur trioxide is then removed by passing the gas mixture through sulphuric acid. The unchanged sulphur dioxide (plus oxygen and nitrogen) is then passed through a fourth layer of catalyst. Because there is so little sulphur dioxide left, there is a very high conversion of it to sulphur trioxide since little heat is produced. The overall conversion is then 99.7%.

A typical factory can produce 300 to 2000 tonnes of sulphuric acid each day. Starting with 650 tonnes of sulphur dioxide each day, 995 tonnes of sulphuric acid would be obtained if the process were 100% efficient. If the process were only 98% efficient, 13 tonnes of sulphur dioxide would be left unused and would escape into the atmosphere. It is now easy to see why the law insists strictly on a minimum 99.5% efficiency.

Answers to Chemistry in Action 8
Mixture I
One tonne will contain: 0.19 tonne of KCl
0.27 tonne of $Ca(H_2PO_4)_2$
0.49 tonne of NH_4NO_3
The remainder will be made up with sand.

Mixture II
One tonne will contain: 0.19 tonne of KCl
0.30 tonne of $(NH_4)_2HPO_4$
0.51 tonne of $(NH_4)_2SO_4$

Mixture III
One tonne will contain: 0.19 tonne of KCl
0.30 tonne of $(NH_4)_2HPO_4$
0.30 tonne of NH_4NO_3
The remainder will be made up with sand.

Costs
Mixture I   19 260 groats
Mixture II   18 550 groats
Mixture III   16 900 groats

Answers to Chemistry in Action 9
Part II
(a) Add a source of calcium ions—probably calcium hydroxide, which is very cheap. The sulphate and sulphite ions will form precipitates of calcium sulphate and calcium sulphite. These can be allowed to settle out. Using barium, lead, or silver ions instead of calcium ions is far too expensive.
(b) The pupil could be given a source of metal ions such as Mg^{2+}, Ca^{2+}, Ba^{2+}, Pb^{2+}, Ag^+. However, the last three are themselves poisonous! A recommended treatment is to give milk of magnesia, which is magnesium hydroxide. This forms magnesium oxalate which, being insoluble, passes through the digestive system without giving any trouble. Any excess magnesium hydroxide is itself fairly harmless.
(c) Bromine could be present in the sea, as most bromides are soluble in water. However, fluorine is unlikely to be present in the sea in large amounts, because calcium fluoride is rather insoluble; silver is also unlikely to be present in large amounts, because silver chloride is rather insoluble.
(d) Treat the bauxite ore with just enough alkali to dissolve all the aluminium oxide, leaving the iron oxide unaffected. Filter off the iron oxide. Add acid to lower the pH until it is near neutral and the aluminium oxide reappears as a

solid (it is insoluble in water). Filter off the aluminium oxide, wash it in water and dry it. A process rather like this is carried out by the British Aluminium Company at Burntisland in Fife.

Answers to Chemistry in Action 10

Fibre	Identity
A	Wool
B	Cotton
C	Silk
D	Viscose rayon
E	Cellulose triacetate (Tricel)
F	Nylon 6
G	Terylene (polyester)
H	Acrylic

Your likely choices might be
Running vest: cotton or nylon
Tights: nylon
Fishing net: Terylene, although cotton and nylon are both possible.

Appendix for Teachers: Practical Work

To keep the length of this book within reasonable bounds we have omitted details of practical work. This should not be taken to imply that we disapprove of practical work; on the contrary, we see it as a vital part of any chemistry course.

Practical work is not a single activity. It is a very complex transaction involving instructions, given in various forms, skills of hand and observation, recording, and interpretation. We do not believe that there is one ideal method nor do we subscribe to the idea that an experiment done by a pupil is, of necessity, a better teaching experience than a demonstration. Our own research suggests that the very act of doing an apparently simple piece of practical work may detract from the message it is trying to convey.

To help teachers to plan a practical course to accompany the book, we have set out, where applicable, references to our other textbook series *Chemistry Takes Shape* (Books 1–5, published by Heinemann Educational Books) in which explicit experimental details are to be found. Teachers might like to know that further research into the methodology of experimental work is currently being carried out.

In due course it is hoped to produce a fresh practical book, based upon this research, to accompany this volume.

Chemistry About Us (section numbers)	Description of experiment	*Chemistry Takes Shape* (volume and section numbers)
4.2	Water gas	Vol. 2, 6.6
4.2	Evidence for hydrocarbon	Vol. 4, 5.2
4.5	Separation of isomers	Vol. 4, 6.5
4.6	Cracking and test for unsaturation	Vol. 4, 6.4
5.2	Distillation of crude oil	Vol. 4, 6.4
5.4	Addition polymerization	Vol. 4, 12.6(c)
6.3	Hydrolysis of carbohydrates	Vol. 4, 7.7
	Chromatographic separation of hydrolysate	Vol. 4, 7.7
6.4	Enzyme hydrolysis of starch	Vol. 4, 7.6
6.5	Fermentation	Vol. 4, 8.2
6.8	Soap making	Vol. 4, 10.3
6.9	Ester formation	Vol. 5, 9.3

Chemistry About Us (section numbers)	Description of experiment	Chemistry Takes Shape (volume and section numbers)
6.10	Ester hydrolysis	Vol. 5, 9.4
7.4	Polarity of water (see Fig. 7.7)	
7.5	Ion detector	Vol. 3, 3.4 and 3.5
8.1	Coloured ions and their migration	Vol. 3, 3.1, 3.2 and 3.3
8.2	Comparison of rates of ionic migration	Vol. 3, 10.4
8.5	Metals with water and steam	Vol. 1, 6.5(i) and (ii)
8.7	Different metals in contact with each other	Vol. 3, 8.3
8.9	Displacement reactions	Vol. 3, 7.6
9.4	Sacrificial protection	Vol. 3, 9.1
10.1	Electrolysis (see Fig. 10.1)	
11.2	Combining magnesium with oxygen (quantitative)	
11.3	Lead iodide from lead (quantitative)	
12.1	Reduction of iron oxide using carbon monoxide	
	Production of metallic lead by electrolysis	Vol. 3, 3.4
	Combination of hydrogen and oxygen	Vol. 1, 6.3
12.2	Reduction of copper oxide using carbon (charcoal stick)	Vol. 2, 3.5(d)
13.3	Behaviour of sulphur when	
	—heated	Vol. 3, 15.3
	—burned	Vol. 3, 15.4
13.4	Sulphurous acid from sulphur dioxide	Vol. 3, 16.1(c)
	Test for SO_3^{2-}	Vol. 3, 16.3
	Making sulphur dioxide	Vol. 3, 16.1
13.5	Reaction between sulphurous acid and the halogens	Vol. 3, 16.3(i)
	Test for SO_4^{2-}	Vol. 3, 16.3
	Burning magnesium in sulphur dioxide	Vol. 2, 3.2 fig. 18
13.7	Forming sulphur trioxide	Vol. 3, 17.2 fig. 79
14.3	Sulphuric acid—a strong acid	Vol. 3, 17.6
14.4	Sulphuric acid—its attraction for water	
	(a) diluting the acid	Vol. 3, 17.5
	(b) absorbing water	Vol. 3, 17.5(i) and (ii)
	(c) drawing out the elements of water	Vol. 3, 17.5(iii)
14.5	Sulphuric acid—an electron acceptor	Vol. 3, 17.6
14.7	Making rayon	Vol. 4, 12.2
15.2	Combination of nitrogen and oxygen	Vol. 3, 18.1
15.5	Laboratory preparation of ammonia	Vol. 3, 19.1 and Vol. 3, 18.3
	Solubility of ammonia in water	Vol. 3, 18.5
	Obtaining a steady supply of ammonia	Vol. 3, 19.1, Fig. 92
	Ammonia burning in oxygen	Vol. 3, 19.1, Fig. 93
	Ammonia and hot copper oxide	Vol. 3, 19.2
	Ostwald process	Vol. 3, 19.3
16.1	Neutralization of nitric acid to form nitrates	Vol. 3, 19.4
16.2	Nitric acid as an electron acceptor—reactions with magnesium	Vol. 3, 19.5

Chemistry About Us (section numbers)	Description of experiment	Chemistry Takes Shape (volume and section numbers)
16.3	Heating of nitrates	Vol. 3, 19.7
	Test for a nitrate (brown ring)	
17.1	Heating proteins with soda lime	Vol. 4, 9.1
17.2	Hydrolysis of proteins and detecting the fragments chromatographically	Vol. 4, 9.3 and 9.4
18.1	Burning elements in oxygen	Vol. 1, 5.3
18.2	Metal oxides and water	Vol. 1, 5.3
18.3	Electrolysis of acid solutions	Vol. 3, 9.4 B
	Acids and magnesium to give hydrogen	Vol. 3, 7.3
	Acids and carbonates to give a gas	Vol. 2, 3.4, Fig. 21
	Testing the gas with lime water	Vol. 2, 3.4, Fig. 21
18.5	Conductivity and concentration	Vol. 3, 3.5, Fig. 15
18.6	Mobility of H^+ and OH^-	Vol. 3, 10.4 (a)
	Mobilities of other ions	Vol. 3, 10.4 (b)
18.7	pH scale 1–7–13	Vol. 3, 10.2 and 10.3
Introduction to Chapter 19	Neutralization experiment	Vol. 1, 5.4
19.1	Conductivity of acid and alkali	
	Trends in conductivity experiments	
	—metal and acid	Vol. 3, 12.2
	—metal oxide and acid	Vol. 3, 12.2
	—metal carbonate and acid	Vol. 3, 12.3
	—soluble metal hydroxide and acid	Vol. 3, 12.3
	Forming a salt from a metal oxide and acid	Vol. 3, 12.1
19.4	Making insoluble salts	Vol. 3, 14.1
20.2	Making condensation polymers	
	—nylon	Vol. 4, 12.4 (c)
	—urea-formaldehyde/resorcinol-formaldehyde	Vol. 4, 12.4 (a)
20.4	Experiments with silicones	Vol. 4, 14.2–14.5
20.6	The removal of hardness	
	—using sodium carbonate	Vol. 4, 11.2 (a)
	—using an ion exchange resin	Vol. 4, 11.2 (b)
	Redesigning soap—sulphonating a hydrocarbon	Vol. 4, 11.3

Index